"An emotional tale of families ravaged by high personal debt and job market transitions due to automation and out-sourcing of jobs under globalization."

MINIMUM PAYMENT

Paul Shona

Copyright © 2018 held by author Paul Shona

All rights reserved.

ISBN - 13: 978 - 1986101264
ISBN - 10: 1986101266

No parts of this book may be reproduced or copied in any form, or recorded on any form of electronics or other devices, without the express permission from the author.

In this work of fiction, all characters, situations, and events portrayed are fictional. Any resemblance to an event, situation, or a person - dead or alive - is purely coincidental and non-intentional.

Identities of lending institutions such as chartered banks and credit unions are protected by naming these as Financial Institution (FI) as FI-I, FI-II, and so on. The names of department stores and commercial places cited throughout, on the other hand, are authentic - even though some of these have been closed, and/or no longer exist.

The author has weaved a story based on his professional knowledge and decades of experience analyzing finances of households in Canada and the United States.

For comments, inquiries, contact with the author, go to

rajchawla6@yahoo.ca

Or at:

www.rajchawla6.com

https://www.facebook.com/RajChawla

https://www.twitter.com/@Rajchawla6_Leve

https://www.linkedin.com/rajchawla6@yahoo.ca

This work is dedicated to my wife, Kam Chawla, and to my daughters, Shelly Chawla and Sharon Salter, and my grandson, Nicholas Salter.

Books by the same author:

Quest for Second Sex (debut erotic romance fiction)

A Writer's Journey Through the Bureaucratic Maze:
A True Account

Minimum Payment

URL for books:
https://www.amazon.com/author/paulshona

I want to sincerely thank my editor for her diligent assistance, advice, and support in publishing this fiction, at:

www.momofemmett@gmail.com

Or at:

www.jancaroleromancenovels.weebly.com

Cover Design by Dar Albert at pistoliqued@gmail.com

Interior format by The Killion Group at www.thekilliongroupinc.com

CHAPTER ONE

"I want us to buy a house," Amy demanded.

"Honey, we don't have enough of a down payment at the moment," I replied to my wife softly, my eyes still fixed on the Saturday's expanded edition of the Ottawa Citizen.

"I don't care. We can always get a second mortgage," she vehemently replied. "Almost all of our friends in our income group live in owned homes. Why can't we? I think we should seriously look into this issue."

"I am not disagreeing with you," I replied softly. "Let's first pay off the remaining debt on my student loan, VISA, and MasterCard before burdening ourselves with a mortgage debt. I think we should wait at least another year."

I paused, removed my eyes from the newspaper, and looked straight at Amy's face to read her reaction. She gave me a blank stare, expecting me to spell out what precisely was on my mind.

"Actually, I was thinking of renewing our lease on this apartment for another year," I completed my sentence.

"No way," she shot back. "I want it as soon as possible. I don't care about your outstanding debts. This is all your debt that you took before our marriage. I am not a part of it. Why should I wait until it's all paid up? I don't want you to renew the current lease. I want us to own a home at the earliest opportunity."

"Granted, it's not your debt, but still I have to pay it before taking any more debt," I reemphasized calmly. I put aside the newspaper and looked at her from the opposite end of the small dining table we were sitting at, as we were in the midst of eating our morning breakfast. I wasn't amused by Amy's response. I finished chewing the last bite of toast and egg, and placed the knife and fork in the middle of the empty plate lying in front of me.

I cleared my throat.

I wanted to remind Amy why I took credit and why it was taking that long to repay it.

"I have told you time and again that after I moved to Ottawa almost penniless, I had to use credit to furnish this apartment," I explained to Amy in a hushed tone. "I don't know why this doesn't sink in your head that whenever someone moves in a new city, one needs to start a life, rent a place, furnish it with all the basic necessities."

I paused for a minute, still gazing at her, and continued, "You moved into a fully furnished apartment. You have no clue whatsoever about what it takes to settle down in a new city, new place. Now be honest. Ever since you have been visiting me, or now living with me for almost six months in this apartment, have you ever found anything lacking or missing here?" I asked her point-blank.

"No," she replied, "but that's beside the point. You furnished the apartment the way you wanted. You bought everything of your own choice. Maybe if I had been with you, I would have gone for fewer purchases, and less expensive too, just to take lesser credit. If it had been up to me, I would have paid all of the debt by this time. Now you are asking me to delay my own wishes just to pay-up for all your thrifty spending. It's not fair."

"I strongly believe in buying good quality kitchen appliances and furniture," I replied curtly, "as these last longer. Not only that, I believe in buying products that look appealing to my eyes as well as reflect good taste and the status of a person. I don't want to see someone coming over to visit us and leaving with any negative or poor opinion about us, our status, home, furnishings – you name it."

"I too strongly believe in these things," Amy interjected, "provided I can personally afford these, or if purchased on credit, be able to pay off the debt in full after the allowable grace period. I hate to carry-over any debt balance and keep paying interest on it. In my opinion, that's a waste of money."

"If that's what you think, then what about the interest that we will be paying for twenty-five years on the mortgage that we will be taking to purchase a home," I snarled back at her, questioning the validity of her argument. "If you think paying interest is a waste of money, then we shouldn't buy a house until we have saved enough to fully pay for it. And that would take a good chunk of our life-time before we owned a home." I looked at her face piercingly.

"Oh! I can't argue with you." She looked exasperated. She took a deep breath and let it out harshly and started to collect hurriedly the empty plates, cups, and cutlery to be washed at the kitchen sink – just a few steps away from the back of her chair.

"Never mind how I view the interest payment," she bumbled loudly. "I want us to own a house. That's it. You can work out the rest of the details."

Holding empty dishes, she walked back to the kitchen.

Realizing that I had annoyed and frustrated my beloved and beautiful sweetheart, my life partner, I followed her footsteps up to the kitchen sink where she had started to rinse the dishes. I stood behind her, firmly placed my open palms on the top of her shoulders,

"I am sorry, dear," I whispered into her ears, "I didn't mean to annoy you. You know your wishes are always a command to me, and I always fulfill those – resources permitting – to the best of my ability. You want to live in an owned house, you will get one. I promise."

I gently kissed the back of her neck, and kept pressing her shoulders.

"I know you will get me one," she turned her face around, looking into my naughty eyes, and uttered, "What's the guarantee that you will be able to pay off all the debt in a year's time. Since we are still living on your income alone, we may incur even more debt over the next year."

"Well, it shouldn't happen," I assured her, and softly kissed her cheek. "I am sure you will get a job after finishing your certification in 'Accounting, Administration and Human Resources' course from the Algonquin College. You just have another few months to go. Am I right?"

"Yes," she replied softly. "That's also the reason I am suggesting that we should make a move and start looking for a house. Very soon we will be a two-income family. I am sure we will be able to afford the mortgage. I don't know about you, but I feel somewhat inferior to others for not owning a house when others making even less than you, are living in owned single detached homes. Just think, if we have children tomorrow, would you like to raise them in an apartment? I know I wouldn't."

She shut off the sink tap momentarily and fully turned around to face me. Now we both were standing in the middle of the small kitchen, my hands still resting on her shoulders. We were sandwiched between the sink and fridge on the one side, and the electric stove and the main counter top with white closets hinged a couple of feet above it on the other.

"I agree with everything you are saying," I nodded my head. "I personally prefer to wait at least until our financial situation improves. Servicing a mortgage debt is a big commitment. I hope you realize that once we own a house on a mortgage, we will likely be forced to make some changes in our lifestyle, budget, travel, you name it. That's why I want to start our life as owner of a home with a brand new slate. Just imagine. Children's presence could even more complicate our lives as we will have to accommodate their additional expenses as well. If you personally ask me, I am quite concerned about all these looming changes."

"Stop being too analytic," she shot back and moved away from me. "I have heard this reasoning before. I want us to buy a house, and soon after that, have children. As a woman, I want a house as well as children for my future security. What's wrong with that? I suggest we should start looking for a house right from today. There's a supplement on new houses in today's newspaper. Maybe we should look at it."

"Well, as you wish," I replied and shrugged my shoulders. "Just remember that I warned you about all the high costs associated with home ownership. Since you still are going to look for a job, we have no clue about the amount of money you would be bringing in. Right now, what we have is just my annual salary of twenty-two thousand dollars. That's what any lender will use for approving our mortgage application." I took a deep breath, and moved away from her.

I opened the sliding glass door of the balcony of the apartment – just to breathe in a bit of cold, fresh air, to calm myself down.

"Don't jump off the balcony," she chided from the kitchen. She had turned on the kitchen faucet to rinse the big double sink made of alloyed steel.

I stood at the seventh floor of the thirteen-storey grey apartment building off Richmond Road and McEwen Avenue, located on the west side of Canada's Capital city of Ottawa. The balcony was overlooking Ottawa's Western Parkway and the adjacent vast Ottawa River. I could divert my attention by watching the Saturday traffic moving on the Parkway. I raised my eyes away from the road to look straight up at the Gatineau Hills, still covered with patches of snow in early April, and then looked at the river with water running openly in parts of the middle and small ice floats were moving, melting as spring was in the air.

"Thank God. We have survived another harsh winter," I mumbled to myself.

I looked down at the open in-ground pool in the vicinity of the building and found it filled with thin layers of dirty green and muddy water mixed with snow. It would be a while before tenants would be able to swim, get together in groups, making the environment livelier and noisier. The bright sun was making it hard to keep looking at all the patches of snow because of their strong glaring effects. The cold breeze forced me to return inside the apartment.

The bright sunshine mixed with a fresh and cooler air had melted some of my anger as well. The more I thought about Amy's insistence about owning a home and thereafter children as symbols of her future security, the more I got convinced that she was simply demanding what every other married woman would. These two basic things were instilled in the psyche of women around the globe. She had married me with such expectations and I, in turn, was obligated to fulfill those. What kind of a husband would I be if I couldn't satisfy her basic wants? These thoughts momentarily evaporated all of my financial concerns pertaining to the purchase of a home and its related indebtedness.

I sat on a two-seat small sofa – placed near the balcony door – in an L-shaped room of the rented apartment, with its bigger area used as a formal live-in, and the smaller, as the dining area. There was a small corridor, leading to the bathroom on the one side, and two bedrooms on the other. The master bedroom shared one wall with the living room area. The second bedroom, with stacks of books and academic journals, was strictly used as a study room, and had an entrance to a large walk-in closet.

While I was scanning the new homes section in the newspaper, I could hear the clattering of dishes that Amy was still putting back in closets. She was likely still upset because I had not readily agreed to her suggestion. I had questioned her demand, which she never ever anticipated because after marriage, I had given her a blanket assurance that I would do my best to provide her anything she ever touched and/or wished for in her life – as long as the fulfillment of any of her desires was within my financially possible reach.

After doing the dishes, Amy walked out of the kitchen, drying her hands with a small white cotton dish towel. She sat on my right and glanced at the open pages containing pictures of new homes under construction in the city. She knew full well that she had conveyed her message, her pressure tactic had worked, and the man she was married to was not going to ignore her wishes. She grinned, and put her left arm on my shoulder blades.

"Have you liked any of the models?" She asked me, pressing her face against the side of my right chest.

"No. All of these models look alike, and from these pictures, you can't figure out anything," I replied. "Here, you have a look and tell me what you like. We can then go and have a look at the site. Just make sure that we stay in the west end of the city. We are so used to this end, familiar with the location of shops, and above all, it's closer to my office."

"Does that mean we are going to buy a house?" she was enthused. She hid her enthusiasm and asked with a superficial serious face, "You are sure we can afford one. Just moments ago you sounded glum and beaten as if I had asked you to buy me a world. I don't want to see you unhappy, or under any financial stress."

She kissed my cheek gently.

"I want to own a house, but not by making you unhappy," she added.

"I understand," I replied softly. I gently patted her back. "I don't ever want to see you unhappy. As I promised you right after our wedding, I would fulfill each and every desire of yours as long as it's in my reach. Buying a house is in my reach. I am young. I can take a mortgage loan. I am sure, over time, my income will increase through promotions and other annual increments, and I would pay off all of this debt. Sooner or later we have to buy a house. Now is as good a time as the next year. We may have to adjust our expenditure, that's all."

"That's my man. I want to hear such positive talk," she replied with a wide grin. "We could go and look at some models this afternoon after doing our weekly grocery shopping."

That afternoon, Amy and I drove in our six-year old Plymouth Duster to see models in areas around Woodroffe Avenue, Merivale Road, and Knoxdale Road. Driving through the unpaved areas cluttered with construction materials all around, we visited several construction sites, their sales centres, picked up the folders containing company brochures, layouts of model homes with details about the total living space, number of rooms, and of course, the main information – the sale price at the bottom of the sheet. The price of a single-detached home was higher than that of a semi- detached, or a garden home (a housing unit in a row of linked four or five units, with a common roof, and two shared walls, unless it was an end-unit with one shared wall). The price difference ranged anywhere between fifteen to fifty thousand dollars.

Since our pockets were not that heavy, we didn't want to take any large amount of mortgage, because we knew we needed money to pay, beside the mortgage payment, other regular utility bills on top of the property taxes and other furnishings and maintenance of the property. I had to convince Amy to focus on semi-detached as a short-term compromise. She didn't like my suggestion, but had no choice. She half-heartedly accepted my suggestion and put her foot down that she wouldn't move in a garden home.

Once the single-detached was ruled out because of our weaker financial situation, and a garden home out because she didn't want it at any cost, we were left to focus only on semi-attached models. That sort of compromise would at least allow her to live in an owned house. I promised her that in a few years time, we would move into a single-detached home, especially when kids would likely be on the scene, if not before.

On our drive back to the apartment, Amy, with her grumpy, but still beautiful and attractive face, kept quiet all the way. She must have been reflecting on her decision to have married me – a man with limited financial means and unable to fulfill her wishes. Or, her tacit silence was a sign of reconciling with the realities about the man she had married. Perhaps, she had made the wrong choice and had to live with it for ever, or at least until she voluntarily abort this companionship.

Her long silence was piercing my heart. I wanted her to talk to me about some of the models we had seen both inside and outside. I could sense that she was still sulking over her unfulfilled wish to live in an owned single-detached home. Even though I kept talking to her about the different models that we had visited, their good and bad layouts, and varying prices, she simply let my words pass through one of her ears and out the other. She was least interested in all such talk. At times she gazed at me, perhaps cursing me for betraying her trust in me. She had no clue what I was going through – totally unhappy and feeling belittled over my choice – but that was the best I could do under the circumstances.

That night when we hit the sack, Amy was no longer lying close to me, as she usually did. She was still fuming with anger, chose to lie near the far edge of the king-size bed. When I tried to pull her closer to me to give a peck on her full cheek, she threw my arm away. She didn't want any of me tonight. She wanted to be left alone to brood or to repent over her choice of life partner.

I lay flat on my back, with my arms half-bent behind my head. I kept staring at the dimly visible muddy white ceiling. In the dark of the room, I could see the light fixture and its ceramic squared-shade hooked on the ceiling. My thoughts were traversing over memory lane.

***

I recalled how close to two years ago, on August 8th, 1974, I had moved from Canada's Eastern coastal city of Halifax to Ottawa. This day had become historic as the 37th President of the United States, Mr. Richard Nixon, had resigned as a result of the famous Watergate scandal. He had passed on his presidency to his vice-president, Mr. Gerald Ford.

I was twenty-six years old, and had just completed my master's degree in economics-statistics from the University of Dalhousie in Halifax. I had gotten a job as a research analyst at the federal government's Department of Consumer and Corporate Affairs, located at Tunney's Pasture in Ottawa. I considered myself lucky that I didn't have to search for a job – I got it while I was in the last semester of my degree. I didn't have to wait too long, or experience any period of unemployment, as was typical for most of the persons aged between eighteen and thirty in Halifax. Since I wanted to pursue a career researching on economic and financial issues faced by households in Canada, I heartily welcomed the opportunity to work in Ottawa – the nation's capital where most of the political actions and nation's business were conducted. I thought I had a good chance to contribute to the nation's economic and social policies, and as a result, make a high profile career – with good earnings and supplementary employment benefits, including a defined-benefit retirement pension indexed to the annual rate of inflation.

I had arrived in Ottawa with bare essentials including a few clothes. After living for a week at the Skyline Hotel in downtown Ottawa, I was able to find this apartment and as a renter, signed its lease on August 15th, 1974. Since I had moved from an Ocean city with a water-front small crowded house, I was keen to live not only in a building closer to water, but also in a more open environment. Since this apartment was overlooking the Ottawa River, I didn't hesitate for a second to rent it – despite its high monthly rent. Moreover, this place was closer to my office in Tunney's Pasture and I could use a public transit to commute – at least until I bought my own car.

One Saturday morning, three weeks after arriving in Ottawa, I went to the Shepherds of Good Hope at Murray Street – a place providing food and shelter to the homeless in and around Ottawa. I wanted to volunteer my time over weekends for a good cause. Since I used to do this self-satisfying charity work at a Mission back in Halifax, I wanted to continue doing it after I learnt that Ottawa had a similar open house for the poor and the homeless.

I introduced myself to the Mission's supervisor, and expressed my desire to help in any capacity. Without a blink of an eye, the supervisor welcomed me on board and handed me an apron and a knife along with one big bowl of potatoes to peel, and another of tomatoes to slice – ingredients required for preparing the lunch for that day.

I joined a few other men and women volunteers of all ages in the big dining hall, containing several rectangular long wooden tables, with small wooden chairs placed on both sides. This hall, now occupied by ten to twelve volunteers, helping to prepare meals, would be filled up to its seams by noon by the city's poor and unfortunate homeless people, likely waiting not only to have lunch on that afternoon, but also to grab extra eggs and cheese sandwiches for their night's, or next day's meal. I picked a corner table, placed the two bowls filled up to their brims on it, and got to work.

While I was peeling potatoes, a young, petite, and attractive girl, with short and pointed nose, thin curvy lips, fully symmetric full cheeks, well-rounded mid-size breasts, with her long black tresses parted in the middle and touching her waist, wearing a printed sleeveless summer dress covered with a white apron, broke my concentration.

"May I join you?" She asked with a smile.

"Please ... by all means," I replied with a broad smile. I saw she was carrying a bowl full of slightly brownish boiled eggs. She had placed her bowl close to my two bowls, and sat on the chair opposite me.

"Are you new here?" she asked. "I don't think I have seen you before, at least, ever since I have been coming here on Saturday mornings."

"Yah," I replied, still smiling. "I came to this city from Halifax three weeks ago as I got a job with the Department of Consumer and Corporate Affairs."

"Oh! The Ocean city ... I love the ocean. Maybe some day I would have the chance to visit your famous Peggy's Cove. My grandparents live in the close neighbourhood – Holyrood area in St. John's, Newfoundland. I visit them occasionally. I must say – every time I go there, I love being near the ocean ... Hi, I am Amy Carson and you ...?"

"I am Robert Vaughan." I extended my hand to shake Amy's. "Pleased to meet you ... You come here every Saturday morning?"

"Yes," she replied cheerily. "I like volunteering my time here and talk to these vulnerable homeless people, understand them and the likely reasons behind their deprivation. Even though I can't do much for them, I feel really bad for them. I have a soft spot for them."

She kept peeling the shells off the eggs with her long thin fingers. She had her clean and trimmed fingernails polished in dark red. As she kept removing the brown shelling, I could see all clean white hard-boiled eggs she was placing back in the bowl.

"Someone else would mash these to make egg sandwiches," she added.

"Do you live close by?" I asked, and stealthily looked at her eye-catching face and sparkling black eyes. Our eyes met for a couple of seconds.

While doing our respective tasks, we occasionally looked at each other, perhaps weighing mutual compatibility of our personas. She blushed at times with a grin. I occasionally focused on her penetrating eyes, small sharp nose, thinner lips with a little bow under the nose, well rounded chin – all fitting well on her symmetric oval face. She had a small cleavage with small well-rounded boobs. She looked cool, elegant, and beautiful. She was talking freely, demonstrating her likely outgoing warm personality.

"I live in a one-bedroom apartment off King Edward Avenue – just a walking distance from here," she replied. "I am an Ottawa girl – born and raised in this city. Even though my parents live in the city, I live alone. I work as a sales representative at the Hudson Bay downtown. How about you? Do you live in the neighbourhood?"

"Not really ... I live in the west-end, off Richmond Road. I have a two-bedroom apartment, with a balcony overlooking the Ottawa River and Gatineau Hills." I bragged about my apartment to impress her.

"Wow! That's interesting. Must be costing you a fortune," she remarked with smiling and intriguing eyes. "I can't afford that sort of luxury. You don't mind me asking you why you are in a two-bedroom apartment. Are you married? Have children?"

"Neither," I replied promptly to keep her interest in me fully well and alive. "I use one bed-room strictly for study as my job involves a lot of reading and writing. That room is full of stacks of books, journals, and periodicals." I gave her a convincing description.

"So you are a book-worm. Have you made any friends in the city in the last three weeks?" she asked.

She took one potato from my bowel and started to peel it. She had finished her task of removing shells of hard boiled eggs.

"None other than my office colleagues," I replied, while peeling the last potato at hand. "Today being Saturday, I have no access to them. Since I used to volunteer my time at a similar Mission in Halifax, I just thought I would come here and keep myself occupied during the morning. Like you, I fully sympathize with all the destitute and the homeless, but can't do much to help them other than simply volunteer my time to feed them."

"I am glad to hear that," she uttered softly, and stood up to carry her bowl of white eggs to the kitchen. "I see you are done with potatoes, too," and lifted my bowl as well to take it inside. "I will be back in a minute," she said, and walked away.

When she came back, she was carrying loafs of bread and a container of butter. She was going to butter the slices of bread to be served at lunch. We had another ninety minutes before noon – the official time to start serving the lunch.

After she sat on her chair, she looked at me, and asked hesitatingly,

"How can I get a government job? I want to get out of this sales job. Since you work for the government, can you help me get in there, or tell me how to get in," she sought my advice.

"The best way to get in there is to learn some marketable skills – skills that the employer wants." I suggested to her without any reservation.

"Such as ..." She gave me a blank stare, seeking some more explanation. She had a slice of bread in one hand, and a butter knife in the other. She had stopped buttering that slice.

"Upgrading your accounting and/or administrative skills. If I were you, I would enrol at Algonquin College to earn a certificate or diploma in either of these fields. Since there's a good demand for people in these areas, I am quite sure you will get an opportunity to get in there. It may take you twelve to eighteen months to complete the course though," I articulated to her.

"Thanks," she replied. "I really appreciate your suggestion. I will contact the Algonquin College and see if it has any such course available in its Eastern Campus, or I will have to go all the way to its main Western Campus."

She had re-started buttering slices of bread.

By noon, the hordes of homeless and the most vulnerable in the city were lined up outside the kitchen. These were men and women of all ages, creeds, and races. Men were mostly in baggy pants with just a dirty vest or sport shirt on, mostly unshaven, with black or grey beards, some had front teeth missing, and others had dishevelled hair. Women, on the other hand, were wearing either cheap knee-long summer dresses or sleeveless blouses with jeans with torn patches. As they entered the hall, they all looked happy, cheery, and talkative as they all were going to eat to their heart's content a free meal.

Not that these persons had no source of income to survive, but whatever weekly/biweekly/monthly financial assistance they received from municipal, provincial, and/or federal government, most of them would likely spend it on booze and drugs either to forget momentarily the pathetic situation they were in, or enjoyed hallucinating themselves with street drugs mixed with beer and other booze. One could see how badly they seemed to have given up any hope of improving their situation. In my opinion, they could have done better, provided they were willing to work hard and do whatever it takes to get out of this dire situation. Since I wasn't there to lecture them, I simply did what I was asked to do: serve them with soft cold or hot drinks.

Amy was asked to act as a server at the food counter serving fried potatoes whereas I stayed in the dining hall serving drinks including tea, coffee, coke, orange juice, or plain water. I could hear Amy's sweet voice as she enthusiastically welcomed each person with a "Hello, how are you ... good to see you again ... want some more fries?" I could sense how warm and out-going she was as a person compared to my more introverted, quiet, shy, and book-worm personality.

After serving food, Amy got back to the main hall and asked me if I wanted to eat there, as volunteers were also allowed to eat after serving the intended crowd. I didn't want to. She didn't either, as she had to go to work.

"See you next week," she said and gently tapped my upper left arm, adding, "take care," and she left the Mission.

***

Amy and I kept meeting at the Mission on each Saturday morning, helping cut vegetables and fruits to be served at lunch that day. We both looked forward to Saturday mornings to meet and chat in order to know each other well.

On the fifth Saturday, I asked Amy,

"Do you think we could meet outside this Mission or on any other day besides Saturday?"

"You are asking me for a date?" She winked and chuckled.

"Very much so," I replied confidently.

"Gosh! I didn't think you would ever ask," she looked astounded. "What's taken you so long to ask?" she questioned me with her totally blushed face. "I was quite willing to date you right after our first meeting. Why do you think that of all people in the room, I chose to sit with you on the first day I saw you. My sixth sense told me that you were well educated, but were shy to sit with others. I liked the look of you and minding your own business. Since I like serious guys, I simply wanted to befriend you. You are a good looking, slim and handsome guy, well-educated, with a compassionate nature, holding a well-paying professional job with potentially good future. What more can a girl look for in her potential date? We now know well enough of each other since we have chatted long on four consecutive Saturdays." She paused for a minute. "When and where do you want to meet?" she asked me and looked into my eyes.

I was totally mesmerized with Amy's forth-righteous response.

***

We kept dating for more than a year. We would go for a dinner, a movie, long walks, or long drives. During this period, Amy continued to work at the Hudson Bay and had also begun her studies to earn her diploma in accounting and administration. She had all the time not only to date me, but also to take care of my emotional and sexual needs, cook for me on weekends, and accompany me on drives outside of Ottawa over the long weekends.

Even though she had had sex before meeting me, she always seemed to enjoy having sex with me. She looked sexually contented after one or two orgasms. She even told me that my soft touch to her body alone was good enough to make her all wet with excitement. I didn't have to spend too much time on foreplay before entering her in any position. One time she even confessed that she always found herself sexually aroused and excited in my company, so much so, that she wanted to spend her life with me. And that, in turn, made it easier for me to propose her.

I remembered how almost a year after our first meeting at the Mission, I had invited Amy to a dinner at the Ottawa's only revolving restaurant at Kent Street. From this restaurant, one could have a breath-taking bird's view of the city, Gatineau Hills, and Ottawa River. While eating at tables, one could, at a pace even slower than that of a snail, encircle all four directions, and back to where one started. Amy had never been to this quite exquisite restaurant. Even though she got suspicious of my moves, she masked her feelings well.

After wining and dining, we went to the dancing area to dance on a slow tune. As we were dancing, wrapped in each other's arms, Amy mumbled softly in my ears, "What's in your sleeve, tonight?" She kept looking into my eyes.

I quietly gazed at Amy's attractive and naughtily smiling face, realized that either the secret was almost over, or I could no longer keep it – whatever the reason – I bent on my knees, still holding her hands,

"Will you marry me, sweetheart?" I asked her.

I released my right hand from her clasp, pulled the engagement ring out of my coat pocket, and waited for her long awaited response.

For a minute, Amy gasped. She didn't know what to say. Her eyes, now full of tears of joy, had unravelled her heart's desire. She bent slightly, and cupped tightly my hands.

"Oh, I would love to," Amy had responded, and she put her open hands on the upper sides of my arms, symbolically lifted me up. She let me slide the ring on the ring finger of her left hand. All other dancers in the room, watching this live show of love and emotion, clapped and applauded in thunder. Amy and I kissed each other passionately. Everyone in the room congratulated us.

Four weeks after the engagement, Amy and I got married at Ottawa's Christ Church Cathedral on Queens Street, and held the wedding reception at the same hotel for our immediate families and friends. And right after our honeymoon, Amy had moved in my apartment.

***

I was still reminiscing that ever since Amy and I had been living as a couple, it had become a routine that we both would go to bed at the same time, Amy lying to my left, wrapping my upper body with her arm, and her face resting against my chest, and my right arm wrapping her back. We both would likely fall asleep in each other's arms. Either one of us was free to initiate sex almost each and every night, indulge into romantic pillow-talks, have penetrating sessions to our hearts content. We both were happy to have found deeper and compassionate love for each other until this issue of scarcity of financial funds and indebtedness had begun to constrain our personal relationship.

Tonight was the first time that Amy was lying away from me. She didn't want me to touch her. It was gradually sinking into my head that my inability to fulfill her materialistic desires was the root cause of her distress, which in turn, had begun to create a gulf in our personal relationship. She was acting no different than any other woman who wants and values a spouse with abundant resources.

CHAPTER TWO

By late June 1976, Amy had successfully completed her certification in 'Accounting, Administration, and Human Resources' from the Algonquin College. After scanning the government job posters on display in hallways and the cafeteria of the college, she opted to apply for a job in the administration section of the federal government's Department of Manpower and Immigration. With her warm and exuberant personality, and good people-oriented skills, and fresh credentials, she got the entry level clerical job in the so-called 'CR-Group' at the lowest starting salary. She was very happy. For her, it was a big success. She had accomplished her mission – to get a government job.

She was no longer going to continue her sales job that she had detested for several reasons, including its shift work, unpredictability of tenure, and above all, had no work-related pension as a future security. At least in this federal government's job, she had that security as she would be covered under a defined benefit pension plan – a plan in which she would contribute about seven to eight percent of her salary, and after thirty-five years of service, would be entitled to receive seventy percent of the average of her last best five years of salary. This pension income was to be adjusted annually by the nation's rate of inflation.

As a federal government employee, I had a similar plan. That meant that after retirement, both of us would have a steady source of retirement income, supplemented further by benefits from employee and employer contributory Canada Pension Plan, and from federal government's Old Age Security program funded entirely by government's tax revenue (benefits from this program were universal at one time, but now are clawed back in part or full – depending on one's total annual income). That meant that we both would have a steady flow of income while retired – a situation that was still moons and moons away. Nonetheless, it still provided a warm feeling that our retirement years were financially secured. How we managed and/or overcame our day-to-day financial hiccups during the course of our work-life was a different issue altogether.

On the first Saturday of July, Amy and I drove back to the construction site off Woodroffe Avenue and Knoxdale Road areas to have another look at model homes being built by local developers. We also visited the site just behind the Nepean Sportsplex. Now that we were specifically looking for a semi-attached house, Amy liked one two-storey house, with one large room to be split into a formal dining room and a living room, along with a small kitchen and a powder-room at the ground floor, and three bedrooms with one full bathroom on the second floor. Since I didn't want to leave our car out in the open during the winter months – because of the damaging effects of snow, sleet, and freezing rain – we made sure that the house we had picked had a one-car garage attached to it. All in all, this house had a live-in area of fifteen hundred fifty square feet.

With a separate driveway, and with enough space between this and those of the adjacent houses, this house looked like a detached house. However, with one shared wall of that large room along with that of the foundation, it was still a semi-detached house. By this time, Amy had reconciled and had accepted with reservations my promise to move in a detached unit in a few years time. This afternoon though, we were there to learn about the total mortgage amount required, monthly payment, and other potential associated costs to maintain that house. I was glad to see her somewhat excited as she looked around the model of the house she was going to own soon. I thought she was over her frustration and would henceforth be normal in her dealings with me including the playful and sensual activities in the bed.

By late July, we signed the deal on that house. It was going to cost us sixty-five thousand dollars. At the time, we had seven thousand dollars at hand, and thought this amount would be fine after paying five percent of sixty-five thousand dollars (that is, three thousand, two hundred and fifty dollars) as down payment.

Lo and behold, we had to pay from the remaining three thousand, seven hundred and fifty dollars, the land transfer cost, lawyer's fee, for sets of keys, and above all, for the movers. The obligatory five percent of the purchase price as the down-payment for the first-time home buyers was a Canadian norm set by the federal government's Canadian Mortgage and Housing Corporation (CMHC). In other words, we could move into a house with 95% mortgage provided by a bank, and this mortgage, in turn, was insured by CMHC. We had to pay the lump sum premium of this insurance, in case we defaulted on the mortgage and couldn't keep the house, for instance, due to the loss of our jobs, drop in income due to sickness or disability, or our untimely death, the CMHC would pay the bank the mortgage outstanding on the house.

Also, we were advised to purchase another insurance insuring our mortgage. This insurance ensured that a family wouldn't lose its house even after the sudden death of its primary breadwinner. We had to pay one hefty premium on this insurance.

And truth be told – the payment of this and several other amounts were totally unexpected and created a big whole in our budgeted funds for the house. This was just a wake-up call – the beginning of spending on essentials not planned at all.

As first time rooky buyers, we were now facing a big financial challenge. All of our enthusiasm about moving into a house had turned into a nightmare. I turned glum-faced, worrying about finding money to finance all of these unplanned expenses. The amount of money we had at the moment was not only limited, but also counted to the last cent on just essential items – items that we could foresee and plan in the process of buying a house. Expenses on essentials, but totally unplanned items had virtually shattered both our plans and hopes to live happily after moving into the so-called "our home".

In the meantime, the sales representative was observing the changing colours of worries and sadness on my face. With his experience, he could likely read my mind how quickly I was doing math in my head about the amount of money I had at hand and what was expected of me to spend. There was a huge shortfall. He could have easily refused us to sell the unit. But he was smart and likely well-trained by the builder, or we were too naïve about the real cost required to buy a house. He didn't want to lose customers who were currently short of cash, but had stable stream of future income with steady jobs.

He offered us a second mortgage of five thousand dollars at a rate of interest – one-and-a-half percentage point more than that charged on the first mortgage. The second mortgage had to be paid in full after five years. In the heat of excitement about moving into an owned home, Amy and I didn't worry for a minute how we would pay back the full amount of a second mortgage in five years. We simply signed the dotted line.

Evidently, we overlooked the reality that if we had no savings by now, how on earth could we save with two mortgage payments and other monthly commitments on paying off bills of utilities, phone, cable, payment on credit cards, and so on? From where this saving would ever come to repay the second mortgage? I didn't want Amy to go through another depression. After all, she had married me with some expectations, and I, in turn, was obligated to fulfill them – come hell or high water.

We instructed the sales representative to go ahead with the deal. He filled in all the forms, detailing monthly payments, including that on the second mortgage, and the estimated annual property taxes, which were roughly one percent of the value of the house.

Combining the main mortgage and property tax payments into one payment was another tactic, followed by chartered banks and other financial institutions issuing mortgages, to ensure that the property didn't fall in City's hands in case of any default on property taxes. Mortgage lending institutions always wanted to have first access, or outright ownership of property in case of any mortgage default.

There was nothing wrong with that. The financial institution had to protect its investment. The bad part of this deal was that those vulnerable and non-savers were being further penalized by being forced to lose the potential interest income on the amount of property taxes, if left as savings in their personal bank account until the payment was due. The way the rep laid out the numbers, the main mortgage amounted to five hundred thirty-two dollars, second mortgage one hundred and eight dollars, and property tax sixty-five dollars, totalling up to seven hundred and five dollars. This meant that of my take-home monthly income of thirteen hundred dollars, fifty-four percent of it would be consumed by these three payments alone. I would have to pay other bills, payments on credit cards, any unexpected maintenance, and other day-to-day expenses from the remaining forty-six percent. That looked like a hell of a challenge to me. I wasn't going to ask Amy for any financial help to pay off such financial commitments.

***

When Amy got her first salary cheque, she gave it to me to deposit it in my bank account. She wanted us to open up a joint account. I complied with her request and added her name to my account, but refused point-blank her offer to deposit her cheque into that account. She was stunned. She gave me a stern look,

"What's wrong?" she asked.

"Nothing is wrong," I replied. "It's your hard-earned money, and you have the full right to spend it anytime, anywhere, on anything you wish to buy. I want you to exercise full control on your money. I, as a man, have the ultimate responsibility to run the house, pay bills, look after your well-being." I strongly insisted upon her.

"But this is family's money too. What's wrong with that?" she persisted.

"Granted, this is family's money, but my manly ego would never accept that I am running this home, or living on my wife's income," I vehemently replied.

"That's a stupid way of thinking," she replied annoyingly. "I think we will do better by having one family account. I don't like your male chauvinistic attitude."

"You have a right to your thinking, the same way I have to mine," I responded coolly. "I suggest you open a separate account under your name. I respect your wishes to pool family's income. But I insist that you fully control your money. Feel free to spend on anything you want to buy for yourself or for the house. As an independent earner, you don't need my permission to shop around for anything. On the other hand, if you insist on alleviating my financial worries, then you can do one thing…"

"What's that," she cut me off. She was too eager to know.

"From now on, you can just buy groceries for home," I completed my sentence. "That way, I wouldn't have to budget for family groceries."

"Are you sure?" she wanted to confirm. "I like your suggestion. That way I can chip in the family's expenses, and also exercise control on my money as you want me to do."

"I didn't suggest that without a reason," I gloatingly replied. I gazed at her. Her anger had begun to fade away, bringing her attractive face to normalcy. "I know you too want to retain your financial independence, as you have always felt bad asking me for over-the-budget money for groceries, or for buying other day-to-day little things. From now on, you are financially independent. Save whatever you can. That also will be a family's saving. It's just that I don't want you to feel that you want my permission to spend on your personal needs."

"Thank you, dear," she replied, and gave me a gentle hug. "I really appreciate your understanding."

On the surface, I was successful in convincing Amy to keep her monetary independence, and spend on her personal needs, and on groceries, as she saw fit. In my mind, though, I was fully aware of my problem of inadequate cash flow to run the house, and wanted any help to improve it, but I refused to let her access my account, or worry at all about paying any bills, or the maintenance of the house. As a man and primary earner, I was responsible to provide her a worry-free life. It was not her job to run the house, or feel stressed out after learning the financial reality. It was deeply entrenched in my mind that a woman, even if she was earning, or even a chief executive officer of a company, she preferred her man take care of household matters including its maintenance, as well as treat her gently with respect, and above all, sexually satisfy her.

Not only did I want to keep Amy away from the heat of any financial worries, I, as a man of the house, wanted to keep an exclusive control on family finances. I wanted full financial privacy. Neither did I want her interference in my financial affairs nor did I want her to know how I was juggling these finances to pay the monthly bills and other committed payments. I wanted her to enjoy her life and not even think how the house was being run financially. She simply had to ask what she wanted. How that wish of hers was to be financed was entirely my responsibility. Because, in it rested my male pride, ego, manliness, position as a provider, and a caretaker of the family, and above all, ability to earn her love, affection, care, and respect. In my opinion, no woman, irrespective of her beauty, nurturing nature, or financial status, was ever happy, or sexually satisfied, with a man unable to provide or cater to her wishes. I strictly believed in my role as a provider and hers as a nurturer, and a receiver.

Also over time, I had observed Amy's spend-thrift habits. Like most women, she would compulsively be buying clothes, footwear, real gold or artificial jewellery. I feared that if she ever had access to my account, I might not even be able to pay the monthly bills – let alone any other expenses associated with the house maintenance.

***

In the first week of September 1976, Amy and I took possession of our very first house. Out of love and respect for Amy, I wanted her to set her foot first in our brand new house. It meant a world to her. Like any other woman, she aspired to live in a house of her own, and now, she was entering it. This house was her castle. And she was the queen of this castle. She could furnish it, set it up in her own way. I could see a glow of some satisfaction on her face.

At that very moment, I knew in my heart the kind of financial stresses and strains I was going to face, but I successfully hid them well, and softly whispered to her, "Welcome to our new house."

She gently kissed my cheek and walked in for a thorough inspection of the house. The delivery van would soon be at the door.

Since we had moved from an apartment, we had some furniture to furnish the living room, enough of dishes, pans, and other accessories to fill-in the kitchen, a bed for the master bedroom, and enough of accessories to furnish a bathroom. But all of this was not enough. We needed to cover the living-room windows with drapes, and other windows with blinds or curtains, to maintain privacy. We didn't want all passersby in that locality to keep peeping into our empty house.

So, after moving in, our first and immediate concern was to cover all of the glass windows and doors, and that required purchasing a mix of shears, blinds, and opaque and good quality drapes. Again to fix and install these things, we needed essential tools like a hammer, screw drivers, pliers, measurement tape, and so on. All of that required a lot of cash which we didn't have. All of our funds had been used by the time we had paid the lawyer, and stepped into the house. The question was from where to buy all of these things on credit and pay back monthly.

We turned to Sears – an average price department store – and invited one of its interior decorators to come, advise us about the custom-made drapes for the living room, and install all of the other required coverings. Everything had to be charged at a high rate of interest of around thirty percent a year. Since Sears didn't accept the regular credit cards like VISA or MasterCard (MC), we had to open an account with the store – that also meant one more monthly debt payment.

I was now making three debt payments a month, i.e., on VISA, MC, and Sears, besides the regular bills on heat, hydro, water, cable, gas for car, telephone, and other expenditures required during the early stages of settlement in a new house – all from the five hundred ninety-five dollars left after paying for two mortgages and property tax.

It was quite a tough nut to crack. All of these bill payments were mandatory, and especially the utility bills had to be paid in full. The only leeway I had was to adjust my payments on the two credit cards, and to Sears.

I started to make minimum payments on these cards, knowing full well how essential these were to protect my credit rating, which in turn, would also make me eligible to apply and get more future credit or loans. I was equally aware that these minimum payments were simply paying the interest on outstanding balances and not reducing any principle. I was simply keeping the wolf away from the door, buying time for a change in my level of income, primarily from a job promotion, or a raise negotiated by civil servants union. I had no other source of income.

Since these accounts were of revolving nature, I could make a minimum monthly payment and still use these sources of credit to furnish our house, pay any bill due to lack of cash, or for other day-to-day purchases, until I reached their pre-specified limits. Amy, on the other hand, was religiously putting food on the table without a worry, and spent the rest of her salary anyway she wanted, or saw fit.

Two months after we had moved into the house, Amy wanted to furnish the dining room. She wanted to buy a proper set including the hutch, buffet, dining table with six chairs. She wanted me to accompany her to some local furniture stores. I had been anticipating about this demand of hers.

"Can't we wait a little longer?" I suggested to her, trying to postpone her demand. "We just took two mortgages, owe money to Sears on customized drapes and blinds, and our credit cards are almost full. How are we going to pay for the dining set?"

"I am sorry I can't wait," she replied furiously. "I want this and other things to furnish our home while I am young. What will I do with these things in my old age? We can get a loan from the bank to pay for it," she suggested.

"You know you are following a typical phenomena what the economists call a 'life cycle' consumption theory," I shot back.

"What's that?" she queried.

"Almost all families (except those affluent and/or those with established well-run businesses, or large savings) use credit extensively when they are young and starting out their lives because their expenditures exceed their incomes. With their starting low salaries coupled with much larger needs to acquire and furnish a home, establish a family unit, they have no source of funding other than to use credit, provided they are eligible to access it on account of their job stability and a steady flow of income. Banks and financial institutions are well aware of it, and they capitalize on the vulnerability of mid-income young and middle-age families in order to maximize their income earned in the form interest charged on credit cards and other secured and unsecured loans. Then as these families age, their needs also decline and they begin to save as their incomes now exceed their expenditures. Mind you, there are a few older families too that use credit either to supplement their low income, or to renovate their older or worn-out homes, etc." I was now explaining to Amy what I had learnt on my job about how Canadian families were using credit. "Using credit isn't bad ..."

"Then what's the problem?" Amy frustratingly interrupted me. "I am simply suggesting that we borrow money from the bank to get the dining-room set. Don't you want to see your house properly furnished like that of others? Since we bought this place, we can't leave it unfurnished. Like it or not, we have to furnish it."

"Indeed we have to," I concurred with her, "but we also have to see if we can make its monthly payment. Right now, we are barely managing. I really would have to squeeze elsewhere to make a payment on this loan." I didn't want to upset her by divulging all the details about how I already was juggling finances by stealing from Peter to pay Paul.

"You know these things better," she commented, shrugging her shoulders. "I just want the dining set, not a big analytic sermon from you on how to use credit or how many are using it."

"To be honest with you," I continued, "I was thinking of getting a small loan to furnish the bedrooms upstairs, have the eaves-troughs installed around the house to avoid any water damage to its foundation, and put a wired fence around the house to stop animals and strangers walking on our property. I thought we were fine for the time-being with our small dining table that we used in the apartment. But if your priority is to fix the dining room before the bedrooms, so be it. I just want to see you happy."

"I know that," she replied with a wide grin of victory. "Right now, I want the dining set. Tomorrow, if I want to invite some friends over, I want to ensure that the house is properly furnished. I don't want to see them leave with any poor impression about our financial status. We make good money."

"Well, that's what you think," I mumbled and left her alone in the kitchen.

***

While Amy was at Algonquin College, she had, by her warm and people-oriented personality, attracted hoards of friends who wanted to invite us at their home for dinner, social get-togethers, and three-card poker games. Some of these successfully ran their owned businesses while others were working as paid workers – like us – either in the public or private sector. Financially, we were quite a mixed bunch with those with businesses with much higher incomes compared to all those paid workers earning from mid-to-high range salaries.

The reciprocation of hospitality was the key to the success and continuity of this social cohesion. To that effect, Amy too had to invite friends for dinners or other ad-hoc get-togethers in smaller or larger groups. That not only put extra pressure on me to furnish the house much quicker with spiralling debt than at the rate I could afford, but also to use borrowed funds to entertain them well. A good, lavish, and warm hospitality never came that cheap. Since we were wined and dined well and treated generously, we, needless to say, had to reciprocate the same – if not more liberally – with our open heart and warmness. How internally and truly we treated or respected each other because of our differences in financial levels, sizes and kinds of homes we occupied, was a different matter altogether and remained buried under the rug. The bottom line was that we were a very heterogeneous group with varied personal interests, tastes, preferences, and above all, vocal skills. I was more or less the quietest member in the group.

Amy, on the other hand, was a social animal – totally opposite to my serious, bookish, and anti-social personality. She always wanted to be in the company of people, at her place or others', so much so that I began to dread weekends. I very much hated to indulge into small talks, or shoot the breeze, or indulge in any pretentious talks. I was in the group strictly because of Amy for whom such social get-togethers were raison d'être of her life. I considered it as an essential marital adjustment to appease my spouse.

***

Banks and other financial institutions are not benevolent institutions. These are in business to sell money to make money as a commodity and maximize their income in the form of interest earned on unpaid credit card balances, and other short and long term secured and unsecured loans. To that effect, borrowers, especially those who carry-over monthly balances, are their easy prey and they do their damndest to keep this group under their thumb. Not only the greater the number of borrowers, but also the longer the time span these are financially tied or under obligations, the better it is for the institution's financial health and the year-end indicators of net revenue and profit.

One of the ways these institutions keep these vulnerable and needy borrowers as their income contributory clients is to keep increasing borrowers' limit on their credit cards and/or access to credit in general. With interest income earned from such borrowers, the financial institutions can further widen their business by attracting more clients by offering credit cards with built-in incentives including points for air miles, travel insurance, cash-back discounts – to name a few. Any additional cost incurred on providing such benefits is largely paid out of all the interest paid by borrowers unable to pay in-full the balances on their credit cards. In other words, those able to pay full-balances on credit cards enjoy such built-in incentives on the backs of those unable to pay-in-full or carry-over balances.

Since I had been one of those who used credit cards extensively and also was unable to pay off in-full the credit balance each month, the financial institution FI-I, with whom I also had the mortgage agreement, must have labelled me as its most valuable client. No wonder that one day I got a letter from this institution informing me that in order to help me meet my future needs, the institution was pleased to increase my credit card limit by another three thousand dollars.

On receipt of this note, I quietly thanked the Lord and the institution for adding a new breath and hope and extended my life at least for the next few more weeks or months –
depending on how much I had to spend on paying bills, or for other necessities at home. I fully recognized that by increasing my credit limit and enabling me to survive on additional credit, the institution was letting me tighten my neck myself with a noose, or push myself deeper in the debt hole from where I could never recover. All of this didn't matter to the institution as long as it was getting its minimum payment on time, and I, in turn, was protecting my credit worthiness, also encouraging the institution to squeeze my neck more. I

would have to increase my monthly payment, which in reality meant simply augmenting institution's interest income. In other words, I would be enriching the institution rather than reduce any of my liability. In standard economic terms, I would simply be paying the cost of using a borrowed capital.

Such ad-hoc increases on credit card(s), unsolicited but essential for my survival, became an intrinsic part of my life after owning the house. Over time, I began to receive letters from several other financial institutions as well inviting me to apply for their credit cards. They all wanted me to contribute to their revenue. From their perspective, I was a good prey, eligible or qualified to receive their credit card because I was young, had a stable job, high income, and above all, owned a home – list of key characteristics of a borrower that any lender would check before approving credit and fixing its limit. Like any other institution, they were in business and looking for more clients. They didn't want to miss borrowers like me. I, on the other hand, was heartily thanking them for providing me with more and more cash I needed to maintain my household.

After almost three years in the house, I had paid back the bank loan on the dining set. Also, by this time, my VISA and MC had reached their enhanced credit limits. Sears' account had not yet reached its limit. Minimum payments had hardly made a dent in the amount of debt I owed on credit cards including Sears.

With these cards now almost blocked and of no use, I was now finding it hard to pay the bills from my salary left after paying the monthly payments on two mortgages and property tax. Even though Amy was working at the lowest clerical position, she was earning enough to bring in weekly groceries. So physically we were surviving all right, and in the eyes of neighbours and friends, leading a comfortable life, but in reality, I didn't have any money to pay the bills and other day-to-day expenses.

With this tightened situation, I decided to take a consolidated loan to pay off the outstanding debt on all credit cards. I thought it would also give me some needed cash flow to manage my life and the house. I could live a little stress free life. I planned to pay off this loan within three years.

There was a financial institution FI-II in Tunney's Pasture – just across the road from my office at Consumer and Corporate Affairs. I decided to seek a loan from this institution rather than go to FI-I, that had provided me with the first mortgage.

***

"Hi, I am Robert Vaughan," I introduced myself to one of the loan managers at FI-II. "I work across the road at Consumer and Corporate Affairs. I want to apply for a consolidated loan."

"Have you an account with us?" she asked.

"No. Not yet," I replied.

"No problem," she spoke with a smile. "How long have you been working there," she asked.

"About five years."

"In what group and level?" she further enquired just to get a feel about my income level.

"I am a statistician, affiliated to the economists and statisticians group, at level five, making close to thirty-four thousand dollars."

"What do you do?" She continued her enquiries about the kind of job I had.

"As a statistician, I research and analyze and write comprehensive reports on personal indebtedness and bankruptcies of Canadians."

"So you must know a lot about Canadians' financial situation including the level of their indebtedness." She was inquisitive.

"Yes, I do," I replied. "I am familiar with the level of indebtedness of Canadians. Right now, I need money to pay off my debt on credit cards."

"How much?" she asked.

"Seven thousand and five hundred dollars," I replied.

"You have any collateral?" She inquired.

"Besides my three-year old house, I have about fifteen hundred dollars in Registered Retirement Savings Plan, and another fifteen hundred in stocks," I replied confidently.

"That's good," she replied with a smile. "Just take this form, fill it out, and bring it back to me. It may take a few days before you are approved and get the money. But I am afraid you will have to surrender your credit cards."

She gave me the form to fill out. I moved to another table while she went back to her desk.

Surrendering the credit cards meant handing over my lifeline. I had been relying so much on these cards, buying time to see a change of tide in my life. I was a bit stressed out, but was quite optimistic about my future as well as my steadily rising income stream. I was young, close to the mid-thirties, and had a full life ahead of me. I was least discouraged to see myself in this messy situation, carrying that much debt. The mortgage debt I owed didn't bother me that much as I knew it was a good debt – used to acquire the most important asset of our life – a house, that would in all likelihood appreciate over time as well as provide the family some future security. I simply attributed this financially dire situation to my life cycle stage where expenses were bound to be way higher than my net income.

Nonetheless, I felt hurt and insulted by the loan manager's demand. This really bruised my ego. The loan manager's voice kept reverberating into my ears,

"You will have to surrender your credit cards."

On one hand, I couldn't afford to lose this opportunity to consolidate my loans by disagreeing to surrender cards, and on the other, I argued with myself about what good the cards were if I couldn't use these any longer? I thought of seeking the loan from FI-I. What would happen if that institution refused my request for another loan, as it already owned my first mortgage? Then I wouldn't have any chance to clear up the outstanding balances on these three accounts.

Since I was familiar with the conditions of credit market and with rules, regulations, and policies of Canadian financial institutions, I knew that all institutions more or less followed similar policies. After rehashing the situation in my mind, I surrendered my two credit cards along with the loan application.

After almost a week, I got the money I asked for. Not only that, the institution had also offered me an open and revolving line of credit worth ten-thousand dollars. I thought it was likely due to the surrendering of credit cards. The institution wanted me to use their funds and contribute to its interest income rather than use credit cards and enrich their issuers. After all, the institution was in a competitive business, and like its counterparts, would do everything possible to attract more clientele.

Now I didn't have any debt on credit cards, or with Sears. I no longer had to pay just the interest on three outstanding amounts. I was making one payment including principal and interest, and consoled myself that after three years, I would be debt free. I was no longer throwing my hard-earned money – simply paying out 'interest on credit' – in a drain. But then again, no institution was forcing me to dole out my money in a drain. It was all my own doing. I had borrowed money from them on my own volition. Thank goodness. I have repaid all of it.

I was now going to pay on the two mortgages, property taxes, and this consolidated loan, besides the regular monthly bills. I also could now save a little for the rainy day.

***

I wanted and tried hard to avoid the recurrence of this situation. I didn't want to live under loads of debt any more. I decided to supplement my income by looking for a part-time job over weekends and evenings.

Since I held a challenging, creative, mentally invigorating, and respectable job with the Consumer and Corporate Affairs, I didn't want to look for any low paying service job at some burger joint or sales outlet. I knew my personality too well. I was fully aware that I would be a complete misfit in any such job interacting and serving queues and queues of customers.

One day, I saw an advertisement that one local Radio Station was looking for a part-time news-reader. That job looked perfect and very promising to me. My intellect wanted that sort of stimulation – something new to deliver each and everyday. No monotony except the rigid schedule. It would not only supplement income, but also make me a household name, which I desperately wanted. I contacted the radio station, and was told to appear for an interview and a voice test.

On a scheduled Saturday morning, I accompanied Amy to the ByWard Market of Ottawa, and met representatives of the radio station on one of its paved sidewalks of York Street. After the formal interview (or chit-chat) was over, a technician held a microphone in front of my mouth, and one of the reps handed me a page containing two paragraphs –each with three short sentences. They were testing my voice, its sound, the pauses, the speed of reading, and the station's reps acted as listeners.

These reps were supposed tell how they felt when they heard my voice, my manner of delivery, pausing at right spots, etc. They wanted me to act naturally, and so I did. Amy kept looking at the whole episode, grinning at times, occasionally exchanging glances with me, and other reps. The Market, as usual, was full of people, including some on-lookers, with no vested interest. For them, it was some sort of a live show.

A month after the voice test, I was advised to take a voice and delivery improvement course from the Association of Broadcasters on weekdays during the regular morning hours at a cost of a couple of thousand dollars. I was not that keen to stay away from my regular job in order to complete this course and that too, at a personal cost of thousands of dollars. I had no money. I was looking for a job to supplement my income rather than enriching the Broadcaster's Association. So my attempt to earn both the income supplement and fame failed.

***

Since Amy was keen to experience motherhood – the innermost desire of almost all women around the globe – she was trying hard to get pregnant. Even though our romantic relationship was steadily withering away partly due to my inability to fulfill her wishes, and partly due the continuing financial stress I was silently suffering, our lovemaking sessions had considerably dropped. Even though she was no longer keen to have such sessions out of any mutual love, affection, or romance – like she was during our dating period, or after marriage until the issue of buying a house cropped up – she was eager to indulge into such sessions at times she thought she had the best chance to conceive – usually on or around her monthly period of ovulation. I could feel her anxiety to have a child of her own.

Even though I personally didn't want any extra mouth to feed under the prevailing financial constrains, I hated to deprive Amy from cherishing her most desired feminine longing. Considering how her attractive, slim and fit body was so tempting and desirous, I was not only always ready to hold her for a good lovemaking session, but also welcomed any gesture of hers to come closer to me and gratify my male hunger. At times, my testosterones were equally eager to impregnate her, but thanks to the pill and condoms, that my dick's invasion of her birth canal had not yet yielded any results to her liking. I had been successful in delaying her impregnation. She kept pestering me about letting her enjoy motherhood.

One late evening, Amy and I were getting ready to go to bed. I had just changed into a night-suit. After she drew the curtains together, she took off her nighty and unhooked her bra. I looked at her full mid-size breasts and wanted to pull one of her erected nipples into my mouth. She read my hungry eyes and perpetual hunger for her.

She winked and said, "Wait 'til we lie down on the bed."

She walked closer to me, put her arms around my neck, and frustratingly asked in a soft voice,

"Why don't you want children? Tonight, tell me the real reason."

"We can't afford them at the moment," I replied calmly. "I don't want to see them grow in poverty, or deprivation. I know how hard it is for a child to grow in that sort of environment, kill his/her desires, develop inferiority complex among friends, or experience other psychological problems. I know all this because I have lived through it. I don't want my children to go through the same mill."

"I don't think we are poor," she disagreed with me. She shook her head side ways. "Granted, we are not millionaires, but not poor either. I firmly believe we can raise them well. Moreover, each child brings his/her own destiny …"

"Just stop giving me that philosophy of yours about destiny," I cut her short.

I had heard her parroting that we were not poor. She had the faintest idea how I was managing financially and maintaining the house. For her, everything looked perfect, and hunky-dory. Granted, I wanted to shield her from all such financial worries, but I didn't want her to live forever with that naivety about the finances of our family either.

"In my opinion," I continued, "a man commits a crime and is totally irresponsible if he produces a child, knowing that he can't provide well for that child. Knowingly, I will not commit this crime," I added. "Children who are raised in poor families with no means to pursue higher education or chosen career paths really have no future. As adults, they likely will be a burden on the society rather than contributors to its well-being."

"What about the woman?" she snapped at me.

She was still not taking me that seriously.

"She's the one conceiving, and giving birth to a baby. She's a partner in crime, too."

"Only to some extent," I replied. "But I hold the man totally responsible because he's the one entering the woman, voluntarily or intentionally, to impregnate her, out of love, anger, frustration, or just to satisfy his manly ego. When a man is determined to have sex with his wife, she is often helpless, hardly has a choice. She mostly gives in to please her spouse – out of either love or affection for him, or simply marital obligation. That's what the nature of committed man-woman relationship is all about. It's the woman who suffers more mental anguish and frustration after giving birth to a child, as she nurtures the baby with inadequate resources. If worse comes to worst, that irresponsible man may even decide to run away from both the suffering mother and the child. He may become totally oblivious that he's the one who had put them into this misery in the first place." I became too emotional, kept dissuading Amy about having a child.

"Calm down, and listen to me," she removed her arms from my neck, and looked straight into my eyes. "Crime, or no crime, I want to conceive, experience the birth of a child, and above all, I want children for my future security. They would, at least, look after me in my old age. So stop lecturing and scaring me. I want you to act as a normal person and face reality."

"And what's the reality?" I snarled at her.

"You know darn well that I have been trying to conceive, and each time I conceive, I experience one problem or the other. I spoke to my gynaecologist about it. He sent me to a fertility specialist at the Civic Hospital. That fertility specialist wants you to accompany me to his clinic so that he could check your sperm count. Can you come with me?"

"No ... never. I have told you I am not that keen to have children under the present circumstances," I replied firmly. "Now, I am really annoyed that you have been doing all this running around without even telling me. I didn't know you were that desperate to have children."

"Well! Now you know," she responded with a shrug, and fumingly walked away to her vanity to brush her hair before going to bed. She had put her nighty back on.

"I'll see what I can do. I have to have your sperm tested," she mumbled loud enough for me to hear her innermost desire.

When she lay on her side of the bed, she was still fuming with anger and turned her face away from me. I too had no more desire left to suck on her nipple. She had killed my craving to hold her or engage in any intimate activity.

CHAPTER THREE

"Welcome to the eighties," Amy and I heard Mr. Pierre Elliott Trudeau on the TV, after his Liberal Party had won the general election in 1980. He had returned as Prime Minister after losing it for less than a year to Mr. Joe Clark, Leader of the Conservative Party.

At the time, the Canadian economy was going through a rough patch. Everyone was scared of looming recession in the country. And, that meant higher inflation, higher unemployment, and higher interest rates on consumer loans and mortgages. Mr. Trudeau, in his victory speech, was assuring Canadians that the new government would undertake measures to soften the upcoming onslaught of recession. I quietly wished the Prime Minister well in his planned strategy.

Since the Canadian economy heavily depended on that of our neighbour, the United States of America, Canada, with its rich resource base, sold close to three-fourths of its raw, semi, or finished products to south of the border. Naturally, any slump in the American economy was bound to slacken the Canadian economy as well. The economic recession that began in the United States slowly engulfed the Canadian economy as well. The majority of families in both countries had entered the eighties with fears about retaining their jobs, incomes, houses, and standards of living. Only a small proportion of families, with large sums of savings and investments, on the other hand, thrived during this period as they earned almost twenty percent return a year – allowing them to double their money in five years.

In the spring of 1980, Amy gave birth to our daughter, named Sarah. She was overjoyed. She had fulfilled her personal wish to experience giving birth to a child, also her long awaited symbol of security in old age. She now was a mother first, and a wife, second. Her role had changed. For me, on the other hand, it meant additional responsibility to help Amy in both the housework and care of Sarah, and above all, to provide for additional mouth to feed, and purchase on credit everything required to raise a newborn baby – ranging from clothes, to crib, car seat, and toys. My resolve not to take any debt for financing my day-to-day living simply melted away under the heat of the family needs of the day.

Amy took a maternity leave for a year, claiming two-thirds of her salary – still good enough to buy family groceries. I was now under more financial pressure to juggle with my finances. Almost every major purchase for Sarah was done on Sears's card. Toys and other day-to-day things were purchased on VISA and MC credit cards which, by the way, were returned to us by the respective banks within the first year of signing the loan agreement with FI-II.

With a new-born infant at hand, and a strong paternal responsibility to provide her not only with all the basic essentials, but also the luxuries, I had no choice other than to reactivate Sears's card, and start making a monthly minimum payment.

Right after Sarah was born, I became obsessed about her future education and with her potential career path. I knew my bleak financial situation. I feared that if my financial situation remained unchanged, I would never be able to provide her any education beyond high school – the latter was being financed by municipal property taxes that I was already paying monthly.

The financial institution FI-I paid such taxes twice annually from my account.

Sarah's education beyond high school was to be financed entirely by out-of-pocket costs. Even though she was still almost eighteen years away from attending any institution for post-secondary education, I had to take a step now to protect her higher education. I didn't think I would have the financial capacity to pave a successful career path for her when she was ready to embark on it.

With my strong belief in the value of higher education, and how it helps one to gain proper skills to have an uninterrupted level of potentially higher earnings, I kept looking for an opportunity to start saving monthly a small amount for Sarah's post-secondary education.

One day, I came across an ad in the newspaper about how Canadian Scholarship Trust (CST) had been helping parents to save for their children's higher education. The ad had invited parents to contact their local rep of CST.

Right away, I arranged a meeting with one of the reps. He had agreed to come over to our house one evening in order to discuss all the details about how funds were collected and disbursed on an annual basis while the child was enrolled at a post-secondary institution.

Since Sarah was receiving a small amount, less than twenty dollars a month, as a child allowance from the federal government's Child Benefit Programme (all families with children under eighteen years of age were entitled to receive such monthly benefits), I evened it up to thirty dollars, and opened a trust account under her name with CST. She would be entitled to get her tuition fee at the beginning of each academic year for four years.

I now felt at ease that the issue of Sarah's annual tuition fee was resolved. I was quite confidant that I would be able to finance her other day-to-today expenses from my savings or borrowings. Our daughter would at least be able to complete her post-secondary education.

***

By 1981, the economic recession in Canada had picked up its momentum and had started to ravage families both economically and financially – especially those living on low and medium fixed incomes. Not only members of a significant proportion of families were laid off, or lost jobs, dropping in turn their levels of incomes, but also the country experienced its highest ever rate of inflation at 12.5 percent as reported by Statistics Canada – Canada's central statistical agency. Not only that, the Bank of Canada's prime interest rate also sky rocketed and fluctuated between a low of 14.66 percent and high of 21.03 percent during the year, averaging to 17.93 percent for the year. These high bank rates, in turn, pushed up rates of conventional five-yearly mortgages issued by chartered banks and other financial institutions – rates varying between 15.50 percent and 21.75 percent, with an average of 18.38 percent for the year. These highest ever rates of interest on conventional five-yearly mortgages forced many home-owners due to renew their mortgages in 1981 to sell their homes as monthly payments became out of their reach, and even forced many to declare personal bankruptcy.

These tough economic times made me very nervous and jittery. Not only my first mortgage was due for renewal in 1981, but also I had to pay back in full the second mortgage – besides the payments on credit cards, including Sears. The thoughts alone about the upcoming mortgage renewal at an anticipated higher interest rate and its resulting higher monthly payment along with the payment of the full balance on second mortgage ran shivers in my body. I was completely stressed out. This stress level further escalated when Amy told me that she was going to give birth to another child just about the time of mortgage renewal.

I found myself in a rather sticky situation. I could no longer eat or sleep that well, or concentrate on work. I was very sad, nervous, finicky, and found totally helpless. Nothing seemed to be under my control. I was simply a victim of several market forces causing this recessionary torpedo blowing and damaging families, their properties, and livelihoods not only in Canada, but in several other countries including the United States.

Amy noticed my sad face and disturbing sleep pattern over days, and then finally asked me, "Is something the matter? Lately, I have been noticing you are tossing and turning, shaking the whole bed."

"I am sorry if I am disturbing you and your sleep," I retorted, "I didn't think you would feel any shakes as you are sleeping at the far end of the bed."

"Never you mind about disturbing me," she replied sympathetically, "just tell me what's bothering you?"

"I hate to mention this to you," I said serenely. "You watch the news, don't you? You know how our economy is heading for a serious recession and how the bank rate is accelerating. Since our mortgage is coming up for renewal, I am just too concerned about the size of the monthly payment I would have to make. Paying extra on mortgage means dispensing out more of our cash income, or cut down some other expenses, or rely more on credit. I have been thinking about all the potential scenarios …"

"Stop worrying about the potential scenarios," she interrupted me. "Just handle the situation as it comes," she advised me. "There's nothing in your control. If worse comes to worst, we can always sell the house. If we can't afford it, we can't afford it. So why keep worrying about it?"

"No. We will keep the house irrespective of the size of payment." I replied forcefully. By raising my tone, I wanted to re-emphasize and assure her that she would not be without a house.

"You know me," I added, "I have an analytic mind. I am looking at all the possibilities and their financial implications. It's a preparatory step, and I want to be ready to face and resolve it within my means. I am not like you who will dig a well when you are thirsty. In life, some planning is essential."

"You know my nature," she replied laughingly, "I don't worry about the future. I believe in living the moment. One person in the family is enough to worry about the future." She paused. "So what have you decided with your analytic mind?" she chided.

"I told you we will keep the house, no matter what," I repeated myself. "It's the only asset we have at the moment. It's one of those assets whose value steadily appreciates over time unless something drastically bad happens – like it's in an area no body wants to live in. Moreover, we can always use it or its equity built over time as collateral to secure a loan for any future investment, or to pay off debts cumulated over time. Above all, now that we are going to have a second child, we need more room for them to grow in a private and open environment. I would hate to see them grow in a high-rise apartment. Just think, an owned house is an asset that can be transferred easily from one generation to another without any penalty – at least in Canada where there are no taxes to pay on the transfer of principal residence."

"O man! I would never think of those things," she was aghast. "Your head is working overtime. For me, it's just good enough to know that we will be keeping this house."

"Yes, we will be, even if I have to live on borrowed money for a while," I confidently stroked her right shoulder. "You don't have to worry about a thing as long as I am around. Considering how the economy is going, we will renew our mortgage on a yearly basis until the rate of interest comes down, or stabilizes. Its current volatility can't go for ever."

"Couldn't you ask your Dad for some financial help to mitigate our potential hardship? We can always pay him back with a little bit of interest," she suggested.

"No chance in hell," I uttered frustratingly. "He couldn't even afford my tuition fee as I had to do multiple part-time jobs to finish my post-secondary education. How can I expect any financial help from him? Moreover, I strictly believe in self-reliance. Don't worry. We will manage."

CHAPTER FOUR

The recession had forced all levels of governments, i.e., federal, provincial, and municipal, to trim their expenditures as well. That meant cutting down primarily their respective wage bills, which in turn, was to be achieved by reducing the number of employees on their payrolls.

The Department of Consumer and Corporate Affairs was no exception. It had to reduce its allotted budget by letting some of its staff go as well, and cut several other administrative and analytic programs. My section on personal bankruptcies was not affected, and neither was the one compiling and analyzing business bankruptcies. I was much relieved to see that my peer, a close female friend, Jennifer Cartwright, working in the business bankruptcies section, was unaffected as well.

Jennifer (or Jen – as she preferred to be called by her abbreviated name) and I had joined the Consumer and Corporate Affairs the same day, nearly seven years ago. Since we both worked on the same floor and with just a couple of offices between us, we had developed over time a close working and social relationship – close enough to share personal and intimate details with one another. Our personal chemistries had blended very well. Right after taking the oath of secrecy and preserving confidentiality of data, and allegiance to the Queen, we started talking as if we knew each other for years.

Jen had moved from Hamilton to Ottawa along with her husband, Peter, who also had a diploma in computer sciences from McMaster University. She and Peter were classmates during their bachelor's program at McMaster, and had dated for few years at the campus. After completing bachelor program, she moved on to finish her masters in economics, whereas Peter headed to finish a diploma in computer sciences. Right after their studies, they got married in Hamilton, and later found jobs in Ottawa. Jen was a slim brunette, with an angelic oval face, cheeks with small dimples, short nose over her not too thin curvy lips, and almond shaped hazel eyes. She was as tall as me in her two-inch high-heeled black pumps. She had dark brown hair, left open, touching her thin waist-line, and falling all over her face. She had a long neck, with medium-size well-rounded pointed boobs that looked eager to jump out of her printed cotton summer dress.

The look of her rather innocent face with smiling eyes and furling hair were more than enough not only to attract my attention, but also to wake up my innermost manly desire for her. I looked at her attentively for a few moments. She looked very sensual. Her sensuality had prevailed all over me. I quietly wished to hold her in my arms right away. But that wasn't the opportune moment. After the formal introductions, I didn't want to miss the opportunity to walk with her to the same work floor.

And, ever since that day, there had hardly been a work-day that we didn't interact largely in connection with our work which, in turn, had too much commonality. It had become almost a daily routine to have coffee or lunch together – unless either one of us was committed elsewhere, absent on a sick or vacation leave, or was away on some official trip outside Ottawa. We both had a vague feeling that we were under the watchful eyes of both our peers and seniors.

One summer afternoon in late May, during the midst of this economic upheaval, we were having mid-afternoon coffee together.

"How's your hubby's job? Has this recession affected his company or his job too?" I asked Jen.

"Yes, his company is going through some changes," she replied, and shrugged her shoulder. "Like any other place of work. The unfortunate part is that the company was already undergoing some changes to fix its internal problems, and now this recession has complicated things, especially in respect to the sale of company's micro-electronic products and telephone switching systems."

"But his job is not affected at the moment?" I reconfirmed, giving her a pointed look.

"Not at the moment," she replied with a deep sigh of relief. "Who knows what's down the line? He has told me that his present company may even merge with its larger competitor simply to dominate the market." She took a sip of her coffee, and continued,
"You know, there's no job security in the private sector – the kind of security we have in our government jobs. I am glad my job is as secured as it can be. At least one of us would be able to pay the bills – even if it meant paying just the minimum payments."

"Speaking of minimum payments, I myself am quite concerned about my upcoming mortgage renewal in July. As the bank rate and its associated mortgage rate are rising so fast, as if there is no tomorrow, I am quite concerned about the kind of interest rate I am going to pay. Is your mortgage up for renewal too?"

I checked to see if she was in the same soup – as misery loves company.

"Not for another year," she replied quietly. "I hope the bank rate will drop by that time, and we get a better deal. Now that you mentioned about your upcoming mortgage renewal, I am really concerned about you." She straightened up her back on the chair, and asked, "How's Amy taking it? Is she still enjoying her maternity leave? How's Sarah doing?" She wondered aloud about my family's well-being.

"Both mother and daughter are doing fine," I replied. "You know that Amy is going to deliver our second child in September."

"I know. You have already told me," she reminded me with a smile. "It's good in a way that you two can raise both children almost at the same time. At least age-wise, they will not be that far apart. Also that's where you apply the concept of 'economies of scale' on many things including clothes, toys, and child care – just to name some. I wish I could do the same. Our son, Josh, is almost of your Sarah's age. When we will have another child, is an open question, because of the hanging uncertainty about Peter's job. He doesn't want to even talk about expanding the family, as he is too worried about his job, his future prospects."

"In a way he is acting wisely and not foolishly like me," I replied and focused on Jen's attractive face.

The look of her simple and angelic face with no make up temporarily soothed my tense nerves.

"Right now I seem to be the only one who's concerned about what's likely to happen in the next couple of months," I added.

"Well, we have to face whatever comes our way," she responded with full empathy. She gently tapped the top of my hand. After a momentary pause, she added, "Don't worry. Everything will be all right."

When I returned to my office, I found that Amy had called from home. I picked up the phone, and called her.

"I just got a call from the developer's sales representative who sold us this house," she informed me. "The company wants its balance outstanding on the second mortgage to be paid back in full by the end of July."

"I ... see," I replied haltingly. "The company has the right to ask."

"How are we going to pay?" she sounded alarmed and really panicked. "Do we have the money?"

"You don't worry." I assured her. I mulled over a pause and spoke in a much softer tone, "We will manage to pay, even if we don't have it."

I had gotten over my initial nervousness. Moreover, since Amy was in an advanced state of pregnancy, I didn't want to see her in any panicky or nervous situation. Her well-being was more important to me than the repayment of the loan. "Did the guy tell you the precise amount of payment?" I asked her in a dim voice, as I didn't want anyone in the adjacent rooms to hear about my financial affairs.

"He did mention the exact amount," she replied, "but I can't remember it now. It's about forty-five hundred dollars. How come in five years we have paid only five hundred dollars?" she queried.

"Well, the way it was initially amortized over twenty-five years, we have paid mostly the amount of interest, and hardly any of the principal," I replied gently. "You remember the sales person asked us the term of amortization – five or twenty-five years – and we picked the latter because we couldn't pay the larger monthly payment based on a five-year term."

"Yeah, I remember," she concurred with me. "Do we have money to pay?" she asked anxiously.

"Yes, most of it," I told her, continuing in a soft voice. "I will withdraw money from my Registered Savings Plans as well as from stocks. That will be three thousand, and the rest I will see how I can borrow from other sources. Now that I have received my new VISA and MasterCard, I can use either card to pay the remainder."

"Let's not do that," she suggested. "I will give you the rest from my savings. Since I don't have any large savings, I didn't offer to pay in the first place. But I can pay about fifteen hundred."

She sounded relieved as if a big burden was off her shoulders.

"By the way, did you request him for a possible short-term extension of the loan," I asked her out of sheer curiosity. "The company should know that families, especially those with mortgage and other debts, are currently going through hard times due to the prevailing bad economic situation."

"I did," she replied. "But the guy said that his company is not in a mortgage business. It sells houses, and provides only a short-term financial assistance to its potential customers – simply to facilitate the sale of a house. He suggested that we go to a proper mortgage company to get this sort of loan."

"Obviously, the company doesn't care once the house is sold. It got its money," I commented with sarcasm. "Don't worry. I just asked out of interest. We have to respect the contractual agreement."

How we will pay the balance of the second mortgage was now all finalized. After cashing in all the savings from different accounts, neither of us would have any money left for unexpected contingency. We would be living from paycheque-to-paycheque received after every two weeks. The only financial security we would have will be the unused money left in my revolving line of credit with FI-II, and on two credit cards.

The mystery about the size of monthly payment on the mortgage finally unfolded in the first week of July when I went to FI-I to sign the mortgage renewal. I was quite nervous. My heart was pounding, racing miles a minute, even throbbing, throat totally dry, with the anticipatory fear of a bullet piercing straight through my heart. I sat facing the representative of FI-I assigned to complete the paper work.

"How are you this afternoon, Mr. Vaughan," the rep greeted me with a broad grin.

I hated to see his grinning face. For me, my survival was on the line. And, here he was, all light-hearted and smiling. It seemed the guy was laughing wholeheartedly on my misery which, in fact, was going to be more unbearable.

"Just fine," I replied curtly. "And you," I asked him out of curtsy.

"Great," the rep replied with full enthusiasm.

Why wouldn't he be happy? He had a customer sitting across him, who was going to enrich his institution by paying way more interest income – a source of revenue the financial institutions thrive on.

"It's time to renew the mortgage," he added, with a much wider grin.

"That's why I am here," I replied nervously, words still coming out of my dry mouth with great difficulty.

I still didn't know how deep the surgical knife was going to plunge into my heart and whether I could survive the resulting deep wound.

"What are the options available," I asked him softly, running my eyes on the papers lying on the table top, searching the bottom line – the rate of interest he was going to charge.

"Well, you can renew it for three, six, or twelve months or anywhere between two and five year-term – it's entirely up to you. We let you choose the term that suits you," he added.

"What do you suggest under the prevailing economic conditions?" I solicited his advice.

"I would suggest a one year-term," the rep replied, "because three to six month-terms are too short and would be quite volatile for your finances, and you don't want to commit to any long-term at the prevailing high rate of interest. I shouldn't say this, but since you are our valued customer, I am here to help you make a right decision."

"What's the rate of interest on one year-term?" I asked with a heavily dried gulp, with my heart now heavily throbbing.

I wanted to see the final chip fall at its earliest moment.

"It's 19.75 percent," the rep finally pulled the trigger. His shot seared through my heart. He continued, "On your sixty thousand dollars outstanding, you will now be making a monthly payment of nine hundred fifty-seven dollars and eighty cents, i.e., three hundred and sixty dollars more than what you have been paying at the old rate," the rep explained in more realistic terms.

I was stunned. My face turned pale. I gasped for a bit of air to breathe. The rep noticed the changing colour of my face.

"Are you all right, Mr. Vaughan?" he asked. "I am sorry for delivering you this shocking news. You know how high and volatile the rates are at the moment. You don't know even this rate is good or bad as this may jump up or down a few notches next week, or next month ... who knows. I just gave you the rate as of today. I understand it's causing a hefty increase in your monthly payment, but you have to bite the bullet. Mind you, you can always sell the house, and move into a rental property."

"Oh no, that won't happen," I slurped out.

I had, by this time, composed myself and gotten over my initial fear.

"Everything is fine, and manageable," I added softly. "Let's just complete the paperwork."

I instructed the rep to carry on with his planned task.

"Since you own this property jointly with your wife, we need her to sign this contract as well," the rep demanded.

"No problem. I will bring this contract tomorrow – duly signed by her. She couldn't come because she is at home looking after our little daughter," I explained in my normal tone. I was over the shock.

That evening, after dinner, I gave the contract to Amy for her signature.

"Where do I sign?" she asked.

"Where the cross is marked," I pointed out the location. "Just look at the amount we are going to pay monthly."

I intentionally pointed it out to her in order to see her reaction about the additional cost of simply owning that house.

Indirectly, I was seeking solace, some words of comforts and sympathy from her.

No such words came out of her mouth. She signed the paper, handed it to me, and added,

"Too bad interest rates are so high at the moment. We have no choice if we want to keep the house."

"Of course, we will continue to keep the house at any cost," I assured her, and put back the folded contract in the bank's envelope, to be handed to the rep tomorrow.

I had made up my mind right after meeting with bank's rep the day before that I would keep the house at any cost. Selling it was never the option. Not just to appease Amy, and let her have her peace of mind, but also this house was going to be our only asset that would appreciate in value over time. And any such increase in value would, in turn, provide a sense of financial security, including using it as collateral to likely secure future consolidated loans to pay off debts cumulated over time. Even if my income didn't increase for any reason, the value of house would, and the rising expenses could always be met by borrowed funds.

I was bringing home close to a thousand dollars every two weeks. The new mortgage commitment would now take away one full pay-cheque, and the family's other expenses, including property taxes being deducted by the bank, had to be paid out from the second cheque. In other words, one full cheque, and a part of second, was going to be spent on just owning and maintaining the house. It was next to impossible to pay off all the regular monthly bills and other day-to-day incidentals, personal and other unexpected maintenance expenses from the remainder of the second cheque. Since Amy was purchasing the family's groceries, I was least worried about this important component of family expenditure – a component essential to survive to face what life had to bring to me and my family.

God Almighty had his own way of helping the poor and the most vulnerable. Now I really thanked from the bottom of my heart FI-II for opening up a revolving line of credit in the amount of ten-thousand dollars. The interest rate to be charged on funds borrowed from this account was relatively lower than that charged by regular credit cards, including the one issued by Sears. Since the account was revolving in nature, that meant, I could make the minimum payment, which was three percent of the balance outstanding, on one day, and withdraw funds on the same or the next day – provided the account had funds available. I had to ensure that this account was always in good standing as henceforth I had to lean on it for any shortfall.

This line of credit became a security blanket for me. I relied on it heavily, taking comfort that whatever I couldn't pay from the remainder of my second cheque could be paid by funds borrowed from this line of credit.

This feeling of comfort, however, came with a price – an additional loan payment even if it was revolving in nature. I still had to pay at least the monthly interest on borrowed funds. This became my fifth monthly financial commitment – the other four being the mortgage and property tax, VISA, MC, and Sears. More debt commitment meant making more minimum payments, which in turn, meant lesser money left at hand from the paycheque.

With the exception of money paid out as mortgage and property tax, all payouts on other revolving obligations including credit cards and line of credit could be re-used or even exceeded in dire circumstances as long as the funds were still available in accounts and these were not defaulted or labelled 'delinquent'.

***

In September 1981, Amy gave birth to our second daughter, named Kerry. She was once again on a year's maternity leave, and receiving only two-thirds of her salary. She was still purchasing the family's groceries, few odd things of her own, without asking me for any money. She now had to spend almost double the amount on Pampers, powdered-milk for babies, relatively more on groceries, and other things required to raise young kids. She was a happy spender on her symbols of security. She managed the essentials from her salary.

For all other goods and accessories required for kids, we had to run regularly to Sears and go on credit binge – even at an exorbitant interest rate of close to thirty percent a year. Besides taking additional debt, I also had opened a separate trust account for Kerry's higher education – by further supplementing her monthly government's child allowance.

As a housewife, Amy was now spending her full time with her daughters, and at night, shared the bed with me – lying still beyond my reach. She was either too tired after spending the day caring for the little girls, or she no longer had any interest in me, or desire to come closer to me in order to have mutual gratification of our physical needs. She was no longer the girl I married just five years ago.

***

Two months after Kerry was born, I left my car for pre-winterization at a garage I used to go for regular fill-ups. The pre-winterization of the car included seasonal change of tires, from regular to special winter tires for a better treading on the road, oil and filter change, checking all belts, battery, and whistles – all necessary for secured winter driving in snow, sleet, freezing rain, and sub-zero temperatures. When I went to pick up my car in the evening, the owner of the garage came running to me.

"I am afraid I have some bad news for you, Mr. Vaughan," he said with a slight grin on his face.

"What is it," I asked him, and looked into his eyes, though somewhat anxiously.

I sounded anxious because I anticipated bad news about the car requiring some costly repair for which I had no cash available other than the access to funds remaining on my credit cards. My reaction was no different than that of any man with no cash or savings who dreaded to hear about any new, unplanned, or unexpected expenditure. Furthermore, such a man could easily be cornered if the expenditure was on something essential, or likely to create any risk to his family's well-being.

With no money anywhere in sight, I was living quite a dreadful life – each and every day fearing about the occurrence of any new expenditure and thinking about how I would manage it.

"You need a new car," he replied casually, as if it was not such a big deal.

"Why? It was running all right this morning," I replied in a shakier tone. The news had raised my heart beat.

"I am afraid this is something you can't see," he explained. "When I put the car on the hoist this morning, I noticed its bottom is very weak, and may fall anytime. If I were you, I wouldn't drive it with two very young children." He had figured out the ages of children from the two infant car safety seats tied to the back seat of the car.

"Oh God, don't tell me that," I sputtered out. I knew I couldn't afford a new car right away.

"I am sorry," he added in an apologetic tone, "I am simply telling you the shape your car is in. The rest is up to you. Since I know you well as you have been my loyal customer, I equally consider it my responsibility to warn you about what could likely happen to you or your kids while driving."

"I very much appreciate your advice," I replied still in a stuttering voice. "Thank you for caring about the well-being of my family. I will start looking for its replacement."

I reached home, parked the car in the garage, and entered the kitchen, all glum-faced.

"Why glum-faced," Amy noticed and snarled. "What's the matter? Is something wrong?" She was standing close to the stove, preparing dinner.

"We need to replace the car," I replied softly. "The mechanic has advised me to replace it as soon as possible because its bottom has worn out, and can fall apart while driving."

"That's too bad," she replied in a mellowed tone. "What are we going to do?" She questioned me with her mouth half-open.

"Do we have a choice?" I replied glumly. "We have to look for a replacement. The only choice we have is to look for a new or a used car. And, I don't have money to buy either."

"Well, we can't ignore mechanic's advice," she replied emphatically. "Now that I know about the condition of the car, I wouldn't drive it with kids on board. I will be scared to death."

"You think I will?" I replied angrily.

Her statement had further fuelled my frustration and helplessness. I already was loathing myself for my poor financial situation. The very thought of driving this car and its subsequent consequences were giving me jitters.

"I didn't mean to upset you," she replied rudely. "Do what you want. You always do that anyway." She turned back to her cooking. "I just want to know what you plan to do rather than hear that we don't have money. I am getting tired of listening this," she added.

I left her alone.

I went to our bedroom to change. I had to resolve this critical problem that had surfaced so unexpectedly. I knew that car was getting old and needed to be replaced one day. But I never anticipated that it would that soon. Nonetheless, my family's safety was paramount. I had to resolve this issue quickly.

I seated the girls in the pram, wheeled them to the playground, which was just about two to three hundred yards away from the backyard of the house.

I snuggled each kid in the safety seat of each of the two swings on the playground.

While I gently pushed the side ropes of my kids' swings, and looked at their smiling faces, my head was working overtime to find the right solution. One thing was sure though: any solution to this problem would push me deeper into debt.

"I have decided to buy a used car," I told Amy at the dinner table after we all had returned from the playground.

"Why? You don't believe in buying a used vehicle," she reminded me, while chewing her food.

"Right now, it's not a question of what I believe in, or like to have," I replied calmly, "this is an issue of our survival at a cost that I can afford at the moment. Tomorrow, we will go to a few car dealerships on Merivale Road, and see if we can find some used car at a reasonable price. Once I know the price, I can take a consumer loan from FI-I."

"You don't want to use your line of credit at FI-II? She pondered. "Those funds are available at comparatively lower rate of interest," she added.

"You are right," I nodded, "but I want to keep those funds for day-to-day or emergency use. Once I spend all of these ten thousand dollars, I wouldn't have any source of funds left to meet any family emergency. We have two young children. We need some financial security, even if it's in the form of borrowings." I put forth a very persuasive argument about not touching funds at hand.

"Do you think FI-I would approve our loan?" She wondered loudly.

"I don't see why not," I replied with confidence, "we paid off FI-I the consumer loan we took to buy the dining room set. We will do the same for a car as well. You don't worry."

"If we are going to buy a vehicle, then I want a station wagon rather than a car, because it would be easier and comfortable for kids to travel." She expressed her choice of the new vehicle.

"That's fine with me," I supported her choice, "as long as it's affordable."

The next evening, Amy and I along with our kids went to a dealership, selling mostly cars made by General Motors. I preferred to buy a Chrysler/Plymouth product, because I was quite satisfied with my current Plymouth car that had lasted for more than ten years. But at that moment, the priority was to replace it at a reasonable price and from a dealer closer to home in order to have it serviced in the same vicinity as well. I hated to drive long distance, or in different ends of the city any vehicle for its post-purchase service and maintenance.

While we were walking and looking at new and used cars, a salesman came over, smiling and greeting us.

"Hi folks, looking for a new car?" he inquired, and introduced himself to us. "We have some very good bargains. Are you looking for a new or a used car?"

"Right now, a used car," I replied, "preferably, a station wagon."

The salesman led us to another lot, full of used cars, and pointed out some station wagons. He showed us one by one, pitching loudly their built-in features and/or accessories, kilometres covered, their expected run, until he pointed out a freshly painted, and shining four-seat deep-blue station wagon. Amy liked that, and wanted to buy.

The salesman wanted to know who would like to test drive that picked wagon. Since Amy had driven way more than me, I let her road-test the wagon. The salesman asked for her driver's license in order to make its copy for his records, went inside the building for a while. On his return, he handed her driver's license and hung a temporary license plate on the rear end of the wagon. While I tended the kids, Amy accompanied by the sales rep test-drove the wagon. After fifteen to twenty minutes, she was back in the car lot of the dealership. She told the rep that she liked the wagon and we would buy it.

What remained between the wagon and its ownership was the mutually agreed upon price. The salesman initially demanded nine thousand dollars, but after haggling with Amy, who was good at it, agreed to sell it for seven-thousand-five-hundred dollars. That was the amount I had to seek from FI-I as another consumer loan.

Next day, I called the loan manager and scheduled an appointment for that afternoon. I told her that it was an emergency as I had to replace my almost broken car for family's safety.

When we met, the loan manager wanted me to complete the loan application, and approved the desired loan at an exorbitant interest rate of close to twenty-four percent. Borrowing rates during the 1981 recession were way out of bounds. The financially vulnerable like me who had no choice other than to borrow to finance their needs were totally crushed under the weight of the large monthly payment of such loans with such high rate of interest.

While working with all kinds of statistics on personal debt and the resulting bankruptcy, I knew I wasn't alone experiencing the crushing pain of indebtedness at such killing rate of interest.

With the purchase of the used wagon, it was now safe to drive the kids around. The old two car safety baby-seats were installed in the rear seat of the wagon. Amy was equally relieved.

However, I was going through a very tense period of my life as I was carrying a mortgage debt at 19.75%, car loan at twenty-four percent, Sears at twenty-nine percent, and VISA and MC, equally at high teens.

I had already squeezed close to four hundred dollars from my monthly pay-check to pay close to a thousand dollars on the mortgage, and now I had to find another close to three hundred dollars to pay for the wagon – at least for the next thirty-six months. In other words, the three components – the monthly mortgage payment, property tax, and car payment – alone took away more than three-fourths of my monthly pay. And over and above these, I had to make minimum payments on the Sears account, VISA, MC, line of credit, and other monthly bills including cable, telephone, heat, hydro, water, and other unplanned incidentals.

And above all, I had to pay for toys, games, and other goods and services for kids. It was a real test of my skills and patience to manage and maintain the house without bothering Amy. I ensured that no payment was ever overdue or defaulted, or any creditor or debt collector was calling or knocking on my door for a monthly payment.

The growing debt load didn't stop here. In the same year, Video Cassette Recorders (VCRs) had been introduced in the market, and consumers got crazy about owning them so that they could watch featured movies and/or documentaries in the comfort of their homes. But these recorders came at a very hefty price – depending on the type of model, playing a regular size, or a compact cassette.

Almost all of our friends had purchased such a recorder, even if some had to go to Toronto or Montreal to buy it at a cheaper rate. We didn't want to be an exception, indirectly giving impression to friends that we didn't have it because we couldn't afford it. We wanted to join the rat race rather than stay out of it or within our financial constraints.

Since we couldn't travel to either of these cities, offering lower prices merely because of their larger market sizes, we looked for such a recorder, playing commonly used regular rather than a compact cassette. Since Eaton's, the relatively expensive department store located at the Bayshore Shopping Centre, was the only one that sold such a model, we bought one from it at eleven hundred dollars compared to, for example, eight hundred dollars that our friends paid in Montreal.

It was not the difference of three hundred dollars that made me depressed after the purchase, but the fact that I had opened a new credit account with another department store. That also meant making one additional monthly minimum payment to this new store that also charged annually twenty-nine percent interest on unpaid balances – similar to what its competitors like Sears and Hudson Bay charged.

Since I worked on indebtedness of households and personal bankruptcies, I was well aware of the pitfalls of using credit for gratifying non-essential personal needs, or for simply keeping up with the Joneses. I had this habit to analyze, or rationalize each and every purchase done on credit – like I was able to justify keeping the house as an asset at a very high mortgage interest rate, purchase of a car for the safety of the children, and now this VCR for family entertainment.

Granted, the purchase of the VCR could have been postponed for a while, but then I rationalized it that since Amy and I didn't go out for any dinners, movies at a theatre, we could at least watch a movie, even few weeks or months old, at home, for a change, and that too, by saving all the money to be paid to a babysitter. Moreover, Sarah was now over a year old, and was in a position to enjoy kids' movies as well. The bottom line was that the purchase of the VCR not only made us join the rat race, but it would help us save money on many fronts for years to come.

The very high interest rates during the recession, indeed, hurt borrowers, but these also helped savers to earn high interest income on their savings and investments. For savers and investors, this was the most rewarding period, giving them an opportunity to double their incomes in five to six years. If borrowers were paying twenty-four percent rate of interest on their consumer loans, savers and investors were also getting anywhere between eighteen and twenty percent return on their savings and investments. It was so ironic that borrowers sank deeper and deeper in debts during this period whereas savers and investors thrived and flew sky high. And, in between these two extremes, many lost their jobs, experienced income losses, drop in standards of living, and many even forced to declare bankruptcies. All of these negative economic forces, in turn, contributed to the dissolution of many family units.

***

At the tail end of this recession in 1982, Amy's department went through some organizational changes, resulting in moving some employees from one department to another. Since she turned out to be one who had to be moved, she had to cut short her maternity leave, and resume work in a different department.

She informed me about her intention to resume work. She wanted to leave for work in the morning without any hassle, and wanted me to look after Sarah and Kerry, leave them at the sitter's house before leaving for work. She could care less if I reached my office late, which in turn, could even prove harmful to my professional career. She simply gave priority to her low-paying clerical job, pretending to be totally oblivious to the fact that I was earning more than three times her salary and held a responsible position. She failed to understand, or intentionally overlooked it, that I was being paid more because I held a more senior job than hers.

"No, I am not going to be late each day at work," I told her point-blank. "You have to come up with a better solution."

"I have already told you what's better for me," she jumped at me. "I have an important job. I have to be in the office on time."

"I realize you don't care about my job, or the amount of money I bring home," I said in a calm voice. "Since you wanted children as symbols of your future security, I thought you were going to raise them yourself, rather than leave them with a strange unknown sitter."

"I wish I could," she sighed deeply. "No doubt, I wanted to have children, but now I want to earn my income to maintain my financial independence. Since I don't depend on you, I don't want to hear a word about quitting my job and stay as a housewife."

"And, I hate to see our kids raised in homes of different sitters," I replied vehemently. "We don't know what kind of cleanliness they would have, the kind of food they would serve, the rigid schedules they would maintain, and above all, I don't want to force my children to walk half-asleep in the morning to a sitter's house. I want them to sleep well in their own beds, both at night and during the day. I would hate to leave them at a sitter's home."

"Then, how do you want to raise them?" she frustratingly yelled at me.

I sensed she was ready for a compromise.

"Arrange a sitter who can come, say between seven thirty and eight in the morning, and leave by four, the time you plan to come home in the afternoon. The other option is to have a live-in sitter. We will have her as an employee, pay her weekly, as well as contribute to her Canada Pension Plan, and Unemployment Insurance. It's a costly proposition. Granted, we will lose a good degree of our privacy by having a sitter in the house, but that's the only way to raise kids in the comforts of our own home. Just pick one of these two options before opting to work outside the home. Our children's well-being comes first."

"I didn't say our children's well-being doesn't come first," she screamed at me, "but work, I will. I have told you why I want to continue to work," she spoke emphatically. "Who's going to pay for the sitter? Pay for her food, for TV in her room, and so on. I don't think you can. We will have another mouth to feed. On the other hand, I can see that any sitter on a daily basis can't be that dependable. Her erratic absence could create problem for both of us. The live-in, at least, will be around all the time, care for children in our own home, feeding them our own food. She could also do some household cleaning, wash dishes, and do some cooking for the children. But it's going to cost us a lot."

"We can always divide the cost," I suggested to her. Seeing her bent to accept my suggestion, I added in a mellowed tone,

"I will pay for her pension and unemployment contributions, and any other expenses, and you simply pay her weekly wage. I am sure you can manage it from the amount left-out of your salary after the family's groceries."

"I wish we had money," she exhaled deeply, giving me a scornful look. "Look at some of our friends who are reaping windfalls from this recession. Some of them are doubling their incomes in five years, because they are earning twenty percent return a year on their savings. And, here we are, who are damn paying twenty four percent on our consumer loan, and close to twenty on the mortgage. Right now, I hate to be amidst them and listen to all their bragging. They all consider themselves geniuses."

"No need to feel that way," I interrupted her. "We are in this situation for two reasons: first, we started our life from scratch, purchasing everything on credit, besides repayment of my student loan; and second, it's the economic cycle we got trapped in. It's too bad our mortgage renewal fell during this period of high interest rates, and buying a car further added fuel to the fire of our financial woes. I am sure people you are talking about have likely gone through similar situations, but they started perhaps on a better footing and in relatively good economic times. They have a reason to brag. I am doing the best I can under the circumstances. I didn't know that five years down the line, I would be in this mess. We just have to have patience, and strength, to cope with this temporary, but difficult, phase. Hopefully, the interest rate would drop by the time we renew our mortgage next year. I am still young, and fully confident, that over time, my income would rise, and I would pay off all of these loans. Until then, you have to bear with me."

"All right, all right" she thwarted at me, "you don't need to repeat yourself. I have heard this explanation time and time again."

She had simmered down. She looked at the rationality of the argument, or was happy that she would have a helper to do some of the daily chores.

"I will speak to some of my female friends in the neighbourhood for a good live-in sitter, but until then, we have to have someone on a daily basis."

Even though I had suggested the idea to have a live-in sitter, I was still quite unhappy. I firmly believed that children should be raised by their mother. A paid sitter could never nurture the child with the same quality of care, love, affection, and devotion as the mother could. For a sitter, it was just a job, but for a mother, it was the sense of endowed motherhood that nature had bestowed upon her to raise her own kids with undeterred dedication, love, and discipline. A hired help was just a hired help, and couldn't be forced to replicate a natural mother's performance.

Knowing Amy's stubborn nature, and above all, my own financial situation, I had to compromise with my ideals. I knew darn well that to have a live-in sitter was a luxury that we really couldn't afford. But I had no choice when it came to the welfare of our children, having them to grow up at our own home, without any undue hindrance, or restriction. What Amy was going to benefit from this arrangement was just an icing on the cake.

CHAPTER FIVE

One afternoon, Jen and I were having lunch at the office cafeteria in our favourite quiet corner. I noticed that she was lost in her thoughts, eating slowly with only a shiny steel fork in her right hand, with her eyes fixed on the food plate containing Hungarian beef goulash, cauliflower, and green peas. This was totally contrary to what I was accustomed to – her soft and gentle way of talking about things about her, her family, work, or about me, my family, besides concepts and details common to our work, and occasionally indulging into a small talk.

"What's wrong?" I asked her. "Is something bothering you?"

"Yes," she replied softly, and gazed at me. She had stopped eating. "It's Peter. He acted a bit weird last night."

"What did he do?" I inquired.

"He didn't do anything in particular," she explained, "he couldn't perform in bed last night. This morning he spoke rather rudely with me. Just thinking why he behaved like that. He has never done that since we got married"

"What do you mean by 'he couldn't perform'?" I continued to gaze and read her face.

I had stopped chewing my grilled cheese sandwich. I was now waiting to hear some juicier details.

"We were lying in bed," she began dwelling in a dim voice, "and were in the midst of having some fun. When the time came for him to perform, he couldn't get it up. It was all flaccid. It has never happened before."

"Maybe he's too worried about his job," I replied promptly. "You told me just a week ago that his company is going through several changes including a possible merger with a much larger company and its affiliates."

"Yes," she nodded, "there's a rumour that the two companies may merge, and as a result, some employees could lose their job. But what does it have to do with his performance in bed? Does that mean that our fun loving moments are over until his company settles its situation, or his job is secured? I neither want him to be in this situation, nor want to be deprived of all the fun."

"To me, it's natural," I replied.

"In what way," she asked, and looked puzzled, with her mouth half-open, still holding the fork in her hand.

"You see, right now he's likely very worried and under a lot of stress," I explained. "His mind and thoughts about the potential job change, or loss have overwhelmed his brain, which in turn, controls the nerves that send messages to his body organs, affects circulation of blood to his genitals. If his blood is not filling the chambers of his main organ, he can't get it up, no matter how hard he tries."

"You talk as if you have experienced this kind of situation," she snarled at me with a momentary grin. "You have financial worries. Have these affected you, your performance in bed?"

"I have my share of worries," I concurred with her, "but I don't let these overwhelm me, my brain. I can separate them easily. I know these are temporary, and just will be memories after a few years. You know all men are different, with different personalities, capabilities to cope with day-to-day challenges, adversities, will-power, you name it. Like women, no two men are alike. Maybe, Peter is more sensitive, too worried at the moment, can't separate his anxiety from sexual arousal. Give him some time to adjust. I am sure he would be a fine sex-mate. In the meantime, keep giving him some pep talk to keep his self-confidence high."

"Thanks for boosting my confidence in him," she replied with a wide smile, and restarted picking up the food from the plate with the fork she had been holding all that time. "I will keep you up-to-date on his well-being. I know, right now, he's in doldrums. Maybe, that's why he screamed at me this morning."

"It was a natural transgression of his frustration on you," I explained as a psychologist. "Since he was upset over not having been able to perform, he was mad at himself, and since you happened to be the first one talking to him after he woke up, he poured out all his anger and frustration on you. So don't worry. It's all normal."

"Thanks," she replied. "You have brought me out of the depressed mood I had all this morning. I had been going over all kinds of negative scenarios about my future life with him. I really don't want to see his worry and/or stress affecting our sex life, depriving me of all the essential physical satisfaction."

I had bragged about my ability to separate my financial worries from sexual performance. Granted, most men could easily separate worries from ability to perform as long as they are sexually too aroused, and want an immediate relief. Women, on the other hand, lack such ability. Any anxiety, physical or mental, would distract their sexual participation and its ultimate enjoyment. For women, sex always starts in their brain whereas for men, it starts with a vision. According to many sex professionals, a simple look or glance at a beautiful and/or attractive woman is good enough to ignite a man's sexual desire.

I recalled many sleepless nights when I played in my head scenarios of making a payment on one loan, then withdrawing the same amount to make payment on another loan, and so on. I had to ensure that monthly credit statements with minimum payments paid were officially stamped before their respective due dates. I couldn't tell Jen that at moments like these, sex was far away from my mind. And, even at times, when I wanted to relieve some of my stress by having sex with Amy, or find solace in her arms, she was beyond my reach. My sex-life was almost non-existent. Perhaps, Jen had just started to experience the kind of sexual dissatisfaction that I had been experiencing for years.

***

By late summer of 1982, interest rates on five-yearly conventional mortgages had not yet reverted to more realistic levels. Last year, I had renewed our mortgage for just one year. I was simply buying time, and waiting for the turn of the tide. With less than one bi-weekly paycheque to pay for all the monthly obligations, I had begun to rely more on credit cards issued by banks, and department stores. Since credit cards like VISA and MC were not accepted by major department stores, I had no choice, but to use credit cards issued by department stores simply to manage my family's needs.

As Sarah and Kerry were growing up, their needs for baby clothes, toys, diapers, shoes, and other accessories were equally growing. And, that in turn, meant driving the family to Sears, Eaton's, or the Hudson Bay on each Saturday morning to buy things for them on credit.

Paying Sears and other stores just a minimum monthly payment and taking several times more credit had become a weekly ritual. At times, it was so embarrassing to face and talk to the same sales ladies, week-after-week. I used to stand in shame in one empty corner, and watch Amy trying clothes and shoes on children before purchasing them. The more she tried and picked up, the more I felt I was sinking in the debt hole.

"Couldn't you make with less?" I once asked Amy in utter frustration, while we sat in our wagon.

"I bought what was necessary," she replied in a flustered voice. "I didn't buy anything for myself. Everything is for the kids."

"You could have bought anything you liked for yourself as well," I said calmly, "I never stopped you for that."

"I realize that," she replied. "I know you have never stopped me from buying anything I have asked for, or even pointed out to you indirectly. But, right now, buying for the kids is more important – because of seasonal changes, and also, they are growing day-by-day. Moreover, I don't want Kerry to wear Sarah's used clothes, or footwear. I want to be fair to both of them."

"You do realize that all this weekly credit adds up," I reminded her. "I pay the store one payment a month, and then we buy many times more of this amount. It's a recipe for disaster."

"Don't blame me, or the kids for it," she snarled at me. "You can't blame the kids for the mess we are in. If you had ever acted wisely, we wouldn't have to purchase everything on credit. It's not the time to worry about sorting out our financial woes. We have a responsibility to provide proper things to our kids. We are not poor by any standard."

"We are not poor, but we don't have cash to pay for things," I clarified and reminded her.

"There's no difference between being poor because of low or no earnings, no savings, and no cash flow, and being poor despite high earnings because of no savings and no cash flow. The key difference between the two is that the latter is in a somewhat privileged situation as it can get access to more credit or borrowed funds, and as a result, is able to fulfill all its needs. Even though high earners can camouflage their poverty by borrowed funds, the fact remains that living on borrowed funds is bad. Cutting down on expenses is far better than increasing debt liability."

"Maybe we should stop eating," she said sarcastically. "I could save all the grocery money for you to pay other bills."

"I didn't mean that," I looked at her red face.

She was shaking her head in disbelief. She had her eyes fixed on the road. I gently patted her left thigh, and mumbled, "I am sorry if I have hurt your feelings."

Every time I tried to speak to Amy about cutting expenses or managing finances well, she would get very defensive, start belittling me, reminding me again and again about my poor handling of finances in the past, or inability to save for the rainy day. She would instantly blame me for all of this financial mess, question my ability, lack of financial skills and street smartness. She was ever ready to degrade me, put me down, order me around as if I was her servant, and shower me with her sharp sarcasm.

I eventually reached a point where I stopped talking to her about anything to do with the family's finances. I decided to communicate with her very little, again, only on non-monetary matters, or on matters involving the well-being of children.

***

On June 12, 1982, Canadians got an opportunity to participate in a national lottery game, called Lotto 649, which would allow them to purchase a ticket for one dollar, at least a few hours before the draw. The ticket contained a row of six numbers between one and forty-nine, chosen randomly by a machine at the vendor's counter (called a 'quick pick'), or personally chosen and tick-marked on the official form by a player, which in turn, was to run through the machine at the counter, printing out those chosen numbers. Anyone with a ticket matching all six numbers drawn randomly from a rolling drum was considered as a winner and eligible to get the full prize of one million dollars. Those with three and up to five matching numbers would get some prize money – the amounts were to be determined by pre-defined fractions of the total money collected and set aside for the draw. This lottery draw was to be held on each Wednesday and Saturday night. In other words, there were two chances a week to become a millionaire. However, the probability of winning on one play was one in about fourteen million. That was a long shot.

Despite such a long shot to win a million dollars – and that too twice a week – I started to purchase this lottery ticket religiously for each draw. Considering the financial mess I was in, I thought investing two dollars a week to win one million dollars was a good bet. And I could afford that.

With this bet, I began to hope to win some day the jackpot and lead a debt-free life like other persons with deep pockets. This ever lasting hope of turning things around became a steady fodder for my survival. Each week would bring a fresh new hope that perhaps this was the week my situation was going to be changed, but alas, weeks came and went without bringing any change in my life other than it made me live under more debts. Put another way, these two dollars a week kept me going and kept my hopes alive for a better turn of events. The hope alone was the only fuel that kept my motor running.

Since Amy wanted to keep her financial independence, she too started to buy her own separate ticket. That meant that as a family, we were now spending four dollars a week, or two hundred and eight dollars a year, on this lottery. Even though the odds of winning were too low, the greed pushed us both, along with millions of others, to keep buying tickets as a weekly ritual. At the start of each week, she, like me, hoped to become a millionaire.

***

The convenient use of plastic to satisfy day-to-day needs, or finance the family's other wants arising from raising young kids made me feel good as a provider, but its long-term cumulative effects were turning disastrous for me. I was passing through a life cycle stage where expenditure exceeded income, not only for me but for the majority in their thirties. I wasn't the only one trapped in this vicious phase of indebtedness which was getting worse by the day and weeks with no end in sight. Since my minimum payments on all accounts were simply paying interest on the respective balances I owed, institutions issuing credit cards also kept raising limits on my cards by simply looking at my gross income, pushing me deeper and deeper into the debt hole with no chance to rebound.

At times, I wondered about this kind of source of financial assistance I was getting to barely survive. To me, living on credit was like living on a corporate welfare. This welfare payable to those with high enough incomes, nonetheless, not only had to be returned in full, but also by topping it up by the cost of using it. It was not like any government welfare, provided at no cost to all those poor with low or inadequate incomes, needy, chronically ill, disabled, and unemployed, living in financially straitened circumstances. During my anguished moments, I wished I was genuinely poor. I would then be receiving assistance from all three levels of government, and that too, without worrying to pay back any amount.

But living on government welfare wasn't going to be that smooth either: first, it was going to be a limited amount; second, it was going to be paid for a specific period; and third, as a welfare recipient, I would have no privacy as I would be stigmatized and my life would be an open book for public scrutiny. As a corporate welfare recipient, on the other hand, I didn't have to face these things and still walk with my head high as long as I was able to make the monthly minimum payment on time.

I was fully cognizant that besides owning a home, my stable job with relatively high level of earnings made me a perfect target, eligible to receive such corporate welfare. The bottom line for all these card issuing institutions and department stores was to maximize their source of revenue – the interest income earned on their respective balances outstanding.

Granted, nearly one-half of their customers paid off in full their balances each month, there still were the other half who carried over such balances, and were an easy prey to suppliers of credit. Suppliers would love to keep this half happy, and suck it to the best of their ability by supplying it more and more credit by raising, without first asking, their credit limits. And debtors, in turn, hungry for cash, would love to spend what's offered to them. This vicious cycle would likely go on unchecked as both parties would keep patting each others back. Both would get what they want, but with one significant difference: lenders would be the beneficiaries and borrowers the victims of their own doing.

***

By late 1982, Amy was successful to find a live-in sitter. Before that, a sitter coming daily between seven in the morning till four in the afternoon was caring for Sarah and Kerry. Amy was now happy. She had not only found a proper and a steady sitter, but also she had someone to share the household chores, including cleaning and dusting, dishes, and washing of clothes.

I was equally satisfied to see the sitter ready to provide round-the-clock care for our daughters. This also enabled Amy to save money she usually paid to sitters hired over the weekends to care for the kids while Amy and I were away visiting friends for dinner and/or social get-togethers.

The only disconcerting thing for me was that there was no longer any privacy left in the house. I had to ensure that I controlled my temper, emotions, dress code, and talked and behaved well with Amy and the kids. The spare bedroom in the house was now occupied, and furnished with a TV set, and other furnishings. Amy had another mouth to feed. That meant, paying more for groceries, as well as for sitter's services. For the next foreseeable future, she would have relatively less discretionary money at hand.

The sitter's arrival as well as the growing needs of children to use washroom facilities created havoc at the day-breaks. Amy, being an early bird, or a morning person, had a set routine – get up between five and five-thirty in the morning, and out of the house by six – come rain, snow, or sunshine. I, on the other hand, a night person, or a night owl, started my day around seven in the morning, and my access to washroom was obstructed by both the sitter's and kids' needs. One washroom in the house with five persons – three adults and two kids – was no longer keeping everyone without throwing temper tantrums.

"I think we need to buy a bigger house," Amy suggested on one Saturday morning. "You can see how the washroom gets crowded in the mornings. Besides that, we have no room to accommodate anyone visiting us for any extended stay. I suggest we begin to look for a slightly bigger house, preferably a detached one this time."

"I agree with you wholeheartedly," I replied. "Could we wait at least until the interest rates are down a little? I am already paying a little over one full bi-weekly paycheque on the current mortgage. I can't afford to take any more mortgage liability."

"I am not asking you to buy anything right now," she snapped back at me. "I am simply suggesting that this house is not big enough for five people."

"Well, it depends how you look at it," I replied softly. "Look at our neighbours on both sides. On our right, one has three grown-up boys, and the other, on our left, has three grown-up girls. They are managing it all right, also likely living within their means. We all have to be careful and do things that we can afford. It's worth living with some inconvenience, or bear tantrums if one can avoid taking bigger mortgage liability, something beyond one's affordability. Because paying more in mortgage means using more consumer credit, if one has a limited income, or poor cash flow situation. With our current cash flow problem, I don't think I can afford to take more mortgage liability."

"Since you are already paying one-half of your salary to pay-off the mortgage," she commented, "let us wait 'til the interest rate falls. Then buying a bigger house, high-priced, requiring higher mortgage, but at a relatively reduced interest rate, will likely not increase the monthly payment we are currently making. We know now we can allocate one paycheque to pay for the mortgage."

"That's how things are at the moment," I replied, shrugging my shoulders.

I didn't want to start a war of nagging words by telling her the personal pain and mental torture that I was presently going through while paying bills on credit cards and using funds from the line of credit of FI-II. She didn't want to hear the parrot repeating the same song.

"Let's wait 'til next spring or summer, and then look around for a new house," I suggested to her. I knew her mind was now set on moving into a single detached house, just to keep up our social status compatible with our gross earnings.

By the early summer of 1983, the 5-year conventional mortgage rate charged by the Canadian financial institutions had dropped to a little over thirteen percent – full six percentage points less than what I was currently paying. That looked like a real bargain, and seemed like a good time to look for a new and bigger house.

Since I was keen to reduce the size of the monthly mortgage payment in order to improve my cash flow, I had to look for a house that required a little less borrowing; in other words, a house with a relatively lower purchase price. Moreover, I had learnt at work that the higher the market or assessed price of the house, the higher would be its property tax. So in the end, I wasn't going to gain anything as whatever little I would be saving in mortgage payout would be swallowed by the increase in property tax.

Comprehending all this detailed math about owning a property was, unfortunately, beyond Amy's head. Nonetheless, I was committed to fulfill her wish. Her beautiful and attractive face had overshadowed my logical mind. Despite our poor personal and almost no-sex relationship, I always admired her as a pretty and attractive woman. I had too soft a corner for her in my heart.

At the time, the City of Ottawa had quite an economic divide among its East, West, and South ends. Since the west of Ottawa was more developed and economically prosperous, naturally, houses in this part of the city were way more expensive because of both higher density of population and land development cost compared to its less prosperous east end. Consequently, houses, old or new, were relatively cheaper on this sparsely populated end of the city.

Now that we were looking for a big and a better new house, I used to read sections of newspapers to look at different models of single detached houses, liveable area space along with its front and backyard area, and above all, their purchase prices. We wanted to purchase a house from the same developer from whom we had purchased the current house as we knew about the kind of service and care it provided after the sale.

Moreover, this developer, compared to others, made neither too fancy nor high quality homes with costly products or finishes, but simply made and sold homes that fit the pockets of middle income families. I thought the developer was smart, keeping prices of houses lower, and attracting large number of buyers, which in turn, was good for the business and share of the city's real estate market. For any new buyer, the price of the house was a critical and a decisive matter – especially the one with limited means.

I gathered from the newspaper ads that this developer had made a particular model of the house with similar living area space and lay out that we liked in both the west and east ends. What differentiated the two houses was strictly the location and their price – the developer was charging more than sixty thousand dollars for the same house in the west end.

That meant that I had to take much higher amount of mortgage if I decided to stay in the west end. Moving to the east end, on the other hand, would enable me to own the house we liked, and that too, at a much lower mortgage amount. Not only that, a lower mortgage would help amortize it in a relatively shorter time span, which in turn, meant saving all the money I was to pay as interest on the mortgage. The only discouraging factor was that we had to move from the bustling, prosperous, developed, and well-familiar west end to totally unfamiliar, thinly populated, and economically depressed east end.

"Would you like to move to the east end?" I asked Amy after doing the math on mortgages, their amortization, and interest to be paid.

"Why are you asking me?" She questioned me as she stood and tucked the clothes basket on her left side. "You know both of us like to live in the west end. I would hate to leave our familiar surroundings."

She headed towards the washing machine.

"Even if you have to take sixty thousand dollars of mortgage extra for the same type of house?" I questioned her in a slightly raised voice just to ensure she heard me right.

"What do you mean?" she asked.

She had stopped walking and turned towards me.

"Come here. I will show you the ad about the house we talked about this morning," I signalled her with my half-bent right hand, and made room for her to sit beside me.

"Look at the sale prices," I pointed with my index finger, "the model's price in the west end is more than sixty thousand dollars than that in the east. Do you want to take that much extra mortgage? In my opinion it isn't necessary."

"I wouldn't mind paying the extra mortgage, knowing that the house will appreciate more in value over time – much more in the west than in the east. I think it's a better deal, and also we wouldn't have to move far," she replied instantly.

"You have a point," I concurred with her, "but right now, I have to see what suits my pocket. The house will appreciate in the east end too. Maybe not at the same rate, but it will. Right now we have to decide between what we can presently afford and the long-term potential home equity." I paused with my eyes fixed on the ad.

"Well, since you know better what we can afford as you are the one going to pay for it," she replied callously. She stood up with her laundry basket, and added, "I just want to move in a bigger house and not have these daily arguments about the use of washroom facilities or lack of space. Kids are growing up and they need to have their own rooms, and a good size backyard to play or have a pool."

She shrugged her shoulders and walked away.

After we reluctantly agreed to move to the east end, we visited the developer's construction site. There was no house built as yet as per the advertised model that we had liked. We simply looked at the lot where our house was to be erected, signed the bottom line after looking at the detailed layout of the house. We were told by the developer's rep that this was the largest model being built in that developmental phase.

We signed the necessary papers pertaining to the land transfer, agreement to purchase with ten percent down payment, principal mortgage, insurance, and property tax. At the time of signing these papers, the rep asked us if we wanted to upgrade any thing including the kitchen's floor or carpets in the house. We had to say 'no' because we had no money whatsoever.

On hearing our categorical 'no', the rep commented that we were the only family who had not asked for any upgrading. We heard him loud and clear, but we could only grin and bear it.

***

Amy finally set her foot in her single detached house in early September. By moving into this house, we had gained more than six hundred square foot of living space, a bigger kitchen, one extra bedroom, one full bathroom, and quite a big backyard – good for a full-length in-ground pool, or a tennis court. The developer had provided a very cheap quality carpeting and kitchen flooring along with three appliances, namely, fridge, stove, and dishwasher. Like the previous house, this too had central air conditioning.

We had sold our semi-attached house at thirty thousands dollars more than its purchase price. Out of these thirty thousand dollars, the only cash we had at hand, we paid ten percent of the purchase price as down payment, besides paying the land transfer tax, lawyer's fee, obligatory insurances, and mover's cost.

Out of the remainder, we paid a bit of debt on Sears account. This was essential as we were regularly using Sears account to purchase goods for the kids as well as for kitchen, lawn, and other accessories required to furnish the new house. We also used some of this cash to buy good quality furniture from reputable shops for the living and family rooms.

Moving into the new house also meant purchasing again customized coverings for glass windows and doors, eaves-troughs to protect the house from the running rain water, fence around the house to protect it from running wild animals in the backyard, security alarm to protect against any break-ins or thefts, and insurance to protect the property from any damage due to fire or natural disaster.

All of these things, essential to securely maintain the property, required immediate access to cash, which I didn't have. Since we couldn't live in an unfurnished and/or unprotected property, I had no choice other than to use borrowed funds from all available sources.

Since I already was living with loads of debt, this move into the new house added more debts and that, in turn meant, raising the monthly minimum payments, and squeezing further my already precarious cash flow situation. These numerous debt loads had begun to crush my life.

CHAPTER SIX

"So, how was the move?" Jen asked me after I returned to the office.

We were on our regular lunch break. Considering it was almost past the middle of September, she was still wearing a knee-length sleeveless summery Raymond dress, with her hair open, parted from the middle.

"It went all right," I replied. "It was quite a job. I am glad it's over," I added with a sense of relief.

"Amy must be happy now that she has moved into a single home," she commented.

"I hope so," I replied, "I have done my best to please her even if that has sunk me with loads of debt. I don't know if I ever will be able to pay-off these debts."

"Did you have to do it?" She asked.

She wanted to reconfirm what I had done was all really needed because of my own volition or due to some marital obligation. Since she was, like me, inquisitive by nature, she likely wanted to know the real reason why I had put myself under loads of new debt.

"Yes, absolutely – if I wanted to keep peace at home and see Amy happy. She can now live with one less tension. She, like most of her friends and colleagues, is now living in a single detached home. She really had a hard time living in a semi-attached."

"You care that much for her happiness that you are ready to lose your own peace of mind?" she shot back.

"As a husband and the primary provider, I will go to any length to see her live at peace and in harmony," I boasted. "One thing I have learnt is that a happy woman can make the house worth coming to in the evening after work, or sleep comfortably with her at night, and even have a mutually satisfying intimate relationship. If a woman is unhappy and discontented, she can not only make her husband's life miserable, but can also be rude to even her children, or make the whole living environment miserable."

"I wish Peter had similar thoughts about how to keep a woman happy," she lamented.

"What's wrong with him?" I wanted to know.

"Ever since his job prospects have been in a limbo, he has been behaving rather strangely," she began to explain. "He comes home, grabs his beer, and sits in front of television. He hardly kisses me either before leaving for work or after returning from work. Never mind our sex life. At times I get mad at him, and as you say, I act in ways to draw his attention. Nothing is working."

"But he still has a job?" I asked.

"Yes," she confirmed, "but with a lot of uncertainty hanging. He's the kind of guy who wants a sense of job security. Right now he is living with fear about losing his job, his only source of income. At times I look at his sad face, and I equally get worried as what will happen if he ever lost his job. I realize he can get a job elsewhere, but would that fit his persona?"

"In my opinion, both of you are presently worrying unnecessarily," I commented as a sage. "You know how the job market is changing these days. Large technological companies are buying out smaller companies in order to reduce the number of competitors, and as result, can also increase their dominance, or the share of the market of their products. The way things are moving, especially for high-tech companies, we don't know if even such large companies be able to survive in their own land as their products could easily be manufactured in another country with relatively cheaper production costs."

"I am fully aware of it as we both read the same newspapers," she replied in self-defence, "but how can I explain and pacify his feelings, his fear. I think what he's going through at the moment is something you and I can't feel. Our jobs are relatively secured."

"I wouldn't bet on that," I counter-argued. "Any budgetary cuts give an employer a chance to cut the deadwood. I am sure people are going to be affected in almost all federal departments in and outside Ottawa."

"You may be right," she replied curtly.

She looked up at her watch and stood up.

"Let's get back to work. And congratulations again for moving into a new house."

On our way back to the office floor, I kept thinking about Peter's job prospects and how he was becoming a victim of job insecurity, and how his family was suffering with him too. I felt bad for Jen, whom I had known for the last nine years as a colleague and a close friend. At times she looked so attractive and innocent that I had a hard time taking my eyes off of her.

In those moments of infatuation, I simply wanted to hold her tightly and just immerse myself into her.

***

Even though I had a full-time job, earning a little over forty-eight thousand dollars when I moved into the new house, I hardly had any money left from my bi-weekly cheque after making the mortgage and property tax payment, other household maintenance bills, Unemployment Insurance premium and Canada Pension Plan contribution for the sitter, and minimum payments on several cards and charge accounts. Even tellers at FI-I, where I used to make all these bi-weekly or monthly transactions, cashing the cheque and then stamping statements of payments used to note that the amount of my cheque was totally wiped out by these payments to the last cent.

On one of such visits, one teller couldn't resist himself and eventually chuckled loudly,

"You don't have anything left to pay for a cup of coffee even."

He laughed ruefully.

He thought he had just joked with me as a familiar patron, but what he failed to grasp was that his sentence uttered as an innocent joke worked as a bullet that pierced my heart and turned me almost into ashes.

At the time I kept my composure, simply grinned superficially after listening to his comment, quietly completed my transactions, without looking at anyone around. I didn't have the courage to make an eye-to-eye contact with anyone in the room. I felt really insulted and ashamed in the eyes of all those standing behind me and on my sides.

I quickly exited the institution with my eyes fixed on the floor.

On my way back to the office, the teller's words kept reverberating into my ears. Logically, he had rightly noted as to how I was going to manage the whole month when I had nothing left from the pay cheque. The more I thought about it, the more emotional in self-pity I became.

My eyes were filled with thick layers of tears, refusing to slide on my cheeks. I felt as if I had glassy eyes as faces of all passersby and trees on the sidewalk – all looked occluded. I had to press my eyelids hard enough to drain my teary eyes so that I could see clearly and not create any nuisance on the road.

The teller had reminded me the kind of fragile life I was living.

"You look all pale and gloomy," Jen remarked on seeing me back at the office, "what's wrong? Let's go to my office for a while." She more or less ordered me as if she had full control on me.

I followed her. As soon as we both were in her office, she shut the door. I sat on the chair facing her with her work-desk separating us.

"Now tell me everything," she said gently, and sat straight with her back against the chair. She pulled all of her hair over her left shoulder, covering mostly her left breast.

"Oh! Nothing," I replied, and shook my head. "Just had a bad encounter with a teller at the bank."

"What happened?" She coaxed me.

"He seems to have been flabbergasted as I had used my entire pay check to pay off my obligations," I finally opened up. "He commented, perhaps jokingly, I didn't have any money left to buy even a cup of coffee, indirectly asking me how I was going to spend the next two weeks before the next cheque. Since he had seen my account with not much balance either, he couldn't resist asking me this question."

"Maybe he asked you this question out of compassion, worrying about your well-being," she replied as a devil's advocate.

"I don't think so," I side-stepped her comment. "He was just mischievous. He was likely having fun seeing my poor financial situation – like everyone else. I felt really insulted."

"I don't get it. What do you mean? Who's having fun with your poor financial situation?" She wanted me to dwell on it more.

"As we all know," I began to expound, "people, including all these tellers and managers at financial institutions, respect, care, and listen attentively to those with deeper pockets. Have you ever heard anyone paying attention to someone with a lighter pocket? That's the world we live in. Those with money have the power to dominate, influence, or walk all over those with little or no money; they can even get away with murder; the latter are simply dead leaves for the former to walk on. It's a universal truth that money is power. You must have observed even at social get-togethers how much more attention an affluent gets compared to a pauper. That's the real world we live in."

"I personally haven't paid that close attention at social get-togethers, but if you have seen or experienced this sort of discriminatory treatment, then why bother attending such gatherings," she asked.

"Well, at times you have to," I uttered softly, "you can't isolate yourself or live like a hermit. Social interaction with friends, colleagues, or peers is essential for your health and sanity."

"Thank goodness! Peter and I don't attend many of such get-togethers," she replied, "but we used to go out almost every weekend. Right now, though, we have cut down our outings because Peter isn't in a good situation with all the uncertainty hanging on his job. He is going through a depression."

"I hope it's not as bad as mine," I interjected. "You have no clue the kind of depression and worries I am going through these days."

"I thought you and Amy are happy as you have just moved into a new and bigger house, have a live-in sitter to care for the young kids. Why are you depressed?" she asked.

"Everything looks rosier on the surface," I began to explain, "but what's really beneath it is all that matters. We have financially over-extended ourselves. You already know the kind of financial situation I am going through. I just now gave you a glimpse of a short personal experience. Even the teller noted my vulnerable financial situation and couldn't resist himself from making some insulting comments. This vulnerability is making me depressed. So much so, that every moment round the clock, I keep worrying about the expenditure that could possibly befall on me – be it relating to the maintenance of the house, or any new purchase required for the kids as both are growing older by the day and their sizes and requirements are changing. And incurring of any new expenditure would mean increasing my debt load which already is way more than my income can sustain. You know each and every evening when I get off the bus, and take a turn towards my house, I take a good look at it first, and then thank God everything is okay and no new expenditure is required. You know I am living a much fearful and on the edge life. This sort of fear about spending more and more of borrowed money has really taken away all the charm of life and personal serenity – pushing me into a deeper and deeper depression."

"If things are that bad, why did you buy a new house?" She wanted to know. "You could have stayed in the semi-attached like we are. I think we bought the house the same time you did in 1976 – just a short distance away from yours in Knoxdale and Craig Henry area. I don't think we will be moving away from this area as we like it very much."

"Amy wasn't comfortable in the semi-attached house," I explained. "She wanted a slightly bigger house to accommodate the kids and their sitter, and have a spare bedroom for any visiting relative or friend. Considering I am still young, have almost a full career ahead of me with potentially a good flow of future income, I thought I could take a risk and purchase a bigger house. I am sure all these debts will be paid one day and I will be able to lead a debt free life. But until then, I have to play safe and take each day at a time."

"If you feel that burdened by debts, or living that fragile and fearful life, you can always declare bankruptcy," she suggested.

"You must be kidding," I snarled at her, "that's something I will never do. I am simply buying time by making minimum payments on my loans, but I am quite confident that I will pay off each cent that I currently owe."

I stood up from the chair to leave her office.

"I'm sorry I didn't mean to hurt or insult you," she apologized, and stood up. "I was simply suggesting you a short and simple way to get out of this miserable depression. As a close friend, I can feel what you are going through at the moment. I don't want to see you in a depressed situation. I live with such depression each and every day. At least when I am here at the office and in your company, I want to be happy and relaxed, at least have some good time. Over this period of nine years, I think we have become good friends – willing to help one another when asked, or whenever needed."

She put forward her happy face, and extended her hand to shake mine in order to pacify me.

"Thanks for letting me vent out," I smiled back and shook her hand.

I placed my second palm on top of our joined hands.

"Indeed we are not only good, but very close friends," I reassured her, and walked out of her office.

***

There was only one way to pull myself out of this financially tight situation. And that was to find a job supplementing my income. Since I was one of those who used borrowed funds strictly because of my inadequate income rather than for any pleasure, travel, or personal consumption, I had to find a source to augment my income. What sort of source should that be was the issue.

I was not afraid of working long hours at the current or the secondary job. Working extra hours or overtime at the current job was out of the question as no employer was going to approve of overtime to conduct analysis or to write its findings, unless these were required at a short notice by some politician, media, or some high authority. Since such research and analytic jobs were secondary to the overall government operations, these always got token budgets and were the first in line to be chopped off if budgetary cuts warranted. And, that meant seeking a second job outside the department.

The job had to be compatible not only with the kind of skills I had, but also with the daily work schedule of the primary job at hand. I had to perform well on my current professional job, which not only paid well, but also carried a lot of public responsibility.

There was no or very little room for any error, misjudgement, misinterpretation of data, or delayed response or information to both the clients of our data or the media. This also meant that I couldn't simply leave my job at any given specific hour in order to simply run to another job.

Under these constraints of the current job, I had to ensure that the second job didn't create any impediments to my current source of bread and butter. Also, I had to ensure that I had adequate time to perform household chores, maintain the property, and above all, to care for our young daughters. What sort of job could I do within these boundaries?

Since I was a professional statistician with special skills to analyse financial data on incomes, assets and debts of households, and had written and published comprehensive technical and analytic reports on these topics, I thought of sharing all of this acquired knowledge by teaching adults interested to learn concepts of financial economics of households.

Since I loved to teach, I contacted one of the school boards in Ottawa and suggested it to include a topic on household financial economics in its calendar of 13-week miscellany of courses on continuing education. The board offered to adults such courses annually at a fee, conducted usually between seven and nine during evenings in both fall and winter. I also volunteered to teach this course.

Since the hourly rate of teaching was good, I thought that was the best professional and dignified way to earn some income without spending too much time on preparing any additional notes. The board turned down my request with an explanation that I didn't have the right professional credentials like that of a general, cost, or chartered accountant. The board refused to recognize my practical knowledge on household finances that I had acquired over the years and was ready to share it with those interested. No, it wanted a certified professional accountant.

The board's response didn't discourage me. I still wanted to earn side income by teaching.

To that effect, I placed an ad in the newspaper offering a course in statistics. My intention was to teach adults the ways to understand, analyze, and get a gist of what is important to know in this rapidly progressing information and digital age. I offered this course at a relatively reduced fee than what the area school boards were charging.

The ad ran for three days. Not a single person responded or showed any interest. That was my second failure.

Failures never discouraged me; rather these made me stronger and challenged my creative mind, and resolve.

One thing was certain though. No body was interested in learning what I was offering to teach. I shrugged it off as their loss and thought of the next move to make some extra money.

This time I went to the other extreme.

One evening after dinner, I put forth this idea to Amy to test her reaction.

"What!" she howled at me, "are you in your senses? You want to deliver newspapers?"

"What's wrong with that?" I replied softly. "The company pays good money for a door-to-door delivery. I can get up a bit early and should be back in time to get ready for the office."

"How early you can get up when you come to bed around or after one at night," she wondered. "How many hours would you be sleeping? Wouldn't the lack of sleep affect not only your health, but the performance at work too? You may jeopardize your main job which right now is your only source of income. You are trying to earn few extra dollars a month by risking your well-paid main job."

"Well, I need extra money to maintain this house and family expenditure," I repeated, "I have no choice …"

"I am not disputing it," she furiously interrupted me. "I want you to consider some of the consequences of your planned move. Just think for a moment. You are a father of two young daughters who will be in school shortly. Just imagine if someone told them that their father delivers newspapers. How would they feel? What kind of respect would they have among their friends? Again, think if you happen to deliver a paper at one of our friends or acquaintances home, what would they think about you, our family's status? You would be telling the world that what we are earning isn't enough. We are poor and need more money. You are going to ruin the family's image and social standing in the eyes of all neighbours and friends. I will not let you do it. In my opinion, we make a decent income. If you haven't acted wisely in the past, that's your problem and the family is suffering the consequences. If you must make some extra income, then think of some other plan." She moved away from the dining table to the kitchen's counter.

"You see the kind of profession I am in, I can't find a part-time work in the evening as many of our acquaintances have," I started to give her the justification. "For example, those in the accounting profession can easily find extra source of income by working, amending, or updating books of others for few hours in the evening or over weekends. Same goes for trades people like electricians and auto mechanics, and not only that, even engineers and lawyers can do some counselling work – all within their professional expertise or speciality. As a mathematical statistician or analyst, I can't find an hourly evening job in my profession. That's the irony. That's why I have to think of other ways, even if these look weird to you. In principle, I agree with you. Delivering newspapers is not that an ideal job, but it still pays well, and that's my bottom line."

I looked at her for her reaction.

"No, I wouldn't let you do it," she replied in rage. "It's a dumb idea. You are going to damage and disrepute the family. As I have said before, you don't and have never acted wisely."

"You can say that," I replied quietly, "but I know in my own heart I did the best I could under the circumstances. You always complain that I haven't acted wisely, or have acted dumb as I couldn't buy any income generating rental property, or purchase any land for future capital gains. I never ever had had enough funds not only to buy a rental property, but also to sustain its maintenance and up-keep in the event it wasn't rented out. I fully understand how different investments work and their subsequent rewards. But to make any sort of investment, you have to have some money available. It's a simple case of money begets money. If one doesn't have money to take even the initial step on this road to prosperity, then one shouldn't hope to experience the subsequent fruits of such prosperity. On the other hand, if I haven't been able to do any investment in the past, that doesn't mean I wouldn't be able to do any in the future either. So, please stop reminding me of my past. The past never determines the future. My life isn't over. I still hope to recover, and be able to offer you a much better life."

"I have heard it before. You sound like a broken record," she said sarcastically.

She left the kitchen. I heard her rumbling in the hallway,

"We'll see."

That was a typical Amy, my spouse, my life partner, always ready to remind me of my shortcomings, how dumb and stupid I was who didn't make any money by saving and investing wisely like others, ready to nag and belittle me at every possible opportunity. Her day-to-day insults, slings and arrows had almost strewn my body. Her attitude had steadily destroyed our personal relationship.

We were two living souls, living under the same roof, eating at the same table, sharing the same bed, but emotionally far away from each other. Other than communicating about our daughters' well-being or the house required this and that repair, or fixing, there was hardly anything left between us to talk about.

Our sex life had touched the rock bottom. If my levels of testosterone and/or her obligatory libido ever compelled us to indulge sexually, we made sure that those winds of arousal passed quietly without making a fury of passion – allowing our hot bodies to cool off quickly. Such winds of union blew no more than four to six times a year, which in turn, were good enough for both of us.

I didn't blame Amy for treating me like dirt. I deserved all of her nagging and belittling. Like any other woman, she had dreams to marry someone well-off and with good enough resources to offer her and our daughters a worry-free and comfortable life. She had agreed to marry me with some expectations about the kind of life, I, as a provider would be offering her.

There wasn't anything wrong with her expectations. I was fully aware that compared to men, women usually married with much higher expectations. I always felt bad, even ashamed that within ten years of marriage, all her expectations had dissipated, turning her into an angry and unfulfilled woman.

With too much of indebtedness and no cash money available, I was totally unable to fulfill her personal materialistic needs as a woman. The scarcity of money not only made me unable to offer her any presents or gifts, even on occasions like her birthday or wedding anniversary, as a token of my affection for her, but also I failed to entertain her by taking her out on any romantic trips. What I had offered her was simply a caged life – eat, sleep, and work.

And no woman living such a punitive life was ever going to be happy with her man – spouse or partner. Amy was no exception. Once I knew the root cause of her unhappiness, I accepted her anger, frustration, nagging, and all the belittling. I thought she was fully justified. She deserved a man who could provide her much more than just a simple roof over her head.

I wasn't even putting food on the table. Whatever she and the family were eating was purchased by herself, with her own earnings. I had no money budgeted to provide food for the family. All of my income was spent on paying the mortgage, property tax, insurances, monthly and other unplanned or unexpected bills, and minimum payments on a number of debts I was carrying.

The only good thing I did to her was that I kept her away from all of day-to-day financial woes.

***

With my financial situation worsening by the day, I was getting quite desperate to find a source of supplementary income. I had not only been unable to find a teaching job in the evening with one of the school boards in Ottawa, but also had failed to assemble a private group of my own for the same purpose.

I was now looking for opportunities outside teaching.

I was so obsessed and hungry about getting any evening job just to make few extra dollars in order to make my life liveable. I would come back from the office, eat my dinner, and then back to reading of the columns and columns of two newspapers - *The Ottawa Citizen* and *The Globe and Mail* that I used to subscribe to – in my study room located in one corner of our semi-finished basement.

At times the anguish and the frustration would force me to walk to and fro the length of the basement, and the overwhelming thoughts of total helplessness would make me strike my head against the drywalls of the basement, hoping that hits to the brain would eventually open it up and yield some viable solution. I would even quietly sob and utter in pain, "God, please help! Help me find a source of supplementary income," as if God had put me into this mess and He was obligated to find a solution for me. I would bang by forehead time and time again against the wall just to vent out my anger and despair.

***

One day in early July 1985, I found an ad in *The Globe and Mail*, under the caption **Business Opportunities.** It read:

STUFFING envelopes at home. $1.00 per envelope.
For details, write Box xxx, The Globe, XXX, Toronto, Ont. Xxx xxx.

I thought God had finally heard my cries of pain and bestowed me with an opportunity to make some extra cash. Stuffing of envelopes at home wasn't going to be that difficult. It didn't require any special skill – just the time and I had plenty of it. The ad injected a new life in me, gave me a hope to recover. I promptly responded to this ad.

A few weeks later, I got a response from a company located south of the border in the United States. The very first line of the letter read:

"How would you like to earn up to $1,000 weekly or more by simply securing envelopes, stuffing them with offers and returning them for payment?"

The letter went on, stating, "… *Now you can earn extra money in your spare time doing simple, pleasant work mainly* *consisting of stuffing envelopes at home. Firms pay you $1 per envelope you secure, stuffed with their circulars and submitted according to instructions. Submit 20 envelopes and receive a check for $20. Submit 100 – a check for $100. Submit 300 – receive a check for $300... No experience needed! We will show you how to start and continue day after day...."*

After making the sales pitch on a formatted letter with all the glittering and inviting details, the company wanted me to send C$46.95, with $5 extra for special delivery. In other words, I had to mail a cheque for C$51.95 to pull myself out of the financial misery I was in.

With all high hopes, I mailed out the payment. I was finally going to earn some supplementary income to a maximum of $1,000 a week.

After mailing the cheque, I took a deep breath of relief. I didn't worry about using more borrowed funds as needed to run the house, knowing that I was going to make nearly thousand dollars a week in my new business. I set up a special corner including a table in the basement to store supplies of materials to be stuffed into envelopes. I had put together all other accessories required to do this job – like the scotch tape, glue, and a pair of scissors, and a wet roller to affix stamps. I was all prepared to see the wheels of my fortune changing.

I kept waiting for month after month for any further news from the company or any shipment of materials and envelopes. Nothing came other than pure disappointment.

In early fall, I contacted the company again, reminding them that it had already cashed my cheque I had mailed in July. How come nothing had happened since then? Then the company sent me a note in late September informing me that it would take six to eight weeks for normal order processing.

By this time I was pissed off with the company. I realized it was all a hoax and I had been duped. Being desperate and needy, I simply focused on the potential dollars return from the ad without even questioning or checking its authenticity.

A few days later I got a letter from the company stating that people might think that an ad like this was a big hoax, but what it did was perfectly true and legal. Stuffing of envelopes is a legitimate business and anyone can run it at home, but to get that sort of business, a person him/herself had to make contact with a company and make the necessary arrangement. The company then sent me a few names of companies in the United States that I could check with.

Now who in his right mind with a business in the U.S. would send any materials for stuffing in envelopes, especially if that someone is living in Canada? So both logically and realistically, the whole issue wasn't worth pursuing. Even though I had been a victim of a hoax and had lost $51.95 in the deal, my resolve to find a source of supplementary income was still alive and well.

I kept looking at the ad columns of newspapers and came across the following:

UNLIMITED income. Home mailers program.
Free details. XXX Mail Order. Box xxx. B.C. xxx xxx.

This time I had to send a cheque for C$30 to the advertiser in order to get more details about what was being offered.

When the pamphlet arrived, its top line read '*How to find your fortune! Earn between $350 and $1,000 by working at home in your spare time. Open up an own, or join some existing mail order business.*'

This pamphlet had expounded on the benefits of opening a mail order business, stating that two factors that determined its success were one's intense ambition, and a real determination to succeed. Since I had both of these traits, I liked what I read and was really inspired by it. Since I was hungry for cash, I was willing to try anything. And considering my preference to work on my own account, I thought the opportunity fitted well with both my personality and the choice of work hours. There wasn't going to be any conflict with my main job. I had to dig a bit more deeply into this venture.

I realized that nobody was going to pull me out of this sinking indebtedness. Granted, any financial institution would be glad to lend me a consolidated loan, but still that loan had to be paid back and for that I needed money.

A little bit of research further showed that the mail order business was quite lucrative in the mid eighties as American and Canadian households spent $50 billion a year, or $137 million a day, purchasing goods and services by mail. This was quite a convincing figure, something real and worth pursuing. Since I wasn't ready to surrender to any adversity, I decided to give it a try.

Luckily, this business didn't require any large investment, or required any special office or work place. I could easily start it from my study room in the basement, and that too, without leaving or affecting my main job. I didn't need any specific business experience other than some simple book-keeping and marketing.

Another good point about this business was that the entire country was my potential market. I thought of people like Hewlett and Packard who started their business in Packard's garage with an initial investment of a little more than $500. Similarly, Mattel, the world's largest toy company, started its business in 1945 in a garage. Kraft foods started its business from selling house-to-house a variety of cheeses. Examples abounded. What I needed was the strong will to put my intentions into action.

Once I had decided to start a mail order business from home, the next question was what type of product I could sell. I knew I couldn't sell any perishable goods, health or hygienic products. I thought of selling a variety of garden-tools and/or other household accessories including telephones, security or kitchen aids, etc., but didn't feel comfortable with any one of these options.

Since I was too bookish, I had a good knowledge of books in print and on audios. Also, as I was always keen to learn and teach, I thought of helping the community to enhance its knowledge and upgrade skills for the rapidly changing job market. To that effect, I decided to open a mail-order business selling skill development products including books, audios, videos, and CDs.

After I made the choice about the products to sell, I had to work hard to find a network of suppliers of these products at a workable discount.

To ensure that I wasn't doing anything contrary to municipality's zoning laws, I cleared with the municipality about using a part of our basement for storing, packaging, and shipping of goods. I paid for a Post-Box number for all business mailings and correspondence. I also got federal goods and services tax (GST) number from Canada's Revenue Agency (CRA) as well as a provincial sales tax (PST) number from the ministry of finance of the Ontario's provincial government. I wanted to make sure that whatever I was doing was within the laws of the land because I was still working as an employee of the federal government.

I was now wearing two hats: A full-time paid worker as well as a self-employed man working on my own account.

"How can you do both jobs?" Jen asked me while we were having lunch one afternoon. "Do you take any rest at all?" She wondered.

"My work is my rest," I replied. "Even if it's hard, I really enjoy it. I don't get any feeling of tiredness." I boasted to impress her.

"Still, I think you need to go easy on yourself," she remarked, "you have a responsible job here and any advertent or inadvertent misstep due to poor sleep or fatigue can prove costly." She warned me in good faith.

"I am fully aware of that," I concurred with her, "especially when dealing with the media. Any wrong words spoken can do irreparable damage. I realize I may even lose my job."

"I don't think you'll ever lose your job," she interrupted me. "You are a good researcher, analyst, and above all a prodigious writer. The media has always accepted and highlighted your reports and papers. Everyone here knows about it. You have earned your reputation." She was likely pumping my ego.

"Oh! Please stop talking like that," I shook my head, and peered into her eyes, "why are you saying all this. You are not reading my farewell speech. What's on your mind?"

"Nothing," she recoiled and rolled her eyes, "I was just reminding you how good you are. I am quite impressed."

"Thank you, good to hear," I said and changed the topic of our conversation. "How is Peter doing? What's the latest on his job?"

"He has moved to another local technology company in order to get away from that job uncertainty hanging like a sword over his head. He is getting a little less salary, but he tells me he has better security and supplementary benefits including the retirement pension. The only trouble is that he's now more miserable and dissatisfied as he doesn't like his job. He thinks he's over-qualified for the kind of job he's doing."

"We all think that way at one point or another," I commented, "I am sure you feel the same at some point."

"True," she replied softly, "but I am really concerned about him. I don't know where he will end up with this attitude. His day-to-day moodiness has begun to affect not only our relationship, but also he isn't behaving well with our son, Josh either. The poor kid used to go out with his father most of the evenings, but ever since he changed the job, he isn't paying proper attention to our son. I can't see the kid whining over Dad's poor behaviour. Not only that, even if I accidently touch him at night, he jerks away from me. Maybe he has had enough of me."

"All of his actions seem normal to me as he's under a lot of stress," I expressed my opinion. "He should know that the labour market is going through a sea of change and a good majority of workers are holding jobs totally incompatible to what they studied and trained for at university. They are in jobs not that well suited to their skills. Considering the prevailing not only the domestic, but also the international economic situation, the job market in each and every developed and developing country is changing. Canada is no exception. As paid workers, we don't have a choice. The only way to keep our job as well as sanity is to adjust with the changes in the labour market even if these required upgrading and/or learning of new skills. The onus is on us, the workers, how we cope with this fast looming transformation."

"I keep telling him that," she replied softly, "the guy doesn't pay any attention to whatever I say. It's so frustrating. We both know how economies all over the world are changing and we need to adjust to the reality of times. Why go too far? I see the example sitting right in front of me. You couldn't find a second paid job to supplement your income. So rather than getting frustrated or blaming the system or the environment, you have opted to work on your own. Not very many people would take this brave initiative. I really admire your guts. You have taken a big step to eventually get what you want."

"Hang on, hang on," I stopped her. "I have just taken the initial steps. I still have a long way to go. I have no clue as to how much of net income I would be making at the end. I had to take this step because I couldn't sit and watch my own slow death. As the main provider, I had to act to protect the well-being of my family."

"I wish my husband would think the same way," she exhaled a deep breath. "The way things are I am afraid one day I will end up as the main breadwinner of the family. The guy is losing his sense of family responsibility. To be honest with you, I think it's all a matter of time. I can see reversing of our roles in the family."

"Oh, please don't jump to such conclusions that fast," I consoled her gently. "The guy may soon regain his sense of responsibility both as a father and a husband. Consider this as a transitory phase. After all, he's a well educated guy and understands well his role as a provider."

"Thanks for uplifting my spirits," she replied with a half-hearted grin. "I hope you are right. By the way, are you coming to the office picnic next week at the Lac Lemay Park?" she asked.

"Yes! I was planning to," I replied. "Do you want a ride?"

"Please, if you don't mind," she nodded with a light grin.

She had likely overcome her doom and gloom.

"That way, you can also drop me home in time to take care of Josh," she added.

***

On the morning of the picnic, Jen caught my eye and made me glance at her full figure for a couple of minutes. This was contrary to my daily routine of casually exchanging 'Good morning' and very few words with her before walking down to my office. She was looking thoroughly smashing.

In stead of wearing her professional outfit – a blouse tucked in a skirt, with an open matching jacket long enough to cover her waist, or a long dress touching her knees, with black pumps, or spike heels covering her stockinged feet – she was wearing a sleeveless white dress with red polka dots, with her hair pinned up, and wearing typical Brazilian V-shaped flip-flops.

"You are all dressed up, ready to go to the picnic," I commented.

"Of course," she replied with a wide smile, and slowly walked to her office.

"I will bring the car in front of the office at twelve-thirty," I said loud enough so that she could hear me before entering her office.

She was already waiting for me by the time I pulled up my station wagon in front of the office building. She opened the passenger door, hopped on the seat, and pulled the door to close it with a bang. She buckled herself. Under the bright afternoon summer sun, we were on our way to Lac Lemay to spend the rest of the day with our colleagues.

"You look salacious in this summary dress," I complimented her. "I wanted to say it the moment I saw you this morning, but then I didn't want anyone else to hear, or misread my comments," I gave her the unsolicited explanation. "You know how people bad-mouth others, or spread wild rumours about them."

"I wouldn't have minded if you had complimented me right away," she replied with a broad smile. "To be honest with you, I would have liked to hear your instant reaction. Tell me if you find me smashing today just because I am dressed differently, or you find me smashing each and every day. Be honest."

She turned her face and fixed her eyes on me.

"What kind of a question is that?" I asked freakishly and gave her an inquisitive momentary look as I had to focus on the road. "As a woman, you can't read my eyes when we meet or talk almost every day?"

"I read you well," she replied bashfully, "I know you like me as your close friend. Right now I am just asking how you like me as a woman. Forget for a moment that we are close friends, work together as colleagues, help and share each other's work. Just look at me as a man. Would you be interested to pursue me?"

"Well, if you really want to know," I turned my face to look into her eyes, "I have found you very attractive since the day we started this job together. Your innocent smiling face and your beautiful almond eyes are more than enough, at least for me, to not only like you, but also pursue you until I got you."

"Like in what sense," she queried, her eyes still fixed on me.

My explanation was still not good enough for her. She was looking for some more specifics.

"Gee! You must be in a mood to play some sexy or intriguing game," I replied churlishly. "After all, we are going to have a fun-filled afternoon."

I gave her a loving look and re-focused on the road.

"Why do you think a healthy young man would pursue a pretty woman?" I asked.

"I know it, but I still want to hear from your mouth," she insisted.

She kept looking at my face, as if she was searching for some clues. After a short pause, she continued, "The reason I am asking this question is because at home, Peter no longer pays any attention to me even if I am standing bare naked in front of him. I just want to know if I, as a woman, have lost all the sex appeal. Do you find me sexy?"

"Of course, I do," I blurted out. "I, as a man, find you sexy enough to arouse my feelings, desire to hold you in my arms, kiss you passionately, and even have sex with you – that of course with your full consent."

I smiled at her.

"Does this answer your question?" I asked her after a pause.

"Yes," she replied. "You have boosted my soul and spirit. You have validated me as a woman who's still sexy and vibrant. It's good to know that I haven't lost any of my sex appeal. I still look attractive to a man, can arouse his desire to hold me in his arms and make love to me. I am sure Peter has his own reasons for rejecting me. Maybe I should stop paying attention to his repulsive behaviour, resulting in nothing but personal grief and utter dissatisfaction. I must take charge of my life and pay more attention to gratify my own needs. Do you think that would be too selfish for me?"

She questioned me, her eyes still tucked on my face, seeking some personally satisfying answer.

"I don't think that would be selfish by any standard," I replied calmly. "As a woman, you have every right to do and act what pleases you as long as you are not physically hurting anyone including Josh and Peter, and/or breaking any law of the land. You are one responsible free soul."

We had reached Lac Lemay.

We parked our car at the marked parking lot.

We all assembled as a group and chalked out our activities for the remainder of the afternoon. We had the choice of playing sports including volleyball, badminton, or football, go on the hiking trails, boat ride, walk on the beach, or do anything that pleases each one of us. And if we didn't want to do anything, we could go home or even back to the office.

Jen and I joined the opposing teams formed to play a few games of volleyball. It was a bit of exercise and a bit of fun playing with colleagues. We both had to remove our footwear to play the game. For Jen, it was easy, as she shook her feet up and threw away her flip-flops, whereas I had to undo the laces of my shoes first before separating them from my feet, and then remove the socks.

Right after the game, Jen and I separated from the group and opted to walk on the beach. We were still walking barefoot, full of sand and light brown mud clinging to our soles and toes.

We were both wearing dark sunglasses but no hats. The sun's heat was too strong. Our faces were beginning to perspire. Since we were walking close to the waters of the Gatineau River, the light cooler breeze was a welcome relief under the hot blazing sun.

While I was walking with Jen, occasionally making comments on the environment –people walking or swimming, or structures of buildings around the lake – I was still focused on the conversation that Jen had initiated in the car.

The more I analyzed it, the more I reached to the conclusion that Jen was one hell of a sexually frustrated woman. She wasn't getting her fair share of sexual satisfaction. Her husband, Peter, was either too engulfed by his worries about his job and the resulting economic insecurity it provided, or likely was involved with another woman. Irrespective of the reason, he was distancing himself from his wife, who in my eyes, was quite pretty and sexually inviting. Since she was in her thirties, she was likely at the apex of her sexual appetite. She was desperately looking for someone to satisfy and cool down her burning sexual desire.

When a woman is in a situation like this, searching for a man with whom she could go to bed, she, first and foremost, looks for someone whom she knows well, likely among her friends or colleagues. With a known person, she can easily express herself, her desire, and be open to other give and take adjustments needed to mutually satisfy each other. The bottom line is that she feels sexually secure with such a person. She would, however, think twice before sharing a bed with a complete stranger, say picked up at a bar or social club, because of the potential risks involved such as catching any sexual infection or disease, creating any ill-will threatening the relationship if the planned arrangement failed to materialize, earning any bad reputation for herself or her family. If stigmatized as a loose sexual character, she can even lose her job.

I knew I was her close friend and worked with her. Over time I had earned her trust. She had tried to open up with me today and initiated this very intimate conversation. She wanted to know how I found her as a woman, a woman good enough to share the bed. She looked very happy and satisfied after listening to what I really thought about her and my long held inner desire to make love to her.

Now that she was accessible, was I ready to accept her and give her what she wanted? I wasn't that certain in my mind. I kept clearing up my foggy mind. The main hurdle was that I still had a family with two young daughters, a wife in name only to support, a house to maintain, and above all, deeply indebted. I had no money whatsoever to entertain her. How could she be happy with me? Sex alone wasn't going to keep us together for too long. And I didn't want her to turn over time into another Amy.

While I was mulling over these thoughts and the possible liaison between us, Jen pointed out one empty wooden layback red chair in the park and suggested we sat down on it. She was likely tired and thirsty after the ball game.

She wanted me to get her a plain soda. While I walked towards the food counter, she walked to sit or lie on that chair.

By the time, I got to that chair, holding a can of plain soda for her and ginger ale for me, Jen had stretched her body on the chair, resting her back against the slanted but raised wooden plank, and her head on it using her pinned up hair as a cushion. The late afternoon sun was piercing her eyes, even if covered by her sunglasses.

She took the can of soda from me and invited me to sit on the foot of that long chair. As she sat up, the bottom of her short dress was furling by the blowing breeze. I could see she wasn't wearing any nylons, but just a white panty covering her vital organs.

I quickly glanced away from her barely naked thighs. Even if I wanted to touch them, I couldn't because we were sitting in a bustling public place. We continued to quench our thirst caused by the sun's heat. This commercially paid small can of drink, however, was not meant to quench her real inner body thirst that only a man's natural reservoir could do. I fully sympathized with her.

We both were quiet and watching the passersby, or those swimming at the nearby shore, or boats sailing at a distance right in the middle or on the far shore of the river. I could see the brightness of the sun was still bothering her. She had placed her bent right arm on her glasses to further protect her eyes from the hot glaring rays of sun.

After few minutes, she changed her direction.

She bent her knees, removed her sunglasses, folded them, and placed these on the long arm of the chair. She laid on her left side, placing her head on top of her joined open palms, and brought her face very close to the outside of my right thigh.

"Lying this way, the sun's brightness won't bother my eyes," she mumbled.

I let her adjust her posture on the chair without making any move.

"Make yourself comfortable," I replied softly. "You can snooze for a while, if you like. We have plenty of time."

She gave me her empty soda can to throw in the nearest garbage can.

She must have dozed off. I watched her move her body's position, moving her right arm from under her left cheek and letting it fall in my lap. I could now feel the pleasant light weight of a woman's bare arm around my waist. I couldn't tell if she knew what she was doing or it was all because she was snoozing.

Even though I had touched her arms accidently during work or walks we had taken together over all these years, I had never experienced such a close touch of her arm, or any part of her body, for that matter. Her bare arm twirled around my waist had sensationalized my body. I simply looked at her right cheek and somewhat pinkish ears.

While I was enjoying the touch of that sleeping beauty, with her nose now touching the outer edge of my thigh, I felt her right hand had gripped more forcefully the front of my waist line. I couldn't tell if she was now sleeping soundly and, to be honest, didn't want to know either what she was doing – knowingly or unknowingly. I simply sat there as a statue.

After fifteen minutes or so, she opened up her eyes, looked at me and said with a broad grin, "I hope you didn't mind. I likely was dreaming and tried to hold on to something tightly. I didn't think it was your waist. I am so sorry."

"Don't worry. That wasn't any big deal," I assured her with a smile. "I am glad you could relax a bit. Do you want another drink or are you ready to leave?"

"We'd better leave as I want to reach home in time for Josh," she replied.

She got up, brushed her hair and dress with her open palms. She wore her flip-flops. We were ready to leave.

On the way to the parking lot, she asked me, "Can dreams turn true?"

"I have no clue," I replied, and then asked in the same breath, "Why do you ask? Has it something to do with what you just dreamt?"

"Sort of," she chided.

I opened the car's door for her to let her sit on the passenger seat.

"It was a weird dream," she continued, "still thinking about it."

"What was it about?" I was now more curious to know.

"I'll tell you some other day," she chuckled, and fastened her seat-belt.

On the way to Ottawa, she smelt some kind of an odour in the car. She inhaled deeply to figure out the kind of smell she smelt. She gave me an inquisitive look.

"What's this smell?" she asked.

"These are the gas fumes that occasionally come from the exhaust pipe – when touched by any bumpy objects on the road," I told her.

And with that, I rolled down the panes of windows on our sides.

"Ever since I bought this second-hand piece of lemon, I have been taking it in for repairs of one kind or another. I have already spent way more on this car than it really warranted. Now I pay attention only to life-threatening repairs like fixing up of brakes, supporting rods, axels, transmission, alternator, etc. The rest I treat as a minor repair and liveable, including the emission of gas fumes."

"But breathing in such gas fumes isn't healthy for anyone driving or sitting in this car," she snarled at me. "This can be very harmful as anyone sitting in the car is inhaling carbon dioxide and carbon monoxide – both have terrible consequences. You are endangering not only your life, but also of those driving with you in this car."

"I am too scared of taking it in for repairs," I replied casually. "You know how these garages rip you off as if money grows on trees. The fixing of this particular problem may not be that expensive, but once the mechanic has a hand on the vehicle, he can tell me several other problems requiring a fix. Then it becomes more problematic: damn if you ignore the mechanic's findings or advice, and damn if you go along with all of his suggested repairs. So the best thing is to go in and get the specific job done. When you are short of money, you skip minor or non-life threatening repairs."

"I hate to agree with you," she replied with all the empathy. "Still, you can't drive a car with leaky gas fumes."

"Well, when you have no savings or cash available, and the only source of funds to fix any repairs on a car or home, and/or meet other needs is more borrowing, then you have to prioritize what's important and not important for survival. You limit your borrowing to sustain just the essentials of day-to-day life, forget all other less important needs or necessities, and don't even think of spending on luxuries or personal entertainment."

I indirectly conveyed her where I stood financially. Even if she knew about the level of my indebtedness, she had not as yet personally witnessed the kind of life I was living.

"I have been fully aware of your financial constraints and the level of your current indebtedness as we have always shared our personal details, but I didn't think you would be that reckless about hurting the lives of others," she scolded me. "Imagine if someone suffered any serious or fatal outcome due to your taking of short-cuts or setting wrong priorities just to save on borrowed funds? You will be feeling guilty, wouldn't you? And this guilt alone will not let you live with any peace or harmony the rest of your life, and may even kill you prematurely. No, I totally disagree with your thinking."

She was now quite emotional.

"I can't be emotional like you," I responded. "I have to live with the reality. Neither the lenders have unlimited cash to lend me, nor I have the resources to pay them back. I have already over-extended myself and barely managing to keep the wolf away from the door. What I now have is simply the ability to make bare minimum payments on cards and other loans. By making such payments, I am simply buying time, hoping that someday the tide in my life will change and I would be able to pay back every cent that I owe."

"I am not questioning your thinking, ability, or the approach to pay off all the debt you owe," she parroted back, "I am talking about your senseless manner in which you are risking the lives of those travelling with you in this car. Need I tell you that indebtedness is very much related to your life-cycle stage? Granted, right now you have moved into a new house with much more mortgage debt, besides all of your other consumer loans. Imagine when children are all grown up, and mortgage is paid out, you have little or no debt left. But in the meantime, if you knowingly hurt or injure someone simply because of excessive debt, that's something that will leave a permanent scar on, even making you care for a sick or disabled person for the rest of your life. So which is the lesser of the two evils? As I see it, avoid risking lives of others. I am not saying you don't spend carefully. You do, but by not causing any hurt to others."

"Lesson learnt," I looked at her, bowed my head in gratitude. "Now that you have learnt much more about my precarious financial situation as well as about my personal thoughts and philosophy, would you still wish to keep my company outside the work environment?"

"Your current financial situation and its related thinking are all peripheral to me," she replied with a shrug. "Over all these years, I have found you a very decent, disciplined, hard-working, and compassionate person. I personally would like to see our friendship grow over time. Financially, you will be all right one day, and who knows, we together might even be reminiscing these times."

"Thank you for having that much confidence in me," I replied with my head bowed. "I wish well for our lasting friendship."

"People have a lasting friendship when they have something in common," she remarked, sounding like a sage. "And you know full well what's common between us? We both have been let loose by our spouses. You, because of too much indebtedness and no cash flow, and me, because of job insecurity brought in by the changing labour market. We two have to find a life of our own within the parameters of our individual families."

I didn't pay much attention to what she had said. But her words *'we both have been let loose by our spouses'* kept ringing in my ears while my eyes were focused on the road. I didn't want to pursue this discussion as I was taking a turn to her house.

I stopped the car in front of her house.

I got out as I saw Peter and Josh standing on the driveway. "How are you? Peter," I asked and shook his hand, "long time, no see. How's everything?"

While I was talking to him, I saw Jen stepping out of the car. No sooner did she get off, Josh wrapped her legs with his tiny arms. She lifted him up and kissed his cheek. Peter, while talking to me, kept shifting his stares at me and his wife.

"Everything is okay," he replied in a soft and depressed voice. "I wish I had a better job that I could really enjoy doing. My current job is too mundane with no mental challenge or stimulation whatsoever. Jen must have told you about how I feel about my current job. At least you and she are working on issues that touch all of us in one form or another."

I could detect an element of envy as well as total ennui in Peter's depressed voice.

I shook his hand and said 'bye' to Jen before getting into the car. I had to inhale gas fumes for another half an hour.

CHAPTER SEVEN

While I was in the throes of setting up the mail-order business, I came across an ad that had invited people to a free presentation by someone who had earned a name and fame and had made millions of dollars from developing, investing, and speculating in real estate including land holdings, acquisition and building of houses for sale or rent. This guy was doing the public a favour by sharing his secrets on how to make money in real estate.

The ad's caption *"Come and learn how to become rich by investing in real estate"* intrigued me. Since I was frantically looking for ways to make money and improve my financial security, and that too, as early as possible, I became quite anxious to attend this free seminar. The only thing I had to do was to phone the named contact, give her my name and phone number, and reserve a place. In other words, the presenter wanted to have all the contact information of all those attending his presentation, in case he had to follow them up.

As I was driving to the advertised venue, I was making all sorts of plans about how I would invest if I were able to make money from real estate, what I would buy, and how I would be out of this painful life without money. I wanted money, money, and nothing but the money to pull me out of my current misery. The ad had given me a glimmer of hope that my bad days were just numbered. My life was about to change.

I reached the venue in time, parked my car in the parking lot, and entered the big hall that could easily accommodate close to two hundred people. There were many people already sitting upfront on rows and rows of folding chairs, laid out in two sections separated by a walkway – about eight to ten feet wide, running all along the big hall.

I walked up to one of the horizontal desks covered with white linen tablecloth, placed right at the entrance to the hall. Behind these desks were young, pretty, attractive, and vivacious women (one of the ways to influence and calm down people entering with any nervousness or apprehension is to have them engaged in a conversation with an attractive smiling young woman) who were to cross check names of attendees, and hand them some material describing the achievements of the presenter, his special skills and qualifications, contact information for more details, and the session's agenda. I had my name checked, and was instructed to have a seat anywhere I wanted to sit.

When the speaker entered the hall, smiling and dancing, he spoke with full throttle,

"Welcome to my seminar, folks. You have done yourself a big favour. Tonight you are going to learn how to make big money by investing in real estate. Just follow the simple rules that I am going to share with you tonight." And with that pitch, he started his presentation.

He was a good orator. He impressed me. *'Maybe everyone whose pockets were deep and full, smiled and spoke that cheerfully with full voice,'* so I thought. I hadn't ever spoken like that in my life. As a man with no money, I had been sad and gloomy all my life, spoken softly and timidly, lacked self-confidence and self-esteem, and felt powerless and useless – like a walking dead, unable to attract or influence anyone. For a moment, I really envied the presenter who was making jokes, laughing and walking with big strides on the floor.

What he spoke could be summarized in few simple steps: once you have saved enough to make a down payment for your first property including your principal residence, i.e. your house, then you were all set to indulge in a real estate market. Over time, as the property created more equity (i.e., its rising market price coupled with a declining mortgage), one would be in a position to take a mortgage close to one-half to two-thirds of that equity value, and along with any other personal savings, or additional temporary borrowings, one could buy another property for rent. Now with equity gains in two properties, and with more savings on account of additional rental income, one was in a better position to re-invest all that in acquiring another property, and so on. Over time, one could cumulate a number of properties and have asset holdings worth millions of dollars, and a horde of cash savings from all that rental income (after paying for all the maintenance, repairs required, and/or property taxes on all holdings).

I liked his key sentences,

"The real estate holdings multiply over time ... One gets rich even while one's sleeping because the market forces are pushing the values of properties largely on account of demand and supply situation ... The value of property varies by city and area ...Very rarely, one loses in real estate unless one buys a property in an economically depressed area ... One shouldn't risk or speculate beyond one's ability to sustain the over-runs or losses ... One should never borrow beyond one's ability to pay, even as a minimum payment ... One can easily succumb to the consequences of over-expanding by taking excessive borrowings, out of any personal ambition or competition ...One shouldn't act recklessly not only in real estate business, but in any business."

Another suggestion he made about making money through sheer speculation in real estate that involved making a down payment on a unit while the building was planned or was in the initial construction phase, and then sell it later to another purchaser at an inflated price when it was all ready for occupancy or even earlier (depending, say, on one's financial situation or level of greed). He cited an example of a person who had pocketed a few thousand dollars in less than twenty-four hours – simply by agreeing to purchase a unit in a new urban development with the minimum required down-payment, and then sold it at an inflated price to another more eager and keen purchaser who was still waiting in the queue while all of the units were sold out. The initial purchaser made cash on a quick flip of real estate.

To us rookies sitting in the hall, this all looked like a magic way of making quick money, but as the presenter re-emphasized, that's all it takes to profit from real estate speculation.

After his one-hour presentation, he got into his sales pitch – the real reason he had invited financially hungry people to his seminar. He wanted to exploit their financial wants and squeeze some money out of them.

He would personally guide all those who would like to enrol in his course on real estate, which was usually offered at three thousand dollars, was being made available at fifteen hundred dollars for those enrolling on the spot that evening. He wanted to be benevolent and didn't want anyone to leave disappointed. He was there to help people get rich by investing in real estate business. He sounded too enthusiastic to share the secrets of his enriching trade.

Since I didn't have fifteen hundred dollars, I didn't volunteer to enrol in his course. Moreover, I thought that he had spoken only one side of investing in real estate property, which in turn, was good enough to persuade money-hunters to follow him and make quick bucks.

He hadn't mentioned the other side of the coin dealing with costs and risks a financially poor person owning any rental property would have to go through. These risks included the ability to maintain the property in good and habitable condition, property tax and other maintenance costs like heat, hydro, water, and above all, the ability to sustain the cost of a vacant rental property. If the owner had bought a property on a financial margin, there was a good chance that he/she could lose that property, if it stayed vacant for a much longer duration. The lender can reclaim it; that means the poor purchaser would lose even his/her initial investment, putting him/her into more financial misery, or even bankruptcy.

And, as far as making any quick gain from real estate speculation was concerned, that too was beyond my reach as it required making the initial down-payment, besides the cost of keeping it at least until it was sold. A person like me who was already drowned in debt couldn't afford to take any such risk. Even though the concept of getting rich by quick flipping of real estate looked simple and straight forward, I could hardly venture into it.

I left the seminar with the intention of not indulging into the real estate market because for me, its risks outweighed the benefits.

"How did it go?" Amy asked me casually after I reached home.

"It was quite informative," I replied in the same manner, "the guy was selling his course for fifteen hundred dollars. Like any other businessman, he's selling a product to mostly those who have the least capability to get into the market."

"How can you make such a blanket statement?" she wondered loudly. "There could be many who were likely there to improve their knowledge about how to delve into the real estate market or exploit it for profit."

"You may be right," I concurred with her. "I know I can't get into it with my current financial situation. I might even lose my initial down-payment."

"That's what I don't like in you – always thinking negatively," she yelled. "How do you know you will lose your down-payment? You haven't tried anything yet. Moreover, there's risk in everything. Try something first before jumping to conclusions." She strongly advised.

I was well aware of Amy's impression about me. She never thought of me as financially smart. Nonetheless, she desperately wanted me to get into this thriving business.

Alas! She knew the reality.

I knew all about this flourishing business, and also was much keener than her to get into this business, but I had no means. I was like a bird who wanted to fly up in the sky, but had no wings. And a bird with no wings was meant to simply find its living by crawling on the hard earth.

"If you so insist," I replied just to quieten her.

I didn't want her to degrade me any further.

"I will look into it," I mumbled softly, and left her alone.

In the following weeks, Amy and I looked and read more carefully the ads on properties for sale. Finally, we liked one and decided to purchase it.

It was a small garden home in the east end of the city. I thought I could own it by using some of my funds available in my line of credit as a down-payment, and the rest would be mortgaged. Even if I didn't make money in the early stages, I could manage it on funds available in my line of credit. We were now ready to purchase a property to generate some supplementary income in the form of net rent.

I phoned the seller and made an appointment to see him as well as his property in question. Although Amy was happy that we were finally going to have a property to rent, and enjoy the benefits of ensuing rental income, I was quite concerned and apprehensive about getting the mortgage approved with my existing commitments on several borrowings. Knowing the possible outcome, I still pursued our plan to purchase the property and applied for the desired mortgage. Since this was going to be our investment property rather than the first principal residence, we were obligated to pay close to twenty percent of its value as a down-payment.

One Saturday morning, Amy and I met the seller at the property in question. We were there to have a first look at it. It was a small, end unit garden home with three bed rooms, and one-and-a-half bathrooms, and required some upgrading including repairs. That was an extra and unplanned expenditure.

After inspecting every nook and corner of the unit, we agreed to pursue the purchase and talked to our respective notaries. I attached a cheque in the amount of five hundred dollars with the initial agreement of purchase as a sign of our serious intention to buy the property. I had decided to take a plunge in the real estate market and take a chance to see where this adventure would take us. I would at least be able to shut Amy's mouth billowing out any more derogatory comments.

I went to a financial institution (FI-III) and submitted my request for the required mortgage amount. Since I had a number of borrowings from different sources, I had to specify their names and the amount I owed to each of them. I personally felt rather uncomfortable and somewhat belittled as I completed such details, so much so, that I intentionally didn't report the source of my line of credit with FI-II and the amount left in it as this was going to be my source of down-payment. I was fully aware that what I was doing was not right as I should be reporting all of my financial details to FI-III so that it could rightly assess my loan application.

A few days after submitting the request for mortgage, I got a phone call from one of the reps of FI-III. She asked me if I had a line of credit with FI-II and what was my outstanding balance there. I had no choice other than to tell her the details. She asked me why I didn't report it in the loan application. What could I tell her? I told her it must have been an inadvertent mistake, and I apologized for it. But then she told me that since I didn't provide all of the relevant details in my mortgage application, FI-III had to reject my application. She apologized for refusing to approve my mortgage and causing any inconvenience to me.

I wasn't surprised to hear her verdict on my mortgage application. I knew it all along. No financial institution was going to lend me that hefty amount of mortgage, especially with my current financial bindings.

My plan was simple: to pay the monthly payment on the second mortgage from the expected monthly rent, and if worse came to worst, I would be paying the condominium fee and property tax from my line of credit with FI-II just to maintain the property. This property would eventually appreciate in value over time and prove financially beneficial to me and my family.

The entire plan crashed with FI-III's refusal to approve the mortgage. All of this angered Amy and as a result, she turned more sarcastic, hurting me more with her verbal slings and arrows, and further pulled herself away from me. Our personal life had touched the rock bottom. Our already cool sexual relationship had chilled even more.

Not only this episode of trying to purchase a second property to earn some rental income and/or improve future financial security turned sour, I also lost money in this deal. When I informed the seller's notary about my inability to secure a mortgage for the property in question, and requested him to return my cheque of five hundred dollars, he, after several weeks, sent me a cheque of fifteen dollars, stating that it was all that was left for me after paying all the administrative and other charges on the deal.

In other words, I paid five hundred dollars for all this humiliation, insults, and degradation heaped not only by the seller and his attorney, but also by my own spouse, who was still sharing the roof with me. The latter's boorishness, in turn, now pushed me to concentrate more on my mail-order business and turn it into a successful venture – just to impress upon her that I was quite capable and serious about making some supplementary income.

Both my life and dignity were at stake.

"You sure you know what you are doing?" Amy asked me, doubting my intentions. "You have no knowledge, no experience of running a business."

"You are darn right. I have neither any knowledge nor experience," I supported her conclusions, "but I can learn everything about running this business from books and other sources." I replied emphatically. "I won't need any bank's permission or loan to establish this business."

"But we will still need some money to establish it," she parroted with a sense of panic.

"How much money could one need to buy papers, pencils, stamps, and other essential supplies?" I asked her sarcastically. "I will manage financially. This is one business that requires no capital whatsoever. The only thing it requires is determination and dedication, and I have plenty of that."

I pacified her worries. Considering our chilled relationship, she was likely happy to see me experience failure after failure.

"Where will you find the material to learn about this business?" she wondered.

"All such material can be found in public libraries," I replied. "Not only about setting it up, but also about selecting the suppliers of one's chosen products, prices, marketing, public relations, you name it. The only thing you need, as I told you earlier, is your ability to work hard with full concentration and dedication. And I will now be spending my evenings and weekends on learning these details, unless I have to go to the office to complete some scheduled paper or report. To fulfill any official commitment is obligatory."

"How long will it take to establish this business and see any actual return in the form of additional income?" She was curious about the realization of the actual bottom line – inflow of extra income.

"It can take anywhere between six to twelve months," I replied with a shrug. "It all depends on what sort of product we decide to sell, time spent in securing its source of supply, negotiating the terms of doing business, delivery times, and on and on. Since we are not going to sell any perishable goods, I have to think of selling something more solid and tangible. I want to sell something unique."

"And what would that be?" She enquired, still showing her cavalier attitude.

She didn't think I was serious enough about my plans.

"A good majority in this business usually sell books, clothes, garden and other small tools, sound recordings including albums of songs, tapes, CDs, small handy kitchen accessories, and so on. All of these things are always in demand. These are all non-perishable and unbreakable things that can also endure shocks and bumps during shipping and delivery, and above all, are affordable for an average household. Buyers can simply order any such thing from the comfort of their home without wasting time on looking for it, or shopping at any shopping center."

"Never mind what the majority of people sell," she rudely interrupted me, "just tell me what you want to sell?"

"I plan to sell skill development products on books, audio tapes, videos, and CD-ROMs. Considering how our labour market is changing and how those presently employed or looking for employment need new skills, I think we have a good potential market or clientele to serve. The only thing is to find the right suppliers and negotiate acceptable terms of doing business, including the discounted rate that we will be getting these products at."

"What's this discounted rate?" She interrupted me again.

"That's the rate we will get the product from the manufacturer or supplier in order to sell it to our potential customer. Say, if the supplier has listed a retail price of twenty dollars for a given product, that supplier will sell that product to us, as its agent, say, at fifty percent of its listed price or ten dollars, then that fifty percent discount is referred to as our discounted price. Since the customer pays the same listed price whether he/she buys from the manufacturer or supplier, or any of its agents like a book store, tool shop, or any mail-order supplier, we as intermediate agent will operate on the discounted value of that product. This discounted value is meant to cover our cost of running the business, and then what's left after paying our business expenses is our net income." I explained to her in simple terms.

"Not only this additional income is subject to tax, but also all these business expenses will be tax deductible?" She wondered loudly, showing her familiarity with concepts of accounting she had learnt at the Algonquin College.

"Indeed," I nodded my head, "you are right. Even if we don't make any net business income or profit from this venture, all of the business expenses can be claimed. That way, we can expect to receive some tax refund – depending on how good, or bad the business is running."

"So we can expect to receive some tax refund each year as long as we are operating the business," she elatedly confirmed. "That will indeed be a help to us – getting tax refund over and above whatever we get in respect to our annual earnings from our job."

"Well, that will be sort of our annual supplementary income," I mumbled softly.

"Since both of us are working for the federal government, I just want you to make sure that whatever you do, do it according to the rules laid out by Canada's Revenue Agency." She warned me in good faith.

"You know me," I quipped instantly, "I don't do any thing against the law. I understand the sensitivity of the situation and what's at stake."

***

With the real estate deal gone sour, I was now focused on learning the ropes of running a mail-order business. I wanted to lift it off successfully.

Each evening during the work week, I would study books after books, borrowed from Ottawa's Public Library, on running a mail-order business, and over weekends, would go there to browse over the reference books (that I couldn't borrow) naming manufacturers and suppliers of books, tapes, videos, and CD-ROMs on a variety of topics. I would note down names and addresses of suppliers – both the key ones and those who sold something even closer to what I had in mind – and then write introductory letters to all explaining the type of business I was running, products I was interested in, and asking for their terms of business including the discount rate they offered. For me, it was work around the clock, sleeping hardly four to five hours, irrespective of the day of the week.

To establish any business takes time. And during all this time, the clock of needs keeps ticking on and on. It doesn't wait for any business to establish, or find source of supplementary income, unless all of a sudden, all needs freeze or cease – like if everyone dies. Otherwise any living soul has wants and needs – essential or non-essential – which ought to be met. Also, this clock of needs doesn't really wait for any turn of events – good or bad.

Likewise, family expenses keep spiralling up irrespective of any change in income. Either one has cash or savings on hand to meet this steadily rising expenditure, or one needs to borrow more funds to do the same. One can only postpone non-essential needs, but the essential and critical ones have to be taken care of without causing any pain of deprivation – especially when children's as well as family's well-being is involved.

In my financially fragile situation, the rising expenditure meant the use of more borrowed funds. As I stated earlier, I wasn't able to save a penny from my monthly salary.

Three years after moving into the second home, I had totally exhausted all sources of available borrowings. My credit cards had reached their limits, Sears account was at the seams, and my supportive line of credit had thinned to a trickle. I was desperately looking for a rescue. The only way out was to take a loan to pay off these smaller loans, and that in turn, meant re-financing the mortgage on the three-year old home.

I saw an ad in the newspaper that one financial institution was offering an opportunity to home-owners to refinance their mortgage in order get funds to pay off their consumer loans, start a business, or pay for children's higher education, etc. I thanked the Lord for giving me this opportunity to seek a new loan, not only extending my life, but also giving me some more time to find supplementary income.

Since I had owned this house for just three years, I didn't expect that it had any substantial equity built in it over such a short period. I knew how much down payment I had paid, which in turn, was my initial equity. However, the real current equity was to be determined eventually by the current market value of the house *less* the mortgage outstanding on it.

Since the house had appreciated in value over three years, offering me more equity in it, I decided to cash some of it. I immediately contacted the financial institution (FI-IV) that had placed the ad in the newspaper. I made an appointment with one of its loan managers.

I was willing to take any cashable portion of current home equity, or say the eligible amount refinanced from FI-IV. I intentionally avoided asking for such a loan from all three financial institutions I had been dealing with: FI-I, because it held my current mortgage; FI-II, because it had my revolving line of credit; and FI-III, because it had refused to offer me a mortgage for rental property.

On the day of appointment, I went to see the loan manager at FI-IV – a middle-aged bespectacled woman – who was sitting in a glass enclosed office, with an entrance from inside the institution. The second glass wall of her office touched the pedestrian footpath at the main street level.

I sat facing her, with the afternoon sun almost blinding my eyes as its brightness warmed her back. I was a bit nervous. The uncertainty about the amount of loan I was going to get, the bottom line for me, had completely overshadowed my senses. My head was fast working on numbers.

After going over the information I had provided on the loan application, the loan manager told me that I was eligible to get sixteen thousand and five hundred dollars of loan. She wondered though that I was refinancing the mortgage that early, and with that she suggested I move my mortgage from FI-I to her institution. In other words, she didn't want FI-I to keep my house as collateral in lieu of my principal mortgage. She wanted to take over the entire mortgage including the amount of loan she had offered.

To me, it didn't matter who held my mortgage. The advantage of moving the entire mortgage business to one institution was that I would be making one monthly payment to one institution rather than two separate payments at two institutions. By transferring the mortgage, she also ensured that she now had the full house as collateral for the total amount I owed.

She also told me how to pay off the mortgage a bit earlier than the conventional over twenty-five years and save some long-term interest as well by making weekly rather than monthly payments on the mortgage. In other words, instead of making the conventional twelve payments a year, I was to make fifty-two payments. This new payment system didn't substantially change the amount I had to dish out from my bi-weekly salary cheque, but it changed the frequency of payments which, in turn, helped reduce the amortization period, and saved me a lot of interest on the mortgage.

The loan manager was a mature and well experienced woman. She had not only helped me by offering a loan, but also helped her institution earn more interest income. Such loan managers are normally rewarded for bringing in new clients and more income to their institution. On the other hand, if such clients default on their loans, resulting in losses of income for the institution, then these managers can equally be penalized for their poor judgement in approving loans. A loan manager may even lose his/her job – depending on the magnitude of the income loss.

This was my second consolidated loan, good enough to pay off balances on credit cards, Sears and Eaton's accounts, remainder of loan outstanding on the station wagon, and part of the line of credit. The payment of these loans gave me some room to breath. I was good to live and take care of my family and house for another few years. I had consolidated such loans for the second time – almost five to seven years after I had sought my first consolidated loan to pay off balances on credit cards and Sears account.

I was approaching the mid-forties mark and I had no cash, no savings at hand. The future looked totally bleak to me. I couldn't see any light at the end of the tunnel. I didn't know what to do? How to make some extra income? I didn't care much about my own well-being. Nonetheless, I was quite concerned about our children's future, their higher education and choice of careers, marriage, and other life events. I was in a real quandary.

The use of consolidation of loans is good for those who no longer wish or plan to use credit during or after the pay-off. For those with no savings or no cash flow at hand and still depend heavily on credit, the use of such consolidated loan is only a transitory solution to overcome their financial woes. For this group, this consolidation adds another monthly committed payment, besides other payments on debts they would again undertake over time. In other words, for those dependent on credit, this sort of consolidation is a short-term gain for a long-term pain.

I lived through this situation. I was now sunk in a much deeper debt hole. My bi-weekly paycheque was no longer enough to pay off all of my monthly financial commitments on the principal mortgage, property taxes, credit cards, department stores, regular bills on heat, hydro, cable, water, phone, and other unexpected maintenance costs of the home. Over and above, I was at such a life cycle stage when children were young and growing up and ready to go to school, or required orthodontic treatments, eye glasses, transportation, and on and on. There was no short cut or any leeway or option open to reduce or cut down such essential expenses. Anyone with any sense of parental and/or family responsibility would have acted the same way I did to ensure to keep up the well-being of family, even if that required living on borrowed money.

In the absence of any supplementary income, the only thing I could do was to juggle ways to make payments of bills and other obligations. Since mortgage and property tax payments, consuming close to sixty percent of my monthly net income, were now being fixed and paid weekly, it had become an uphill battle to discharge other obligatory and non-obligatory commitments from the remaining forty percent of my income. I would make the minimum payment on each and every credit card issued by financial institutions or department stores in order to have my statements stamped that I had made the payment simply to protect my credit rating and allowing me to continue using credit. I was fully aware that these minimum payments were not helping me to pay off any of my outstanding balances. These were just slowly prolonging my totally listless and empty life. I was leading the life of a walking dead.

Since it was not in my personality to throw in the towel and accept defeat, I was still thinking and working hard on ways to generate supplementary income. I had not been successful to find a teaching job with any of the local school board's program of continuing education, nor in purchasing any rental property, nor in obtaining permission to work overtime on the job. Also, the mail-order business was still in the process of development. I had to find some other way to earn income.

Since I still had my rotten to the core station wagon in a driveable situation, with its colour peeling, emitting unbearable gas fumes, non-functional passenger door, I thought of opening up a courier business – i.e., delivering commercial mail. I planned to operate it during evenings and over the weekends.

Again, to start this business, I needed no capital investment – just the time and a dependable vehicle. Since the station wagon's back seat could be folded, I had plenty of room to carry lots of heavy brown boxes, big envelopes and mails to be delivered in and around the city of Ottawa. I simply had to let people know that there now was a new, efficient, dependable, and affordable courier service available in the city.

Under the '*Office Support*' heading, I gave the following ad in the local newspaper:

Mailing and processing services available for business correspondence or advertisement. Reply Xxxx, Box yyy.

Since Ottawa was, and still is the hub of federal government, along with private companies and corporations of different sizes, software and computer companies, lobbyists, etc., I thought there was a good opportunity to earn money by delivering mail from one end of the city to another. I had seen not only special vans marked with big company names, and non-marked regular vans/cars engaged in this activity, I thought of earning a little bit by sharing in this business. I was fully confident that this scheme of mine would be successful. I simply had to wait for a few favourable responses to my ad.

I waited for weeks and weeks and hoped that very soon a big brown envelope containing responses would be delivered at my door, bringing in some sanity and stability to my financially turbulent life. Unfortunately, I didn't get a single response.

My hope of a better turn in my life had washed away, leaving me with a bleeding defeat. I was deeply wounded, but not dead yet. I had to pull myself as a real strong and determined man. Such men never cry in defeat, no matter what. In each and every defeat, there was always something to learn.

This failure further fortified my resolve to make my mail-order business much more successful. That was the only source left to earn any supplementary income. I wanted to launch this business at the earliest opportunity as I was slowly moving to a graveyard where I would eventually be resting in peace.

By this time, our daughters were in a primary school.

According to their school curriculum, children, accompanied by their teacher(s), had to go out a few times during the year, visiting some national sites, museums, parks, and galleries. The annual cost of such trips was to be shared equally by parents and school.

At the beginning of one of the school's terms, both Sarah and Kerry wanted me to give each one a cheque in the amount of fifteen dollars covering the cost of such out-door trips. Since I had no money in my chequing account, I told them that I would give each of them the cash, put it in an envelope with their name on the outside flap of the envelope.

"No!" Sarah yelled, with tears in her eyes, "that's not the way the teacher wants money. You have to give us the proper cheque."

"Do as the teachers want," added Amy angrily, supporting our daughters' demand.

How could I explain to Amy as well as my daughters that I had no money in the bank account, and as a result, I was unable to comply with their teachers' wish? I felt really ashamed, belittled, and worthless in the eyes of my family.

My daughters were too young to comprehend the reason why I was unable to issue them the cheques they wanted. To them, both of their parents were holding decent jobs, providing them with new toys or games each week, fulfilling their each and every need, even providing them a live-in child care. What was this fuss about giving each one a cheque for fifteen dollars? Was their father serious – offering them cash, but no cheque?

The innocent age they were at, they weren't in a position to understand all these concepts of savings or no, low, or high cash flow. As kids, they simply wanted to comply with their teacher's wish. Whether I, as their provider, was able to do what they, in turn, wanted was a different story. I was a prisoner of my own financial circumstances. How could I tell them I don't have any money sitting in my bank account at the moment? Or, my bank account simply facilitated making monthly payments to the last cent of my paycheques. I didn't want them to grow with any fear or anxiety about money or family's finances.

"I am doing what the teachers want," I yelled back at Amy, "I am giving them the money they want. It's just the way I am giving is a bit different. Money is money – whether I pay as cash in an envelope or by conventional cheque."

"But the teacher wants a cheque so that she can easily identify our family name while she checks her list as to who has paid and who hasn't," Sarah squealed.

"I understand that, honey," I spoke to her softly. "I will clearly write your name and other particulars on the envelope so that your teacher would know you have paid. You don't worry."

"Why can't you give a cheque?" Amy frustratingly yelled at me.

She then looked at Sarah and Kerry, patted their backs, and instructed them to go to their rooms.

"Because I have no money in my account," I told her gently after the girls had left the room. "I don't want any cheque to be bounced back as I would have to pay penalty for that. I would draw thirty dollars from by line of credit tomorrow and then put fifteen in each envelope with their names, grade, classroom number, and teacher's name."

"So you are using borrowed funds," she asked sarcastically. "Tell me something new."

She shrugged her shoulders and left the room with her red face.

Left alone in the room, I began soul-searching the cause of my messy financial situation –something I had done many times without fruition. Was it all due to poor planning, or did I over-extend myself by buying a single detached house? Sixty percent of my monthly income was consumed by just two items related to home-ownership: mortgage and property tax. There was no way I could manage to run the house as well as fulfill other needs of my family on the remaining forty percent. I had no choice: I had to use borrowed money. Damned if I did and damned if I didn't.

I kept sitting alone in the room, sweating over my helplessness until my brain got all fogged up after hashing and rehashing the current dilemma. There was no way I could cut down any expenses – monthly payments of regular bills were almost fixed; minimum payments on credit cards, however, varied, and that too only in one direction – creeping upwards. There was no way I could cut down any other family expense – especially when it involved the well-being of Amy and the kids.

The end result each of such soul-searching sessions was the same: I had to keep living on borrowed money. The only way out was to find a source of additional income. At this point, my thought process stopped and shifted its focus on how to run successfully the planned mail-order business.

***

"Nothing is working," I softly mumbled and exhaled while Jen and I were putting our food plates on one of the corner tables of the office cafeteria. "It's really frustrating me."

"What's it? You sound so depressed." Jen was inquisitive. She sat on her chair and sternly looked at my face. "What's bothering you?"

"You know people don't want me to even deliver their mail." I blurted out in frustration. "I put an ad in the newspaper about my courier service to deliver commercial mail in and around the city and I got no response whatsoever."

"I didn't know you had started a courier service." She was startled. "I know you have started a mail-order business, and now you are mentioning about your courier business. How many businesses you want to run besides this full-time job that requires a lot of concentration on analysis and writing?" She wondered aloud.

"It takes quite a bit of time to establish a mail-order business and actually make some income," I softly explained to her, hiding my inner anxiety about the slow progress I was making on it. "But this courier business would help me earn some quick cash."

"Gee! That's quite clever and ambitious," she chortled. "Now Amy wouldn't object to delivering of mail? As I recall, she stopped you from delivering newspapers. Now where's her concern about protecting family's social status?"

"To be honest with you, I haven't spoken a word to her about my courier service," I poured out. "I will be doing this business during evenings and weekends. She doesn't have to know. I could always tell her I have some extra work to do at office, or visiting some friend. She doesn't have to know all about my whereabouts. What she's interested in is seeing me run and manage the house without causing her any personal distraction or problem – financial or non-financial."

"I wish I could live that carefree," she lamented. "Peter unloads all of his problems on me. What a guy! Not only he feels insecure in his job, he's demanding more and more of my attention. I already have Josh to take care of and his daily activities including swimming, hockey, and soccer. Rather than help me run the house, my husband is really becoming a burden on me." She languished.

"Peter has moved to another bigger local technology company. Hasn't he?" I asked her. "Why he's still feeling insecure?"

"Because this company is also planning to merge with, or outright buy, another company to increase its dominance, or share of the market. You know how these technology companies operate – fast pace, competitive, minimizing production costs, expansion outside the country, and on and on. Peter and other people at his level have no long-term job security. Each and every day he comes home with a new story about the upcoming possible expansion, merger, or internal changes which, in turn, cause him all this anxiety about his job and future career path." She exhaled and rested her back against the chair.

She looked beaten. With her reversed palms flatly placed on each side of her food plate, she added in almost inaudible voice, "I really don't know what to do."

"Don't worry," I said softly, and gently tapped a couple of times the top of her right hand. "Everything will be all right," I reassured her. "Cheer up. Let's finish our lunch. Remember, we have a staff meeting this afternoon."

"Speaking of the meeting," she asked me in a relatively stronger and clearer tone, "are you going to attend the upcoming conference in Toronto, focusing on *'The Role of Credit in Our Society'*? I have been instructed to go."

"Yes, I have been too," I replied excitedly. "What a coincidence? We both have been instructed to attend the same conference this time. Usually we have been attending such annual get-togethers on a rotational basis – one of us is always here to handle the media's inquiries on personal and business bankruptcies."

"Maybe the department's thinking has changed or it thinks this conference would benefit us both," she guessed. "At least I will be away from the ghastly environment of home for few days. I need a break to charge up my batteries." After a pause, she added, "Actually it makes sense because when you come to think of the conference's focus, we two are not only quite knowledgeable on issues relating to indebtedness, but also analyze and control the national data on bankruptcies – personal and business."

"You are likely right," I supported her hypothesis.

She was right as far as the analysis and control of data on bankruptcies were concerned. But in my own mind, I was now focused on something else – spending few full days with the attractive woman sitting in front of me.

I knew she was not presently happy living with her husband, who, instead of helping and loving her, was demanding more of her attention and driving her nuts. I myself was in no different situation as I also wanted to get away from Amy's daily nagging and chilled behaviour.

In my opinion, both Jen and I were victims of the poor treatment, insults, and nagging of our spouses. She was suffering from her husbands' frustrations resulting from his job insecurity, whereas, I was from my inability to provide enough cash flow to satisfy my family's needs. We both were looking for a way or some kind of solution that would keep us healthy, physically fit, mentally alert to function well on our jobs and continue earning to maintain our family units. Put simply, we were looking for a way to keep us invigorated to fight our daily battles.

While I was still mulling over my inner most thoughts, my eyes were still roaming all over her beautiful face. I made her too conscious.

"Why are you looking at me like that?" She snickered at me.

"Oh! Nothing," I blurted out. "I was just thinking about this coincidence of spending a few full days with you away from this city. I was just thinking about how it all will go. Even though we have known each other for years and years and have become close friends, we never ever have travelled together or been in one another's company away from this city."

"Don't fret much on it," she replied with a sly grin. "Everything will be all right. We know each other well enough that even if we ended up in the sack, it wouldn't crash our world. I am sure we will have a good time."

"So do I," I quipped.

CHAPTER EIGHT

On the scheduled Tuesday morning at six o' clock, Jen and I met at Air Canada's ticket counter at Ottawa's airport. Jen was wearing a light purple full-sleeve blouse, with a purple open light cardigan, dark purple knee-length skirt, legs covered with nylon stockings, and feet with black pumps with an inch and a half high heel. She had her dark brown hair tied in a ponytail, touching her waist. She was wearing purple crystal earrings, with a thin white chain necklace with a matching pendant resting in the center of her cleavage. She wasn't wearing much makeup. She had left buttons of her purple coloured fall coat opened for the time-being. She looked very pretty in her purple attire.

"You are looking fabulous ... radiant ... in your all purple outfit," I complimented her.

"Thank you," she replied with a broad smile. With her face blushed, she quickly added in self-defence, "I seldom dress up like this. You see me how I usually dress."

Evidently, she didn't want to hear any words of praise.

I could read her mind.

Each of us had reached there by taxi. Since our travel arrangement including hotel accommodation and itinerary were arranged by our administrative department, who also had paid us advance money for taxis and day-to-day incidentals, we didn't have to do much other than to show up with ticket vouchers at Air Canada's counter, registering passengers flying to Toronto by eight o' clock flight.

Since tickets were booked under separate names, naturally, when each of us presented our ticket at the counter, the rep assigned us a separate seat number. He had placed tags on our suitcases and pushed them on top of the conveyor belt in order to send these to the loading area near the aircraft.

Jen and I had to clear the security area after showing our tickets and other pieces of identification. We sat side by side on the long red seat in the waiting area and glanced over the local newspaper.

After boarding the plane, we occupied different seats. We both placed our fall coats in the overhead horizontal cabins. I sat three-rows behind her on the same side of the aisle. I was sitting in a seat from where I could admire her open visible neck as she had moved her ponytail upfront partly covering one of her breasts. Her bare visible neck was really inviting, likely seeking a soft touch or a kiss from a man none other than me.

Since the flight was on time, we reached Toronto by nine-thirty. Once we were off the aircraft, I knew we would now be together until we were back in the plane for a return flight to Ottawa.

We headed to the conveyor to pick up our suitcases. We rolled these and exited the terminal while speaking about the conference we were going to attend. We hired a cab and were on our way to Hotel Sheraton at Queens Street.

We headed to the registration desk to report our arrival and showed our documents confirming our already booked rooms. Although the check-in time was three o'clock in the afternoon, the hotel had made a special arrangement with the convener of the conference to let participants check-in before noon so that the conference could start after lunch. The proceedings of the conference were to last 'til Friday noon.

The receptionist at the counter looked at our documents and assigned us the rooms on the twenty-second floor – almost in the middle of the tall hotel tower in downtown Toronto. While handing us the keys, she quipped, "You are going to be neighbours – next to each other."

She pointed us to the elevators to take to get to our rooms.

We rolled our suitcases up to the elevators and got into one of those waiting on the floor. After we exited at the twenty-second floor, we walked together in the narrow hallway until Jen reached her numbered room and opened it, while I went to the next door.

I placed my suitcase on the folding luggage stand in the closet near the entrance and walked into the washroom opposite to relieve my bladder. I looked around the room, removed slightly the big heavy curtain in order to have a peek at the deserted outside pool and the adjoining streets full of traffic moving in both directions. I was in one of the most bustling cities of Canada.

All of a sudden, I noticed there was a door that separated me from Jen's room. This must be a big two-room suite to accommodate families with children and/or older relatives with a door separating a couple from others. The door seemed to have locks on both sides. That meant that it could only be opened, if mutually desired or warranted for any particular reason, by occupants of the rooms on both sides. I wondered if Jen had noticed this removable barrier between us for the next few days. I wanted to meet her at the earliest in order to talk about this door – and its possible role to bring us together, or keep us apart.

After I freshened up, I knocked on Jen's door. She quickly opened the door and invited me in with a mysterious smile. She had just finished setting her accessories on the washroom counter, with a full wall covered with a mirror. I closed the door of her room and stood outside the washroom – with its door open.

"So how do you like the room?" I asked her out of curtsy.

"It's good," she replied, "can't complain."

"Did you notice something in particular?" I continued while looking at her face, wanting to know if she had noticed what I had.

"Yah, there's a door that separates our room. I believe it's closed on both sides," she replied casually, and came out of the washroom.

She sat on her king size bed while I took my seat on one of two wide red chairs in the room.

"That means we are free to open the door in the evening if we want to have each others company, or talk even in our more comfortable night clothes – something we wouldn't have been able to do even if we were next door. Neither of us could walk in night clothes in the hallway." I took the initiative to explain this most rudimentary detail.

"I know that," she replied pensively. "I know what you are alluding to and I thought of the same too. But life is not that simple as we wish to perceive it. We can easily open the door, but what will that accomplish?" She gave me a piercing look. "Nothing really – at least until we both first figure out what we want to do after we open the door." She paused for a while. Then she got up to fix her portfolio that she had to carry to the meeting this afternoon. "Have you prepared yours?" she asked, trying to change the topic.

"Not yet," I replied pronto.

She had, however, touched my inner-self. Her words, 'What we want to do after we open the door' were reverberating in my head. I serenely continued on the topic she had intentionally balked moments ago.

"As two mature adults who have known each other for years, it's up to us to decide what we want to do. Not only when we let this door open, but also when we face any of its consequences afterwards. I am glad we are here together, away from our families and work, and have enough time to decide what we both want to do to re-start living our lives." I kept looking at her pensive, but attractive face.

"We'll continue this discussion in the evening," she suggested. "Let us now get ready for lunch and the big meeting ... I am sure we will find some mutually satisfactory solution."

She opened the door for me to leave.

After I exited her room, I heard the loud bangs. She must have slammed shut her main door as well as the washroom door. She must be perturbed.

When she walked out of her room, all refreshed for lunch, to be followed by the meeting, I noticed she hadn't changed much of her purple attire. The only difference that I could see was that she had opened her long hair, parted in the middle, covering her back. She had clipped her manes with small hair pins placed behind her ears so that these wouldn't cover her eyes anytime she bent over on something. She looked a bit pre-occupied with herself as she didn't utter a word when she came out of her room. She simply started walking with me to the elevator.

We had a quiet lunch. The only time she spoke was when she had to order her meal. Obviously, she was either thinking hard about the upcoming meeting or about our earlier conversation in respect to our possible future together. I was almost certain that it was the latter that had overwhelmed her.

When women are at such crossroads where they have to choose whether or not to indulge into any extra-marital affair, most tend to get too emotional and sentimental, and even get nervous and scared to take any risk involved in the step they are going to take. They think about its impact on children, family, its likely dissolution, finances, property split, friends, and on and on.

I could understand the kind of inner struggle she was going through, but the time wasn't right to open that sort of conversation. After all, we were there to attend the meeting not only as professionals, but also as representatives of the federal government. We carried a highly sensitive public responsibility. Our conduct was under a public microscope.

There were sixty delegates attending the conference. The afternoon session was meant to 'get-to-know each other'. After each of us introduced ourselves, the chairperson of the session added that we were the custodians of national data on personal and business bankruptcies. He cited the reports and the kind of monthly/quarterly/annual data we released and its significance to households, businesses, chartered banks, and other financial institutions, and above all, how these data were used for further research on consumer and business behaviour. These words from the chair not only justified all the reasons that we were there in the first place, but honestly, also inflated our ego about the kind of work we were doing.

While sitting side by side, Jen and I exchanged glances and grins as the chair spoke about us, our work, and our affiliation. I was relieved to see her faintly smiling. She seemed to have come out of her depression.

In the evening, we attended the happy cocktail hour followed by the dinner hosted by the convener of the conference. I started with scotch whiskey followed by white Ontario wine with dinner; Jen, on the other hand, with gin and tonic water followed by red wine.

By the end of the dinner, I felt my head was a bit heavy and I was likely under the influence of alcohol. I was sure Jen was likely feeling the same. We had eaten a heavy dinner comprising of baked salmon and vegetables, followed by 'strawberry short cake' as desert, and a hot cup of coffee.

We left the gathering, and headed to the elevators around ten o' clock. I was feeling a bit tired or perhaps somewhat intoxicated. It has been quite a long day.

Inside the elevator, Jen and I stood facing each other, pressing our backs against the long walls of the elevator. We quietly kept staring at each other, likely reading each others mind.

As soon as we got out of the elevator, I finally broke the silence.

"You want to come to my room for a while?" I asked her while looking into her eyes. "Or, you want me to come to yours."

I gave her the choice.

"We can sit in your room," she replied without any hesitation. "That way, you can at least sit comfortably by removing your suite and tie. I am quite comfortable in my clothes." She justified her decision to sit in my room.

I opened the door of my room and switched on the light. I let her walk in first. After entering the room I locked my door. In the meantime, she had moved one of the red wide chairs closer to the foot of the bed and sat on it.

She had rested her back on the soft layer of her hair pressed against the back cushion of the chair. While she was making herself comfortable, I freed my neck from the noose of the blue tie, and took off my jacket as well. I hung both the jacket and tie on a hanger in the closet. I opened the top two buttons of my shirt and walked over to sit on the foot of the bed, still covered with the cottony multi-coloured thick bedspread.

I sat closer to her.

"Feeling better after dinner?" I asked her.

"A bit woozy after all those drinks," she replied unhesitatingly. "And you?"

"I am fine," I replied. "My head was a bit heavy for a little while. Alcohol doesn't get to me that easily."

"I wish I could say that for myself," she griped.

She had begun to gently tap the wide arms of the chair with her fingertips.

"Why were you so quiet and gloomy this afternoon?" I swiftly asked her.

"You made me think about our future relationship." She replied in all honesty.

I already knew the reason, but I wanted to hear it coming from her mouth.

"And has all that thinking helped you reach any conclusive decision?" I asked.

I was now more anxious to hear her. I kept peering into her eyes, with my hands half bent and pressing the edge of the thick mattress.

"I am still not sure what I really want." She started to dwell on her predicament. "I am all confused." She paused for a moment. "As a man, you see, think, and do things differently than a woman – especially a married woman with a young son.

I am concerned about him. My indulgence into an affair may hurt my son's upbringing, besides all the hurt and damage I would be causing to my family as a unit, my relationship with Peter, even if it's dead at the moment. I tremble at the very thought of facing my family as the person responsible for all this emotional upheaval and break-up of family. I have to do all this simply to have a man's companionship, someone to lean on, and satisfy my sexual starvation. I know for sure, you are not in a position to marry me because as the main provider of the family, you have to take care of your family. Even though your relationship with your wife is almost non-existent, you are still there because you are too good to leave them on their own. So I don't know what to do. I am open to your suggestion."

"You have nicely summarized the problem we both are facing at the time," I confessed and patted the top of her left knee. "We can't marry for sure, but who says we have to live in sexless marriages? The only way we can sanely face the current misery is by re-energizing ourselves by nature's bliss brought only by the mutually consenting sexual satisfaction. This should nurture stability of our mind, body, spirit, thoughts, and some personal contentment. This should also energize us to face our day-to-day battles. Granted, such a union is illicit, so be it. In the end, it will be helping us to continue to live with our current spouses. Just because they are problematic – Peter's job insecurity and Amy's dissatisfaction with inadequate cash flow – we can't live too long in the kind of uncaring, unloving, and sexless lives we are currently living. We also have the right to live our life – fully and contented. If we don't, and continue to live with this unhappy situation, then I am afraid, one day any serious distraction caused by these awfully disturbing circumstances would make us lose our job as well – the only current source of stable income we have. So which is the lesser of the two evils? Losing our livelihood or having an affair to keep our sanity and job. Imagine if we lost our jobs, how more badly our families will suffer. The way I look at it, since we like each other, have enjoyed each others company in both good and bad times, provided emotional support to each other, there's no reason why we can't give each other what we each furiously want. You do want a good and enjoyable sexual satisfaction. Don't you?"

I paused, still searching her eyes for an honest answer. She had stopped tapping the arm of her chair.

"And, so do I," I pranced.

"See how good we are," she rhapsodized. "I summarized the problem and you the options available to us. What a problem-solving team we make?" She unloaded herself.

"How about making it a sex-mating team? Would that work out, you think?" I quipped.

"That! Time alone will tell." She was enthused. "I always liked your company. I think you are a good and compassionate man, always lending me your shoulder to cry. There are times you really put me on with your creativity, productivity, how fast you analyze and write, the way you dare taking risks like opening your mail-order business or courier service. Peter can't even think of these risky ventures, never mind running these. Right now I don't know your sexual prowess. However, I am sure you know my sexual incline towards you. You remember how I laid close to the side of your thigh and put my arm around your waist during our last outing."

"Yah, I recall that," I mumbled with my face somewhat flushed. "Your soft touch ignited a strong desire in me too to touch you in return. But there wasn't a thing I could do in an open environment. Right now, I can do what I couldn't on that day."

I got up and sat on the right arm of her chair, my feet touching the carpeted floor, and placed my left arm underneath her soft hairs on the back of her neck and spread it on top of her shoulders.

"As far as my sexual prowess is concerned," I continued, "it all depends on how you and I act, react, and reciprocate to each others way of fondling, stimulating, and eventual entangling. You know well that any sex act culminating in mutual satisfaction requires both partners to engage without any inhibition. A man can be a stud with one woman and a complete dud with another – depending on how that woman engages and reciprocates – as a hot nymphomaniac or a cold fish. So you will not only whip the horse to run fast, but also will enjoy a fulfilling and delightful ride to the destination."

I was now running my fingertips softly on top of her shoulder.

"Oh! That feels good," she squeezed her shoulders, and exhaled.

She had rested her face on the left side of my torso. As I pressed her shoulder more firmly with my arm, she finally busted out, "It has been more than a year since I placed my face on the side of a man's chest. I really miss such intimate moments … you don't have to tell a sex-starved woman how to be participative to have fulfilling sex. My acceptance of your proposal alone should tell you not only my burning desire to engage in sex, but also to have totally uninhibited sex."

I sat there quietly, my finger tips now roaming on her shoulder as well as on her upper cleavage, touching at times her purple pendant. She had her eyes closed. She had not only accepted my proposal, but also had surrendered herself.

After twenty minutes or so, she got up and straightened up her dress. She gave me a good full smile. She thanked me for the evening, gave me a parting soft kiss, and walked out of the room to go to her own room.

The physical barriers between us were now opened. I had a feeling that she would likely have the door between our rooms open tomorrow.

***

The next morning, sharp at nine o' clock, the convenor formally opened the conference on the role of credit in our society.

In his opening remarks, he stated that the access to credit, if used wisely, can benefit all – from users and non-users of debt to the growth of the economy. He wanted participants to split into six groups, each looking at a specific facet of credit: (i) use by persons and/or households; (ii) by business; (iii) its impact on consumer spending and economy; (iv) health issues associated with use of credit; (v) role of banks and institutions supplying credit; and (vi) the plight of those not eligible to get credit from the conventional sources like banks and credit unions.

I was assigned to group (i) looking at persons and/or households as users of credit whereas Jen was to look at businesses as users. Each group had to prepare its presentation until noon, then after a sixty-minute lunch break, each would make the presentation to all participants for further discussion or follow-ups.

This group formation meant that Jen and I had to work away from each other almost all day including lunch as each group preferred to have lunch together in order to give finishing touches to its presentation.

Even this morning, when we were together at breakfast just for a short while, we didn't have time to discuss anything about what had happened last night, or what we had agreed upon. Even though I was quite keen to pursue the conversation on that topic, Jen's continued silence forced me to stay silent as well.

I had simply said 'Good morning' to her and complimented her attractive look and her attire. Today, she had her hair tied in a French braid. She was wearing her casual blouse and skirt, with a light coloured pink cardigan. She was wearing earrings and pendant matching with her cardigan.

I was the lone talker this morning. I didn't even know if she was paying any attention to what I was saying. I wondered if she was thinking of her son Josh at home or at school at the time, or she was still in the thick of our last night's discussion. One thing was certain though: she wasn't thinking about her husband, Peter, who had pushed her away.

After lunch, I had the honour of presenting the work of our group. We all had agreed with the convenor's opening statement that credit, if used wisely, could help persons and/or households to acquire tangible assets like a home, vacation home, vehicles, etc. as well as could help persons or their off-springs acquire higher education and/or upgrade skills to improve their marketable skills for a better flow of earnings, resulting in a better quality of life and future security.

Mortgage debt taken to buy a house, the major asset that a typical Canadian family would have, or any vacation or rental income-generating property, or student loans taken to finance higher education were all considered as good debts. On the other hand, debts taken on credit cards or borrowings from secured and unsecured loans and lines of credit were considered as bad debts – if spent compulsively or frivolously on day-to-day consumption, travel, pleasure, or for any quick gratification of desires including the desire to meet up with the Joneses. All such debts, categorized as consumer debt, were considered as bad debts.

It was recognized that the use of consumer debt was 'essential for survival' for all those with no or little cash flow at their disposal. The use of such debt would help keep afloat persons and/or households with no savings or cash flow. This sort of debt provided a 'life line' for all those living in financially dire circumstances. If for any reason, the supply of this debt were to stop, many persons and/or households would starve to death.

The bottom line was that inability to pay back in full the debt outstanding would force persons and/or households to declare bankruptcy. That meant turning to an agency or the so-called 'trustee' and surrendering one's assets and liabilities. That trustee, in turn, would negotiate with all suppliers of credit the terms of repayment of debts, depending on debtor's circumstances including his/her flow of current and future income, and any potential savings including pension savings in registered and unregistered pension plans, or those still held by debtor's employer. The bankrupt debtor wouldn't be entitled to access any credit for at least the next five to seven years.

On the business side, Jen too initiated the discussion. She mentioned that besides using personal loans, credit cards and other sources of revolving credit, businesses would have other sources of debt supplied by government and non-government sponsored financial institutions. These debts were meant to help businesses with start-up or venture capital at relatively low or government subsidized interest rate because such businesses were supposed to provide jobs, which in turn, would help the economy grow, bringing in some brownie points, including some tax revenue, for the government.

However, businesses with heavy debts coupled with inability to pay back for reasons including no or little net income, or returns to their investments would run the same risk of bankruptcy like any other debtor. Once declared bankrupt, a person would lose business and surrender all personal and business assets and liabilities to a specially assigned trustee who would be delegated to manage temporarily all of the financial dealings pertaining to that business. That trustee would devise the means and ways to discharge all unpaid or outstanding financial liabilities. And the businessman would also be barred from seeking any business credit for the next few years (the precise number varied with the prevailing circumstances).

A representative of the group speaking on debt as part of consumer spending highlighted the importance of debt and its contribution to the nation's economy. Personal consumer spending of households was one of the key factors contributing to the nation's economy –accounting for roughly sixty percent of the total value of goods and services produced by the nation in a year. Although the households spent largely their disposable income to make their day-to-day purchases, they also purchased goods and services on credit cards issued by banks and other institutions, revolving credit from lines of credit, and on cards issued by department stores and other businesses.

The use of credit cards and easy access to other sources of debt not only facilitated financial transactions, or payment for goods and services bought right on the spot, these also enticed a person to spend way more – impulsively or compulsively – even if that item of purchase was not that necessary or needed at the time.

Credit cards and access to revolving credit encouraged spending so much so that a consumer might not even realize that he/she had overspent, crossed the borrowing limit on cards, or had overextended his/her wants to the extent that making even a minimum payment was no longer possible. That's why it's been emphasized again and again that one should use credit wisely. Credit, if used unwisely, could create several personal and health problems. The bottom line here was whether spending on credit was an issue of compulsive consumer behaviour, requiring some personal discretion or willpower to control it, or it was simply that essential to survive.

Overspending or overextending on credit beyond one's financial capability could really be hazardous to one's health and well-being. As the member of the team dealing with debt and health issues put it, persons living on credit, or overextending themselves on credit very rarely thought of the consequences of using credit when doing all the purchasing, travelling, or pursuing pleasures. The stressful crunch surfaces when such persons have to make payments to pay back their balances outstanding.

A debtor's inability to pay back would likely cause him/her a lot of stress, anxiety, frustration, resulting in a poor sleep or total sleep deprivation, making the debtor lose concentration, focus, pay attention to work and family, and could also develop suicidal tendencies or actually commit suicide. This sort of stress could also lead to a heart attack or a stroke, eventually making the society to pay for debtor's expensive medical treatment – the same society that offered him/her the credit in the first place.

This shows how as a society, we first create the problem, i.e., by allowing persons to load up with too much debt, and then we resolve the problem by paying for all the medical care and medical treatment these debtors need to cure their ensuing debt-related ailments.

The banks, financial institutions, and department stores offer generous credit to middle to high income groups. For these institutions, low income people carry a much greater risk of defaulting on payments on credit and loans, which in other words, translates into financial losses for institutions. Such institutions are averse to losing money.

These institutions can also push debtors into a deeper debt-hole. As the spokesperson of the group who worked on this issue pointed out, all financial institutions kept a good track of the most vulnerable group, i.e., the one who extensively relied on credit and paid monthly a partial or only a minimum payment, which in turn, simply covered monthly interest on outstanding balance owed. Institutions would love to have more and more of such debtors under their wing because they pay the bulk of their interest income with hardly any change in principals owed. Any time an institution noticed that such a debtor was close to or had exhausted his/her credit limit, the institution would increase the limit on credit card encouraging the debtor to spend more, and subsequently contribute more to its interest income.

The institution could care less if the principal owed was also mounting and likely pushing the debtor in a deeper hole with no possible exit. It would get some of its money back after the loaded debtor declared bankruptcy.

Another way that institutions would draw more interest income from this debt-dependent group would be to charge them comparatively higher annual or monthly interest rate on the premise that this group of debtors carried a high risk of defaulting on payment of loans. The more interest income the institution makes from this core of debtors, the better it is not only for its year-end profit, but also for attracting new customers by offering them cards with all kinds of incentives including travel insurance, free air-mile points, cash back discounts, etc. – all at no cost to the institution, but on the backs of those heavy users of debt with insufficient means to pay back in full each month.

The low income group in our society is even more vulnerable since this group is usually refused credit by banks and other financial institutions. As a result, this group turns to private lenders who lend money on exorbitant rate of interest. There is very little legislation – provincial and federal – that controls or administers financial business of these private money lenders.

According to the presenter from the group who worked on this issue, this group of low income borrowers – needy and marginalized and with meagre resources – would likely remain indebted to private money lenders for the rest of their lives. They were likely to pay one loan with another, and would be trapped in this vicious cycle of loans. Lenders were simply there to optimize their money. Only a few borrowers would ever get out of their lender's clutches.

After each of the group had made its presentation, the convenor opened the floor for discussion on all six presentations. An interesting discussion ensued.

By the end of the day, the consensus reached was that in a free market economy, debt played an important role for citizens, government, and the nation's economy. Banks and other financial institutions would continue to sell their product, i.e., lend money, at interest rates guided by the weekly bank rate set by the Bank of Canada.

How much of funds to borrow and where to spend these funds were strictly at the discretion of borrowers. Quoting the latest data from Statistics Canada, the convenor stated that as a society, we owed one dollar and fifty cents for each dollar of disposable income we made. In other words, we owed more than we earned.

The convenor finished the evening with the same statement he used while opening the morning session: 'we should use credit wisely'.

While rapping up the session, the convenor outlined the topic of discussion for the next day and a half: six analytic papers prepared by banks, other financial institutions, and private research organizations, along with some deliberations on their key findings.

After we all exited the conference room, I just rushed to join Jen. I had missed her company all day.

"You did a good job this afternoon." She remarked as I stood in front of her.

"You did too." I replied with a smile. "Let's go and have a cup of coffee. It has been a tiring afternoon," I suggested and began walking with her to the coffee counter.

We poured black coffee in our mugs and then I took two little packets of cream since I preferred cream over milk. Jen, on the other hand, took milk.

"How were you personally feeling when you were talking about indebtedness of persons and/or households?" She was inquisitive. "Considering you are so heavily in debt, how did you feel mentioning that we should use credit wisely?"

"I was quite comfortable speaking those words," I defiantly replied. "Don't forget I was speaking as a professional, not a borrower. I take pride in my professionalism and say the right thing, irrespective of my own situation. Granted, I am heavily in debt at the moment, but this situation isn't going to last for ever. But my professionalism is going to. I am in this mess because I am currently at that stage of my lifecycle where my expenditure exceeds my income and the difference is all made up by borrowed funds," I added hurriedly.

I gave her a cursory look. I knew I wasn't telling her something that she wasn't already aware of.

"Oh! I was just kidding," she blinked smilingly. "You took it so seriously".

"Sorry, for a minute I thought you were serious," I snapped back. "To you, my words may have sounded somewhat hypocritical, but trust me, these were from the bottom of my heart. I still strongly believe that many of the debtors are in the debt-hole, not because of their choice, but largely due to their financial inadequacy. Either these are not earning enough to pay in-full their current expenses, or have no cash flow to pay for their day-to-day expenses. As I stated earlier, for these debtors, debt provides a life-line. Those deeply indebted are the living dead, leading very unhappy and insecure lives. I feel bad for these people. My heart goes to them. On the other hand, only a small number of debtors use debt for fun, pleasure, entertainment, and travel. These debtors are voluntarily in the hole. I have no sympathy for this group". I paused and started to fidget with my portfolio.

I was looking askance toward the hall. I didn't want our eyes to meet. She had touched my soft nerve, even jokingly.

"Are you all said and done?" She chuckled. After a brief pause, she chirped to clear the air, "Come now, look at me. What time are we going to have dinner? Are we eating at the hotel's restaurant or someplace out?"

She began showering me with question after question. She wanted me to come out of my grumpy emotional state as she was too familiar with my nature. She likely felt guilty for knowingly stirring my messy situation.

"We can eat out, if you wish," I mumbled.

I glanced at her grinning face. I looked fiercely into her eyes. She was too attractive to avoid looking at or pay attention to. Moreover, we were the sole company to each other, at least for the next two days.

"Why spoil her mood or upset her while we are here. I better behave," I said to myself.

***

We dined at one of the restaurants close to our hotel. We both had white chicken with some fries and green peas on the side. I ordered a beer, whereas she ordered a glass of red wine. She didn't want to eat any dessert, telling me that she was very diet conscious and wanted to keep her picture perfect figure. I, on the other hand, ordered some as my dinner wasn't ever complete without having a sugary dish, followed by a cup of hot tea or coffee.

After the server left mugs of coffee at the table along with a plate full of packets of milk and cream, she lifted two creams and poured one after the other in my coffee. She slightly stirred the coffee with a spoon and passed the mug to me.

"Thank you for nurturing me tonight," I remarked as we walked out of the restaurant.

"What do you mean?" She asked and looked at me in all innocence.

We were now slowly walking towards our hotel. The fully lit street was still bustling with people walking and vehicles running with head lights on.

"I mean," and slightly bent my neck and whispered in her ear, "I enjoyed watching you how lovingly you poured cream in my coffee and stirred it. I want you to nurture my body and soul as well."

"Oh, you ... *are* being naughty," she giggled loudly.

I wondered if any of the passers-by overheard her remark.

"Honestly, I am still going over our last night's conversation. I am really all messed up at the moment as I am pondering over several ifs and buts. You know I couldn't sleep last night after our conversation. I had a tough time making the presentation today. I think we need to talk a bit more about ourselves."

She suddenly stopped talking and kept walking, keeping her steps aligned with mine.

"What are these ifs and buts? Tell me. Maybe I can help." I tilted my face on her side and asked her in an empathetic tone. "You know I am and have always been there for you. Tell me what's on your mind. Don't ever think you alone have to resolve issues that affect us both."

I suddenly clasped my right fingers around hers left. She didn't object, and kept walking with me.

"I am with you." I slightly tightened my grasp of her fingers.

"We can't talk such things while walking," she turned her eyes on me. "We could talk these over tonight. We are out just for one more night." She drawled.

"I know. Just drop in to my room at your convenience," I warmly suggested.

"Can you just open your inside door after you get to your room," she suggested. "I will come over to your room when I am all done before going to bed."

"*What?*" I stuttered somewhat loudly, and stopped walking.

Our eyes were now fixed on each other.

I was hoping that nobody on the sidewalk had heard me. The jolt of her suggestion had run a strong current in my entire body. I didn't even know when I let her fingers free from my clasp.

"Did I say anything wrong?" She asked nervously. "I was just hoping to come over in a more casual manner as I want to change into more comfortable clothing. I had been in these business clothes all day long, which really is getting to my nerves."

We had started to walk again.

"I understand," I nodded. "I am sorry, I acted that way. For a minute, you surprised me."

"What's there to be surprised after what we talked over last night," she asked innocently. "I bet you too were expecting to have the door between our rooms open in order to move around freely."

"You're absolutely right," I responded without further skirting the issue. "To be honest with you, I thought you would leave it open after you went to your room last night."

"No, I still have some concerns about breaking any barriers between us," she asserted. "Hopefully, we will resolve these tonight."

We entered the foyer of the hotel. We walked up to a notice board to ensure there was no change in our conference program.

"See you later," she gently patted my left arm. "Let me know if something of interest is there."

She walked away from me towards the elevators. I continued to browse other notices on the bulletin board.

By ten-thirty, I had unlocked my side of the door separating our two rooms. I removed the top cover of the bed, placed one pillow on top of the other, and lay down in my pyjamas. I had the table lamps on both sides of the bed switched on in order to read the latest issue of the Maclean's – one of the popular current affairs and news magazines of Canada.

No sooner had I started reading it, I heard the clicking sound on the other side of the door separating our rooms. I knew it was Jen who was unlocking her side of the door.

She gently pushed the door open and stood at the threshold for a minute or so, looking around my partly dark room lighted by only two light bulbs of the table lamps, placed a few feet apart from one another. She was likely still vacillating about crossing the threshold.

I could understand why she was hesitant. Any married woman in her position would have done the same. For a woman to cross a threshold in order to surrender herself to a man other than her husband or boyfriend meant a lot of hurt to her pride, womanhood, self-esteem, self-confidence – all coupled with deep anger and frustration with her current husband. Crossing the threshold and falling into the arms of another man also meant cutting off ties with some or all members of families and friends.

As a woman standing on the threshold, I could feel Jen was somewhat nervous, not knowing what sort of life she was about to enter – better or worse than she currently has. She really didn't know if she would get what she was looking for. She was going to take a chance not with any stranger or some casual acquaintance, but with a person she had worked with as a colleague, a peer, for the last several years. She must be at some ease, considering she was taking a chance with a person whom she knew very well – almost inside-out.

She slowly walked up to the long edge of the bed and drew my attention.

"Are you sleeping? Am I interrupting?" She uttered softly and teetered around the edge of the bed.

I glanced at her and quickly placed the magazine near the table-lamp and jumped out of the bed. Since I was in pyjamas, I grabbed the chair in one big stride, and pulled it near the edge of the bed where she was walking back and forth.

"Oh! Please have a seat." I looked at her and pointed my open hand to the chair. "Feel free to sit on the chair or bed – your choice."

I waited for her to take a seat.

She opted to sit on the chair.

I sat back on the long edge of the bed, facing her, sitting on the chair.

"I am really delighted to see you tonight. You are looking sexy and beautiful," I remarked ecstatically.

I wanted her to feel at home.

She had just a touch of makeup, that too invisible, but I could smell the musky fragrance of perfume she had sprayed on. She was wearing a short black laced nighty – held only by two thin strings on top of her shoulders, covering her torso from upper curves of her breasts to the middle of her thighs. She had her long hair open, simply parted in the middle, with no hair pins or clips controlling their fall. While she sat on the chair, I could see her black lace underwear shielding her womanhood.

No sooner did she sit, she pulled all her hair around her right shoulder, partly covering her right breast.

"So what's on your mind?" I asked her warmly, poring over her.

"A lot," she finally cracked. "Although I have agreed to your suggestion to keep my sanity, my job that I love, and sexual satisfaction by indulging into a no-bar extra marital relationship, I am still concerned about the possible consequences of our relationship. Right now, we are working side by side as colleagues. I wonder what will we do, or what will happen to our jobs, if our affair became a public knowledge, a common topic of discussion at water coolers, grapevine rumours, or the top brass didn't approve of our relationship, or say in the near future, one of us became the boss of the other, or one of us jilted the other for one reason or another, or our spouses came to know and wanted legal separations? Have you thought of these possible side effects of our relationship and their eventual consequences?"

She clammed up, gave me a blank look, and rested her chin on the open palm of her half-folded right arm resting on the side arm of the chair.

"These are all legitimate concerns," I piped up. "But these are all your anticipatory fears and anxieties. As a human being, you are afraid of all possibilities that can doom our planned relationship. Fear is something that freezes people, even to death, from taking any action even if that action is meant to improve their life in general. Fear also causes many unnecessary and unwarranted anxieties. If you are already that much afraid before taking any actual step to improve your life, then I would strongly suggest to you to refrain from taking that step. Faint-hearts can't take any daring step. And, to have an intense and sexually engaging extra-marital affair is a very risky venture. Maybe you like the status-quo and don't mind living with your current state of affairs."

"Would you take it though?" she interjected to me.

She raised her legs in order to place her calves on the bed. She was now resting her back against the seat of the chair and her legs below the knees on the bed.

"I would," I responded haughtily, "without any doubt. I have a different personality. I don't live with any anticipatory fear. However, when it comes, I face it with full tenacity. If I have to try some thing new, or venture into some new direction, I will indeed give it a proper thought and look at its possible pros and cons. And if I do decide to take the step forward, then I don't look back. I would persist and persevere until I get what I want. In other words, once I embark on a journey, I try to finish it no matter what. Maybe as a man, I have a different personality. "

"How come you always tell me that you fear your currently growing indebtedness, or your current no cash flow situation, etc., etc. You do fear 'fear'. Don't you?" she courtly reminded me.

"The kind of fear I talk to you about is way different than the one you and I are currently talking," I expounded on it. "The financial fear that I live with each and every day is something that is the outcome of say, the cumulative effect of my day-to-day spending needs over the years, children's demands, or maintenance of home. Even when I am confronted with any new or unexpected expenses, I do use borrowed funds without any hesitation or fear. It's something I have to do without any fear whatsoever. What I really fear here, and that's what I talk to you about, is that the use of more and more debt is eating away my income at hand, leaving me with no or very little cash flow. I haven't yet surrendered to this fear either. I am trying hard to beat it by finding a source supplementing my income. I am sure one day I am going to find it. Comparing day-to-day financial fear with one associated with romantic liaison doesn't make any sense. We are comparing apples and oranges."

"I get it." She breathed a sigh of relief. "What you are telling me is that once we are in a relationship, nothing would back you off. That's exactly the kind of assurance and support I am looking for before coming to any decision. As long as we are in it together, I am fine with it."

While she moved both of her bare feet with brightly polished red toenails closer to the side of my left thigh, she threw another question at me, "How are we going to handle ourselves at work? Don't you think people could smell something is going on between us?"

"Not really," I replied to alleviate her fear, "if we both acted strictly as professionals like we have been for all these years. We don't have to sneak behind poles or closed doors to purposely touch each other or steal kisses. We will act normal and deal with our peers and colleagues in a business like fashion, like we have always done. Once we are in an intimate relationship, we just have to exercise some self-control and play it cool in public. I am sure you will be able to do it."

"And, where would we meet to have our private moments?" she blurted out. "We can't meet at either of our places."

Her eyes were walking all over my face looking for an answer.

"I haven't worked out such details as yet." I replied in all honesty. "I didn't know if we would ever agree to intimately engage with each other both physically and emotionally. Now that we officially know we will, henceforth, be travelling together at least a few times a year, we will have no problem outside Ottawa. While in Ottawa, we will likely get together after office hours at a cottage owned by one of my colleagues located in Aylmer that we can make it in ten or so minutes from our office. And if that cottage is not available, or closed during winter months, we can always rent a room in one of the motels closer to our office. There are many that provide a room on an hourly or half-day basis as their management is fully aware of what's going on around in this day and age. Adults are free to engage in extra marital affairs with consensual sex as their prime bondage. Motels make good money by short-term renting of a room to sex-hungry adults – provided there's no ensuing scandal to follow or print by the media ... And, as far as our families are concerned, each is well aware that as analysts-cum-writers, we work long hours, mostly leaving the office much later than our colleagues. So our families won't be suspecting anything if some days we were to invigorate each other before returning to our uncomfortable nests. Mind you, we are not going to have such trysts on any regular basis. We will play it by ear, or as our libido would dictate."

"Wow! Good thinking! I am impressed." She crowed with her face all smiling, with an added touch of rouse. "You have already planned the critical details."

"Doesn't it tell you that I have been quietly working on this idea? I was just looking for the right moment to present it to you." I unravelled my long hidden thoughts.

"I have one more thing to clarify, if you don't mind," she pleaded.

She raised the index finger of her right hand. She had her fully stretched left arm all the way on the chair's long arm.

"Shoot," I happily allowed her to speak what was on her mind.

She looked much more relaxed and enthused now than when she had walked over to my room.

"I was just wondering," she paused, then gasped. "Since you are currently going through quite a bit of financial stress, which in turn, may have been affecting your health ... including body functions and ... your main organ ..., you ... think ... you ... can ... satisfy ... a sex-starved woman? We are getting into a relationship meant to sexually satisfy us both. What ... if ... you ... can't ... satisfy ... me, or perform ... the ... way ... I ... want? The reason I am asking this question is because sex being the raison d'être of our newly budding relationship, I want to make sure you have what it takes to sexually satisfy a woman. Since you have told me that you and Amy hardly have any sex life, I just wonder if your dick is still strong and functional."

"That's all, or is there something else you want to clarify, or be certain about?" I giggled and added, "I don't blame you for ensuring if I am the right sexual fit for you. That time alone will tell. Nonetheless, always keep in mind that a woman's satisfaction doesn't exclusively depend on a man's performance. Both have to engage in uninhibited sex to achieve a mutual satisfaction. A stud can't satisfy a cold fish lying under him no matter how hard he keeps hammering her with his thrusts. In the same way, a sexually hot and fully engaged woman can't sexually please a shrink, no matter how hard she tries. You know the old expression, 'good input means good output', or 'the end-result of everything depends on one's quality and quantity of effort put in'. If you really want to enjoy sex with me or anyone else for that matter, you have to fully participate in it."

"Since you know so much about attaining mutual sexual satisfaction, have you ever talked to Amy about what you just told me?" She scraped me purposely.

"The reason Amy and I hardly have any sex is because we no longer have desire or passion left for each other," I replied calmly. "She seems to have written me off as a loser with no money, no cash flow, and no savings – and you know, a loser can't ever sexually excite his wife. Even though I am physically fit and make good income, I am just worthless for her. She's always ready to nag and belittle me with her acidic remarks likely out of her personal frustration. This behaviour of hers has turned me away from her. There's no spark left between us. I am sure, as a frustrated wife, you yourself are in the same situation – having been repulsed by your insecure and temperamental husband."

"You have hit the nail on the head." she replied emphatically.

She stood up from her chair, turned it around to sit on my right on the edge of the bed, and declared, "I don't want to hear a word about that creep."

She flung her bare arms around my neck – resting her half-crossed elbows, one on top of another.

"I don't want to talk or hear anything about him," she re-affirmed.

She rested her face on the right side of my chest.

"Hold me and kiss me," she whispered in her low seductive tone. "I have been longing for your kiss since last night."

I wouldn't say she had taken me by surprise. I knew she was vulnerable. She was standing on the ledge of a high slope, just wanting a gentle push to slide all the way down into the fold of my arms.

In the half-lit room, I looked at her partly closed eyes, nuzzling her face on the side of my chest, just below my right shoulder, finding a more comfortable spot to rest her head. She kept pressing her face against my chest, almost digging into it to find some extra room to hide her face. I placed my right arm on her partly clothed back.

"You sure you want to be kissed?" I teased her.

"What do you think?" She murmured.

She had opened her eyes. She lifted her face few inches away from my chest, looked at me with her seductive eyes, and gently shook my nose with her soft thumb and index finger. She was teasing me back.

"Why do you think I wanted you to keep the door open tonight?" She asked wickedly.

She brought her face closer to mine.

I gently rubbed my closed lips on top of hers. Neither of us was in any hurry to indulge in kissing with fully opened lips. Her loose long hair was falling on my crotch, and some even found the way to touch my still flaccid dick through the open frontal slit of my pyjamas.

The steady touch of her soft, silky hair had eventually begun to spark some life into my dick as it had been awakened. Our bare feet were still resting on the carpet, and upper calves pressing against the long edge of the bed.

We gently began pampering closed lips of one another with shifting stealth looks, slowly combing each others hair with ours fingers. She jerked her body up to straighten herself so that she could bring her lips more in synch with mine.

Realizing her legs must have been tired in that half-upright position for that long, I moved her head from the right to left side of my chest and slipped my right arm underneath the lower portion of her legs in order to pull these all the way on the bed. No sooner had I placed her legs on the bed, she raised her hips and placed them on my covered crotch. She also pulled all of her hair around her left shoulder. She was now lying comfortably in my embrace.

The pretty and attractive woman I had worked with and earnestly longed for her body for all these years was finally lying as a sex kitten in my embrace.

I felt my body was all charged up with the electric current that her body in my arms was generating and transmitting to my brain and body. My heart began to pulsate, blood running fast in my arteries as well as in chambers of my dick – stiffening it up a bit. I was too ecstatic.

In that over-charged ecstasy, I placed by open lips on top of her still closed lips and lightly began to suck them. I was now signalling her to part her lips for good frolicking. No sooner did she do that, our lips got the best of each others – playing, rubbing, licking, and sucking. We really enjoyed the thrills and delicacies of warm, affectionate, and deep French kisses.

While we were engaged in French kissing, deeply roiling our tongues in each other's mouth, I moved my hand on her still covered breasts and the wide bare cleavage. She held my hand and slid it under her nighty.

She wanted me to touch her naked soft skin around her breast and nipple. She badly wanted me to hold and suck her breast.

She pulled her breast out of her laced nighty and brought it closer to my open mouth. She wanted me to play with her full boob and suck her nipple.

I wanted to feel the warmness of her supple and soft skin. I furiously longed to see and feel her fully naked body.

I gently lifted her hips and tried to roll back the lower hem of her nighty in order to pull it over her head. She stopped my hand; gripped it tightly with her right hand.

I thought she was simply hinting that she was not yet ready to be fully undressed. She likely wanted some more warm up, more foreplay.

I had no problem in complying with her wishes. The longer the foreplay, the better it would be for her to reach a satisfactory climax – so I thought.

I didn't want to give her the impression that I was too eager to impale her. On the other hand, I also didn't want her to conclude that I was a slow pusher. This was a critical moment. I had to act and perform wisely. After all, this was our first 'sexually get-to-know each other session'. I still had to know all about her body, especially her hot buttons, or sexually sensitive areas of her body.

While I was sucking her nipple, I tried to slide my open palm under her underwear in order to move my hand all over her crotch including her lips of vulva, clitoris, and the opening to her jade garden. She again stopped the movement of my hand, tightly holding my wrist.

And foolishly, I still thought she perhaps wanted more of kissing and hugging before letting me touch her pubic area. She was likely too hungry for foreplay.

We were in a tight embrace. We kept kissing each other, at times too deeply, including swallowing each others saliva. At times we would be totally motionless.

She had thus far let me touch, lick, suck, or nibble only on one breast that she had exposed, or pulled out of her nighty. I made several attempts to remove her nighty and her underwear and each time, she would grab my wrist and stop me from defrocking her.

She had stopped me every time I tried to undress her completely or touch her genitals below her waist. Her actions were now really frustrating me. I quietly gave her a penetrative frustrating look.

As our eyes met – lo and behold – I noticed she was likely crying in silence as the corners of her eye lids were wet – leaving visible watery tracks on her temples. It was evident that she was crying as she lay quietly in my embrace.

She glumly kept staring at me with her wide open eyes for a couple of minutes, forced a momentary grin on her face, and then abruptly got out of my embrace.

She got off the bed and slowly walked up to her room. I heard the clicking sound. She had put the bolt back on her side of the door.

I got up and folded the thick bedspread halfway. I opened the bed, heaped two pillows in the center of the bed, and lay on my back. I switched off both the table lamps.

While I lay on the bed in the pitched dark room, my head was still working overtime, trying to find the answer to the question: why was she crying? Did I say or do anything that hurt her feelings or body? Did I force myself upon her?

As far as I knew, she had come to my room on her own volition. She herself had told me that she wouldn't mind having an intimate affair with me. She looked all happy and equally participative in whatever we did this evening. To me, she looked perfectly normal. Then why on earth was she crying?

My thoughts took a turn from self-examination to everything from her perspective rather than mine.

She was a happily married woman at one time, adored and loved by her beloved husband with whom she had attended university, and also bore a son. Now that she was no longer desired by her moody and temperamental husband, she must have been feeling a sense of rejection, which in turn, had been instrumental in her agreeing to engage in an affair strictly to satisfy her natural physical hunger. As a woman, she wanted sexual satisfaction in order to not only preserve sanity essential for her professional career path and its associated flow of income, but also to act as a good mother to her young son. These tears of hers were likely a sign of personal remorse, rejection, and defeat.

This scenario about 'being rejected by her husband' seemed far more the real cause of her tears. If that were to be true, then I would have to have another compassionate talk with her before making any move on our plan. With all these thoughts running in my head and trying hard to pin-point the reason behind her tears, I didn't know when I fell in deep sleep.

The next morning around seven-thirty, I was almost ready.

I recalled that just yesterday, Jen and I had breakfast about this time at the hotel's cafeteria. I didn't expect us to have breakfast this morning, considering the way and the situation in which she had left me last night. Initially I was quite angry at her as she had left me dangling in a huff, but when I saw her leaving with wet eyes, my anger mellowed into pure empathy and I wanted to comfort her by lending her my shoulder. She always had and could continue to use it as a pillar of support.

I knew I would be meeting Jen for a while in the conference room at nine o'clock at the start of the day's business – to be conducted in groups created yesterday. That meant she and I wouldn't have a chance to get-together until the closing of the day's session.

I picked up my portfolio and was just about to leave my room that I heard a gentle knock on my door. Who could that be? I was quite certain that it wasn't Jen. I opened the door and who did I see?

Impeccably dressed and smiling Jen, holding her portfolio in one hand, and her handbag in another. She had her hair fixed in a French braid – the hairdo she knew I always liked on her. I had always told her that this hairdo suited her very much as it enhanced her beauty and attraction – especially in my eyes.

"Good morning," she said cheerfully, "ready to go for breakfast?"

"Of course," I mumbled softly.

For a few seconds, I stood still and kept looking at her beautiful smiling face.

I exited my room and then locked the door for almost the entire day.

"I am pleasantly surprised to see you wanting to have breakfast with me this morning." I commented, as we walked up to the elevators.

"What's there to be surprised about?" She questioned. "We had it together yesterday. Didn't we?"

"True." I replied. "Considering how and the condition in which you left me last night, I wasn't sure if you would join me this morning," I explained.

"Don't dwell on what happened last night. It's all passé." She simpered.

We were quiet in the elevator. My eyes were focused on the flashing numbers of floors we were descending, occasionally glancing over her cute face. She looked normal to me, free of any sign of tension, guilt, or bad behaviour. Once out, we kept walking to the cafeteria.

"I am sorry. I can't help it. I just want to know why you cried last night." I queried her after we sat down at one of the middle tables with our breakfast spread all over its glass top. "I must know. Otherwise I won't be able to focus on today's proceedings." I insisted.

"If you must know," she exhaled. She pensively gazed at me and explained, "Those tears were of personal remorse, defeat, and worthlessness. There are times I feel I am no longer attractive enough to draw my husband's attention. That's why he has turned away from me. Often I cry over good times we have had. You saw me in tears just last night, but for me, it's been a while. No one sees my silent tears."

She was no longer smiling. All of her joviality had evaporated. She looked heart-broken. She sluggishly started eating her breakfast in total silence.

"Cheer up," I chirped to bring her back to life, "this self-pity or remorse isn't going to help you or take you anywhere. You have to take charge of your life because if you don't, no one else will. Always remember you have to keep your career going, manage your home and personal life, and above all, be a good mother to your young son. Not getting proper attention of your husband shouldn't mark the end of life for you. I have told you time and time again that people like us not getting any attention from our spouses have to find ways and means to improve our life. These may not be ideal in the eyes of many around us, but ultimately it's our life. We have to manage it the best way we can."

I stopped harping as the clock was ticking and marching to hit the ninth hour.

"Thanks for re-booting by batteries." She curtly replied. Chewing the last bite of her toast and egg, she added, "You won't understand the woman's view point. It's not that easy for a woman to accept rejection and move on to a new way of life. A woman is more emotional, and usually takes a bit longer both to leave the current or to adapt or adjust to any new situation, relationship, or mode of living. You know well that I have already accepted your suggestion about us engaging into a new relationship. It's just me still fidgeting. Don't worry. I will get over my anxieties."

Her tone had reverted back to normal. She gave me a re-assuring smile. She picked up both her portfolio and handbag.

"Now that's the kind of attitude I want to see in you," I proclaimed exultantly. "Cheer up. Be good to yourself. Enjoy the rest of the day. We will get together at dinner."

We silently walked to the conference room.

On this third and the last evening at the hotel, we dined at one of its in-house restaurants. I was thinking that this was going to be our last opportunity being together on this trip. Tonight was the night we both could possibly start engaging in our agreed upon intimate relationship. She had already told me on the first night that she had had no sex with her husband for almost a year. And I myself had been deprived of any physical satisfaction for quite some time – even if it was under a year.

I desperately wanted to have sex with Jen, but only if she also was willing to have it.

I was thinking what a shame it would be to miss this golden opportunity to screw Jen tonight. I was anxious to know how she felt about our potential indulgence.

Considering her mood swings of this morning, I wasn't sure about her desire to have sex tonight. I had to find out where she stood.

While I was musing over these thoughts and sipping white Chardonnay wine with her sitting upright on a chair facing me, she unexpectedly ordered, "When you go to your room, just keep the door unlocked from your side."

She was holding her glass of wine close to her left cheek. She kept staring at me with her seductive eyes.

"Why? You want to repeat what you did last night?" I asked inquisitively. "I really don't see any point in keeping the door open. To be honest with you, I didn't like what you did and the manner in which you left me."

I opened up my heart to her.

"I am sorry," she replied softly and twitched on her chair. With her twinkling eyes, she continued, "It shouldn't happen again. I told you the reason this morning. You are not a woman – and that too married, with a young child. You won't understand why I acted the way I did, even if it annoyed you and put you in an uncomfortable position. Tonight … you won't be uncomfortable … that much I can assure you."

"What's on your mind?" I peevishly asked her. "What has changed overnight?"

"No more questions. Just finish your wine." She commanded with a broad grin. "I will explain it later, if needed."

We both gulped the last few remaining sips of wine.

We slowly walked out of the restaurant and headed towards the elevators. She was now walking a bit ahead of me.

CHAPTER NINE

Right after watching the news at ten, I walked up to the door separating us and unlocked it from my side. I walked to the washroom to change into my pyjamas, floss my teeth, and empty my bladder for a good night sleep.

While I was in the washroom, I heard the clicking sound from Jen's room. I knew she had unlocked her door. She could be here in my room any minute.

The clicking sound had triggered my thoughts about the kind of night we were going to have. Despite her tacit assurance, I still wasn't certain if she was coming over for a real fuck or simply to tease me like she did last night? If she was coming for a real fuck, then I might as well think of how best to satisfy her. My imagination began to run wild scenarios with me pounding her hard in different positions, enabling her to experience the orgasm of her life.

No sooner had I started flossing my teeth by leaning somewhat my upper body, with my left open palm resting on the edge of the white washbasin, I could see Jen's full reflection in the mirror that I was facing. She was standing right behind me in the same nighty she wore last night. She had left her well-combed manes open, partly covering her mostly bare back. She had a wide open smile. She was showing her white sparkling teeth.

Our eyes met in the mirror frame. She looked sensuous and inviting.

"I thought you would be in bed by this time with your dick anxiously waiting for me," she said teasingly.

She slowly ran her right hand on my covered crotch.

Her soft touch had sensationalized my entire body.

"Why would my dick be so anxiously waiting for you?" I teased her back. "It's not going to debut hammering a pussy."

"Still, it's a new pussy." She replied laughingly. "As I understand, a man is way more excited to fuck a new woman than his wife. He doesn't even need any aphrodisiac, including Viagra, to screw a new woman as she ignites his libido. I don't think you are any different from other men."

She was now cavorting with her right open palm my crotch not only a bit faster, but also applying more pressure. She was likely trying to wake up the sleeping monster.

"Good to see you quite ebullient tonight," I remarked.

I turned my face to look over her gorgeous body. I wanted that kind of bubbly woman, full of life and libido, demonstrating her desire to be fucked.

"Yes, I am," she crowed. "I want to have all the fun tonight. Last night, I got too emotional and felt guilty about what I was getting into. Then I thought that now that I have decided to be intimate with you, why show any reservation or personal inhibition. Sexual engagement is the raison d'être of our agreement. Also, I know for men, sex increases intimacy; no sex, no intimacy. For women, on the other hand, it's the emotional involvement that leads to intimacy followed by sex or simply a platonic relationship; no emotional attachment, no relationship – sexual or platonic. An uninhibited sexual relationship is a must for an intimate and lasting relationship between a man and a woman."

"You know full-well that our relationship isn't going to end up in tying a knot unless something happens to our respective spouses," I interrupted her speech on the importance and necessity of sexual engagement to maintain an intimate relationship.

"We both are fully aware of that," she shot back.

She came closer to me and lightly whispered in my left ear, "I don't care how long it's going to last. I just want you to fuck me tonight, and fuck me hard."

She slid her hand through the frontal small slit of my pyjamas to hold my still largely flaccid phallus.

"That I will, now that I know what you want and how you want it." I assured her, and straightened up my body.

I dried my wet face with a small white bath towel hanging on the nearby horizontal steel bar fixed on the wall. There were a few small face towels too, along with a box of large Kleenex tissues.

I turned around to face her.

My dick was now free from her light grip.

She raised her arms and put them around my neck. Her eye lids were half closed. Stuttering, she ordered me, "Let's go to bed. I am too excited."

"You sure you are good to go?" I asked her.

I had encircled my arms around her neck.

"Yes. I have taken the pill." She opened her eyes and gave me a naughty look. "You don't have to worry about it." She shook her head sideways. "Do you think I would put us into any risk – tonight or anytime we are together? We simply want to enjoy and play with each other – totally risk-free."

"Good to know." I exhaled and took a breath of relief. "By the way, do you carry pills all the time in your handbag?" I chuckled.

"Not really," she responded. "I don't know; I had some inkling that since we have been close friends, enjoying each others company and trust for all these years, we might fall for each other while staying together on the road trip. I simply prepared myself for this moment."

"Good thinking should indeed be rewarded," I said softly.

I pulled her closer to me and kissed her lips softly.

"I want a better reward than this petty kiss," she replied haughtily and moved away from my fold.

She grabbed my left hand to walk me out of the washroom.

She led me closer to the bed.

She pulled me all the way back to the foot of the bed, its top cover, light blanket, and the white sheet underneath. She re-arranged the four pillows placed on the head of the bed – making two piles, each with two pillows, and ensured there was no room left between the two. The room was still fully lit

As a married woman, she knew which side of the bed to lie on – left of me – as most women married to right-handed men lay on the left of their husbands, leaving their right hand for better manoeuvring and gripping on their wives' bodies for both the sexual foreplay and a mighty fuck.

Before she lay down on her back, she sat on the edge of her side of the bed and removed both the engagement ring and wedding band from her left ring finger. She shook her head while removing these rings.

"What's the matter?" I enquired.

I just wanted to insure she was all right and nothing was bothering her. I didn't want her to have any kind of distraction – internal or external – as it would have affected her participation in, and eventual climaxing pleasure from the sexual engagement.

"Nothing," she blurted, "I didn't want to have sex wearing my engagement and wedding rings. It would have made me guilty, too conscious about what I was doing – something contrary to what I had vowed at the wedding. I just shook my head as I was telling my inner-self that 'hell with my namesake husband and the world. I have to live my life.' I really don't want to entertain such thoughts, but then again, as a human being, I can't help it. Don't pay any attention to these momentary distractions. I am happy to share the bed with you. That's all that matters."

She turned her neck and looked at me. She was looking for some moral assurance.

"I am in no different position than you are." I replied. "I equally feel guilty, but hell, we have to take charge of our lives. Let us not dwell on it. Once we have agreed to look after the sexual needs of one another, we have to free ourselves of such momentary guilt traps, and make the best use of the time spent together."

I held her left arm, just above her elbow, and pulled her to lie on the bed.

She was now lying beside me on her back, partly cushioned by her soft hair.

I lifted my head, rested it on the palm of my left half-fold arm, and pulled her on the side, closer to my chest.

She nestled her face further close to my chest and enveloped my upper torso with her left arm.

She was now in my fold, as a willing partner, likely waiting to experience the most satisfying and exhilarating pleasure – a pleasure she likely had been yearning for years.

She lay quietly in my embrace. I began to run my fingers through her long hair – from her head to waist. As I ran my fingers through her smooth, soft, and lustrous hair, I could smell the fragrance of her hair and that of the perfume she had sprinkled on. This fragrance slowly scintillated my body.

While running fingers through her hair, my fingertips also touched softly the bare and delicate skin of her upper back, causing her to twitch her body. Every time she twitched, she pressed her face more firmly against my chest, and tightened her arm around me.

"Let's switch off the lights," she murmured, with her eyes closed. "We have enough of the street light filtering through the curtains."

"Not until I have fully seen your gorgeous and adorable body," I lightly nuzzled my nose against hers, "and that won't be for a while."

"I don't think I have that adorable body," she said softly, with her eyes still shut.

It was a typical womanly modest response – happy inside to hear praises of her body, but open denial outside.

"I just want lights off because too much of lighting is getting to my eyes. You can keep your side of the table lamp on, if you so wish," she offered a compromise.

I didn't want to upset her mood on such a trivial issue. I complied with her wish, even if that meant interrupting for a couple of minutes the brushing of her hair with my fingers. I wanted her to stay quiet in my embrace as my mind was wandering about some more critical matters and seeking the right answers.

We had just started our sexual liaison. Since I was lying and stimulating her for a real plunge for the very first time, I had no clue what she liked and didn't like during the foreplay. Or, did she even like the foreplay? And if she did, did she like short or long as it varied from woman to woman? Or did she just want me to enter her as early as possible and let her warm up gradually?

I, as a man, on the other hand, firmly believed in the importance of foreplay as this not only relaxed, but also stimulated the woman well enough for an easy entry. Again, the foreplay had to be performed right as any wrong move could turn the woman cold. And, to perform right, I needed to know her individual hot erogenous zones. I couldn't presume that she and Amy would have the same such zones and would warm her the same way as I did Amy in my good times.

Again, I wasn't the kind of man who believed that 'fucking a woman simply meant giving her few hard thrusts, ejaculate, and leave her in whatever situation she was in because I was all done.' To me, 'fucking a woman meant to first stimulate her by foreplay, oral sex, or whatever else pleased her, and then enter and thrust her to achieve full orgasm, even if it meant slowing down my own momentum'. I knew there were women who never reached orgasm by sheer thrusting, but by additional manual stimulation of their clit, or other erogenous zones.

I had to know Jen's specific chargeable buttons to help her achieve a full and satisfying orgasm.

There were likely two ways I could find out her hot buttons, but unfortunately, both were flawed. For instance, the trial and error approach, including say, too much of rubbing at a wrong spot, could have hurt or irritated her and completely piss her off, depriving her of all the anticipatory sexual fun and pleasure. On the other hand, asking her directly about what pleased her in particular would have demonstrated my ignorance to lead her to satisfaction.

The best option was to try both approaches in a subtle and loving manner. I had to know for sure what activity or position pleased her because that would have made it easier for me to lead her to a satisfactory climax. After all, she was a married woman, had been poked for years, and had likely found her favourite niche. There was no better way to lead a woman to orgasm than initiating, titillating, and eventually screwing her the way she wanted.

While I was mentally roaming through these details in order to figure out a way to bring her to orgasm, I had started skimming slowly my fingertips along her jaw line, occasionally kissing her closed lips, cheekbones, forehead, eyelids, nose, and chin. She was still quietly lying in my embrace.

No sooner had I decided to solicit from her the vital information I wanted, I released her from my fold and moved on top of her, resting my body weight on my elbows, and legs spread beside hers.

Our crotches were now kissing each other. She could easily feel my bulging rod on top of her clit still covered by both her nighty and underwear. I gently brushed my lips against hers as I lightly pressed my palms against her cheeks. I was raptly focused on her still posture.

"Since I am intimately holding you for the first time," I whispered to her and kissed her still dry lips, "do you mind telling me any one sexual activity including physical touch that you most enjoy during love making?"

"I enjoy each and every activity," she whispered back. She tightened her arms around my body. She briefly opened her eyes, and urged, "I just want you to fuck me right now," she added, "I can't wait any longer. I am too hungry."

She gave me a full-hearted kiss with her open lips.

"Still, there has to be one particular activity that you like the most, or a spot you want to be touched, rubbed, or licked."

I returned her kiss by sucking hard on her partly open lips. As soon as I released them, she exhaled and muttered, "I am like any other woman who wants to be hammered well until she bursts out."

She tapped my mouth with her palm, in a way telling me to stop talking. She paused momentarily and slurred,

"Let's ... not ... talk ... right ... now ... just ... fuck ... me ... I ... am ... hungry ... very ... hungry... make ... me ... come ... I ... want ... to ... see ... milk ... drip ... from ... breast ... my ... cunt ... flow ... like ... an ... uncontrolled ... fountain."

She kept slurring haltingly in soft whispers.

She had partly released me from her fold by unclasping her arms around my neck.

She moved her right hand into the slit of my pyjamas to hold my dick.

She held it in her closed fist, slowly moving it up and down,

"I ... want ... it ... right ... now."

I could understand her haste to have my dick fill her long dry hole. She hadn't had any sex for almost a year. She could no longer bear her internal itch.

Her eagerness for coitus had equally excited me.

I could see her body shaking like a leaf.

To calm her down, I rolled back on my side, resting my head on the palm of my left half-fold arm.

I slid my right open palm under her underwear and brushed it at a snail's pace all over her crotch. I felt my palm was moving over coils and coils of her pubic hair. Evidently, she wasn't one of those women who shaved her pubic area. Or, maybe she didn't have sex for almost a year she didn't care to keep this area clean.

This also made me conscious about ensuring that I didn't swallow or gag on any of her hair if I decided to go down on her.

I placed my hand first on her clit, then on the opening of slit between her legs. My hand felt the wetness.

She was too excited. She had surrendered to my dick.

Although I welcomed her cool submission, I wanted to see her agitated more with her burning desire to have me inside her. The more agitated she would be, the better reception my dick will get, and consequently, the more easily and quickly she would orgasm.

I kept her busy talking, even if haltingly.

"You ... haven't ... told ... me ... yet ... the ... preferred ... position ... you ... want ... to be probed," I whispered softly in her ear closer to my mouth.

"Any position other then the conventional missionary," she whispered back, with her eyes shut. "I have enough of that in my darn rotten marriage. I want to experience something new, something that will deeply sensationalize me, make me happily flow, make me even forget this very moment. You know what I mean?"

I could see her half-opened eyes in that dimly lit room. She was looking for some novelty, some excitement, and some real joy to climax.

"I get it," I whispered back and planted a kiss on her cheek.

I began to roll back her nighty. She lifted her head, stopped fondling my cock for a moment, and quietly helped me pull it over her head.

I could see her mid-size full boobs with fully erected nipples. While she sat to have her nighty removed, she pulled all of her hair around her neck and let these fall on the side of her boob and part of her stomach.

"I won't disappoint you," I assured her.

I licked her left hard nipple, and pressed her other swollen tit. My hand was back brushing her crotch, including her fat lips, clit, and honey hole.

I slowly rolled down her underwear and over her feet.

She was now lying bare naked. I could see her full body the way I had been longing to see. I wished I had seen her in a fully lit room.

She hurriedly unbuttoned my shirt first, and then my pyjamas. She wanted our skins to rub against each other.

She was in one hell of a rush to have my dick feed her sex-starved pussy.

I placed the thumb of my right hand on top of her clit and let my four fingers gently rub up and down her point of entry. I gradually increased the pressure on her clit by rubbing it with my thumb in a slow circular motion.

I was now busy working on her three hot buttons – her breast, clit, and cunt hole – all at the same time.

As her clit swelled by the rising pace of rubbing, and breast by my deep sucking of her nipple, she had begun hitting the bed with one of her toes.

She began to whine and quiver, with her eyes fully shut. She placed her hand on my waist to pull me on top of her. My thumb and fingers were fully wet as if I had immersed these in a pot full of honey.

I moved my hand from her drenched crotch and tried to place my four fingers in her open mouth. I wanted her to taste her own juice.

She held my wrist and blurted, "Yuk. I don't want your wet fingers in my mouth. It's for you to taste. Tell me how do you like it?"

"That I will tell you a bit later after I go down on you and run my tongue all over your crotch," I replied promptly. "Right now you are not letting me do anything what I want to do with your hot buttons."

"Because that's not necessary at the moment," she shot back. "I am darn hungry and ready to swallow your cock alive. Just give it to me in any way you want ... I really don't care. Let it calm me down first. You are going to have all the time to press my hot buttons."

She held my hard and rocking rod in her fist and gently brought it at the entrance of her wet yoni.

I finally let my hard pulsing cock slide into her starving wet pussy.

I lay quietly on top of her body, supporting my weight on my elbows.

I wanted her to savour the moments entertaining her new visitor to her private garden.

I wanted her to feel at ease at welcoming the visitor who wasn't going to be that nice and gentle for too long.

I wasn't going to scare her by moving too quick and fast.

Once my dick found the place to walk and run comfortably inside her jaded garden, I pulled her on my side. We were now lying face-to-face, in complete unison, with our arms wrapped around each others back and legs straddling on top of each others.

I held her in a spooning position, face-to-face rather than from the rear.

I opted for this initial position for a couple of reasons: first, since we were having sex for the first time, it had to be lovingly warm, simple, comfortable, and truly open; and second, this position gave us an opportunity to fully look at each other, freely kiss and hug, move our hands freely to further sensationalize each others body, and talk freely, even if dirty and sexually stimulating. Above all, it wasn't a missionary position – a position she didn't want.

She exhaled a sigh of relief, uttering, "Gosh, it feels so good. My body has been badly aching to have it."

She had tightened her hold on my body, rubbed her crotch more vigorously against mine, and tightly squeezed her legs.

We lay, at times motionless, likely enjoying the beginning of our long, intimate, and mutually satisfying sexual union.

We were no longer peers working in separate rooms. We were now united into one. There wasn't any gap – personal or physical – left between us.

Now that she had calmed down a bit, I stretched out one of my hands to pull one of my pillows. I lifted the side of her bums and slipped the pillow underneath. Her bums were now comfortably placed on a softer white pillow, also raised a few inches above the bed sheet.

While my dick was still roaming inside her, I made her lie flat. I kneeled between her legs, held her calves and raised her legs back towards her face.

"What are you doing?" She whispered nervously.

"Just changing your body posture for a deep fuck," I whispered back. "You wanted to experience a flow, and that too in a position different from the conventional missionary, I am going for a deep penetration. Have you ever tried this position?" I asked.

"Are you kidding me?" She chuckled. "I have no clue about any position other than the conventional missionary. The person I live with is not that adventurous or thoughtful."

She relaxed her legs and helped me raise them. Her body was in a reversed-L position.

"Let me know when you feel a hit inside."

I began thrusting her gently, slightly bending more of her legs after each thrust, until she screamed out,

"Yes ... yes ... your ... dick ... is ... touching ... hitting ... me ... all ... the ... way," she whispered loudly.

With a firm hold on her bent legs, I increased the pace of thrusting. With each hit, she jerked her body, and moaned, "Ah ... um ... ah ... um," showing her tacit acceptance to be slammed that way.

Her jerking body, the sight of her swollen lips of vulva, and the sound of "ahs" were equally enhancing my excitement. I started to hit hard her sexually charged hidden gem until she screamed out,

"Please ... let ... me ... straighten ... my ... legs. I ... am ... getting ... tired."

She raised her hands and tried in vain to free her calves from my grip.

I kept hammering her with full force.

She was sweating, breathing heavily, and stuttering, "That's ... enough ... enough ... now ... please ..."

"You wanted to see your cunt flow? Don't ... you ... don't ... you ... don't ... you?"

I began to stutter while slamming hard her pussy until it virtually busted as a fountain sprinkling all over the pillow and the sheet.

My dick too had sprayed and fed her long sex-starved oyster.

I slowly removed the grip of her calves.

She threw her legs on the bed with one loud bang.

Her legs were finally free from the paws of a hungry man who had likely put her in an uncomfortable position, but for a good reason – to give her what she wanted; to sexually satisfy her the way she longed for.

She placed her legs around my body. She hit her bums again and again on the wet pillow, kept quivering, and with her eyes closed, murmured, "Oh … God … oh … God … That was … awesome."

I lay on top of her, placed my arms closer to her head.

I let her squeeze my dick by her pulsating and contracting walls of her secret flesh.

She ran her fingers through my hair, kissed my forehead and cheeks, and hissed, "That was nice, really nice. I wanted that kind of sex – potent, exciting, and really satisfying."

"I'm glad you enjoyed it," I replied.

I turned on her side, and gently tweaked her nose.

"It's just the beginning, dear," I said, "just think the kind of sex we are going to have."

I put my arm around her back.

"Is that the way you fuck Amy?" She abruptly broke the silence.

"Not really," I hushed, and tightened my hold on her. "You don't have this kind of sex in a sexless marriage. To have a good, enjoyable and satisfactory sex, you need an equally interested and participative partner. For a couple in almost a sexless marriage, sex is always obligatory rather than out of any love or affection, and is all done and over within a few minutes."

"I understand." She replied and rested her head against my chest. "Thank goodness, we aren't going to be that sort of a couple as long as we are together. I can tell you that right now. I will be one hell of a happy participative player."

She stretched her hand to wiggle my soft cock.

"What are you up to?" I asked her, pretending as if I didn't know her intention.

"I want another deep fuck but in a different position," she demanded.

She had my cock on her flat four fingers, and started gently rubbing it with her thumb.

"There's a better way to activate it to do its job," I chided with a sly grin.

"I know that," and she started to slide her body down in order to bring her face closer to my crotch.

"Wait," I held her body, and quickly reversed my position.

We were now lying in opposite directions.

"Oh! I know what you are going to do," she burbled.

"I told you I will taste your juice," I parroted. "Didn't I?"

We lay side by side, facing each others crotch. She held my cock in her hand and started massaging it gently. I, on the other hand, had my thumb placed on top of her clitoral hood. We both were now in a comfortable position to do what we wanted: she was keen to prepare my cock for the next deep fuck, whereas I wanted not only to taste her juice, but also to help her achieve another climax by oral stimulation.

Her massaging was working as my cock was getting harder and harder, at times even slipping from her hold.

She softly caged it in her wet mouth. She started rolling her tongue all over its gland.

"I ... won't ... suck ... it." She tattered. "I ... want ... it ... to ... stay ... hard ... for ... a ... good ... poking ... Don't ... bring ... me ... to ... climax ... by ... rubbing ... my ... clit."

"As you wish," I pattered and stopped massaging her clit.

She looked down on me and moved her crotch away from my face.

"Your cock is all ready for action." She released my bulging cock out of her mouth. "How do you want me?"

"From the rear," I replied promptly.

I lifted myself up on the bed. I made her lay on her stomach, with her face down on the pillows. I made her kneel on all fours.

I knelt behind her.

I opened the cheeks of her ass and brought it closer to my vibrating cock.

"I don't want anal." She firmly commanded.

"I wasn't going to," I replied, "we are not there yet. I will simply enter your pussy."

She slowly moved her right hand back to hold my cock in order to bring it closer to her hot point of entry.

I gently brushed the opening of her pussy with my cock before sliding it into her soaking wet slit. She moved her arm back, folded it to support herself. She was all quiet. She occasionally held her breath. She was likely preparing herself for good rams.

I held her upper outer sides of her thighs and gently slid the cock into her cupid's door.

I stayed motionless as I wanted to give her time to adjust her body's posture. She lowered her ass a bit more in order to comfortably accommodate my hot rod.

I took my boner out and then slid it back in.

I continued thrusting her by increasing both the speed and force.

She turned her head, looked at me how I was hammering her that I heard her small voice while she was panting, "Hit me hard ... harder ... more ... harder ... come ... on ... don't ... hold ... back ... I ... want ... you ... to ... hit ... me ... I ... am ... still ... hungry ... I want ... a ... good ... beating."

With each of her whimper, expressing her innermost cry for much harder and forceful thrusts, I pumped and pumped and pumped her with full intensity.

Her stomach and back had begun to sweat badly from likely the strained posture she was in and hits she was taking, and so was my face and hands. This wetness was gradually softening my hold on her body.

She eventually dropped on the bed, with one side of her face sunk on the pillow. She straightened her legs, with my cock still inside her and sandwiched between her bums.

"Let's finish now ... I am tired," she pleaded.

"Okay," I silently concurred with her, and gave her a few more vigorous hits before exploding inside her.

"Thanks for all the sprinkling all over my dry soil," she hummed into my ear, and slowly brushed her soft fingers through my hair.

"It will no longer be dry as long as we are together," I assured her.

I lay on top of her still quivering body.

I pushed my hands underneath her to hold and press her hooters. I kissed her cheek and rested my face on her nape covered with her soft hair.

I could smell her hair, the fragrance of which had always acted as an aphrodisiac for me. She was breathing uncontrollably. My cock was now shrinking inside her and was on its way to exit her sacred garden.

It didn't take that long for it to pop out and lay flaccid between her arced cheeks.

No sooner had she collected her breath, she opened her eyes, and touched my head,

"Can I get up now?" She whispered.

She was seeking my permission to leave me after all that mighty and satiable hitting.

"Of course," I stuttered as if I had woken up after a long sleep. "I am sorry you had to bear my full body weight for that long."

I turned over and moved to one side of the bed.

"Thank you," she hissed seductively, and kissed my lips. "I really enjoyed it."

"Me too," I replied.

I brought her face closer to mine to give her a long, deep, and passionate parting kiss. A kiss – the warmth of which would stay with us for quite a while, at least until we got together again.

She slipped on her nighty and not the underwear. She carried the latter in her hand as she walked to her room. I kept watching her back in the dimly lit room until I heard the clicking sound – she had locked her side of the door.

What a change the last twenty-four hours had made for both of us. It had changed our lives.

The conference ended by two o'clock the next day. We had to pack and get ready for a return flight to Ottawa at six in the evening.

We took a cab together, sitting closely in one corner of the back seat of the cab.

Since we were moving together in the queue, inching forward to Air Canada's counter to drop off our luggage and pick up our boarding pass, Jen asked the receptionist if we could sit next to each other. She wanted to feel the warmth of each others' bodies 'til the last moment of our separation at Ottawa's airport.

Since we still had an hour before taking off, we headed to a coffee bar and sat on one of the corner tables.

"You know I hate to admit it," she glinted, "I had the best ever sex last night. I am still feeling shivers of ecstasy just by thinking about the kind of pounding you gave me. I never thought sex could be that pleasing, soothing, and both physically and spiritually satisfying."

"Thank you." I replied with a flushed grin. "Since you were fully participating in it, you seem to have enjoyed whatever we did to please and satiate each other. Neither a man nor a woman can have a fulfilling satisfactory sex if his/her partner isn't fully participating in it. As I have already told you, it takes two to have a mutually satisfying sex. Right now, we both are sex-starved because of the reluctance of our spouses to engage in sex with us. Since we had had sex after a long time, and that too willingly with a burning passion, we both are feeling high, living in a heavenly and fantasy world."

"Speaking of fantasy," she goggled and added, "I have this fantasy to have a rough sex."

"What do you mean?" I pretended to be ignorant.

"I mean I want to have sex where someone ties me, hits me, or do something to make me feel that I am a woman being loved and passionately probed, not mauled. I want someone to bring a real woman out of me, awake my womanhood. So far I have had almost a cold sex without any excitement. As I told you, Peter is neither aggressive nor adventurous. Sex with him puts me to sleep as it doesn't last for more than few minutes – not enough for me to even warm up, or even just prepare myself for him to enter me. I feel obligated to offer myself, as his wife, to him. There isn't any love or attraction left between us that leads me to have sex with him."

"Love and sex are entirely two different concepts," I interrupted. "You can love someone without having sex, and you can have sex with someone you don't necessarily love or even hardly know. You can have a wonderful sex with even a stranger, or someone you picked up from a bar, or met during one-night stand – provided you liked that person and got excited to the point of no return, culminating in 'my place or yours' as the leading charger."

"I know all that stuff." She proclaimed. "Let's talk about us. Do you think we will continue to have the kind of sex we had last night? I would pay any price to be with you, no matter what, to get the sort of physical and sexual pleasure I now have experienced with you. I think we will be a good company to one another."

"Indeed, we will be," I concurred, "as long as our circumstances will permit. We both know well that we are not going to leave our families or shrug our family responsibilities. So from that perspective, our relationship is going to last for a specific period; how long, nobody knows. What I can assure you right now is that I will never leave you sexually disappointed – provided you are fully in it with me."

"That's all I wanted to know. For me, it's like a dream come true. In fact, it really has." She pushed her back against the high chair. She had emptied half of her coffee mug.

"What do you mean?" I inquisitively asked. "Which dream of yours has come true?"

"You remember when we were at the office picnic at Lac Lemay Park? I had placed my arm around your waist and tightened it. I told you I was likely dreaming at the time. In that dream, I saw you were screwing me and out of excitement, I was clinging strong to your body. Last night that dream turned into a reality. Isn't that something?"

"Quit dreaming,' I remarked, "enjoy as long as our sexual affair lasts."

We still had to spend twenty more minutes.

"Well, there's one thing I am really curious about." She leaned forward and continued, "How can you have that kind of aggressive sex when your personal life, as I know it, is under so much financial pressure, even keeping you awake some nights. I thought depression of any kind would affect one's sexual performance."

"You are right. Depression does affect one's sexual desire and performance." I supported her view point. "I have loads of debt, but that doesn't mean I have no sexual desire, or I am unable to perform or satisfy a woman. Same way, Peter is depressed on account of his job insecurity, but that doesn't mean his sexual wants are finished, or he's unable to satisfy you, assuming all else is physically well with him. Peter and I may be depressed on account of our individual reasons, but what counts is how we cope with depression. Some men, including me, have the ability to compartmentalize their feelings, emotions, disappointments, frustrations, and live on a positive hope that this low tide in life will come to an end one day. With such positive outlook on life, we perform our day-to-day tasks and responsibilities, including sex, well and to the best of our abilities. On the other hand, there are men, like Peter, who are simply unable to compartmentalize their emotions, and end up as victims of stress and depression, and consequently show signs of withdrawal from day-to-day life, including shirking off their responsibilities. The bottom line is how we men handle depression: win it over with a right approach in conjunction with a hope for a bright future, or simply surrender to it and accept it as a fate-accomplice. Coping with depression is a mental issue. Some can handle it better than others. For the optimistic, depression is transitory, whereas for the pessimistic, it can be perennial."

"I am glad to hear that some men, including you, can be that optimistic even under most depressive situations and can lead normal lives. I wish I were married to one of such men. In that case, I wouldn't be looking for any romantic liaison to satisfy my sexual needs."

"Don't keep sweating on it," I commented gloatingly. "Let's face life as it comes."

I got up and invited her to join me in a walk to the departure lounge.

In the aircraft, we sat on a two-seater on the right of the aisle. Jen sat near the window and I next to her.

During an hour long flight, we both were mostly quiet. She had dozed off, resting her face on top of my right shoulder, which at times slipped on top of my chest. She seemed way more comfortable and contented travelling with me on her way into Ottawa than she was on the way out.

After we picked up our luggage from the carousel, we walked up to the taxi stand – a point of our temporary separation after a night of very intimate, passionate and mutually fulfilling sex.

"I will always cherish the time we spent last night," she hushed.

She squeezed my left hand tightly as she sat on the back seat of the cab.

"See you tomorrow." I slammed the door.

CHAPTER TEN

"Have I told you about a guy I work with?" Amy asked me out of the blue one evening at the dining table.

Her face was radiating and she was speaking more confidently. I knew I hadn't done anything to cause such a radiation on her face.

"He's a manager in the 'Pay and Benefits' section. He's so good looking, handsome, smart, and lively, talks to everyone in the section, listens to their complaints, even resolves administrative issues in no time. I think he's really smart and a genius."

"What's his name? How old is he?" I asked with indifference.

"Carlos Ricci. He's Italian, born and raised in Ottawa. He's a few years older than me," she chirped.

"How senior is he to you?" I asked her out of curiosity.

Also, I wanted to know if he earned more than I did, something common in a man's psychology – measuring others exclusively in terms of their financial strength.

"He's four levels senior to me in the AS (administration and supervisory) group. He earns the same or a bit more than you."

"Is he married? Has children?" I asked.

I wanted to know the full profile of this man. He seemed to have made my wife happy and likely drawn her attention.

"No, he's divorced and has two children, who live with their mother," she replied. "He owns a house in the Greenbank area, about fifteen to twenty minutes drive from the office."

"So he's paying alimony and child support." I commented. "That must be taking a good chunk out of his salary. How's he managing financially?"

"He seems to be doing well," she replied in a defensive tone. "I don't ask him such personal questions. But he doesn't mind talking to me about his personal life. Like he told me that he has hefty investments in stocks and mutual funds, or he even drove a cab in his financially difficult times. He always stops by at my desk to say 'hello' to me. Even though he holds a much senior job, I don't mind talking to him. In fact, I feel very comfortable in his company. He seems to like me. He really appreciates my work. We are good friends."

"How good of friends are you?" I asked with my fully calmed exterior.

"We have coffee and/or lunch together at the cafeteria in the building, and some days we could even be at each others office. He doesn't mind," she replied gloatingly.

"So you found a good company for yourself?" I retorted.

"Don't worry. He's no threat to you." She sneered at me and stood up to clean the table. "Don't jump to any conclusions," she instructed me in her loud tone, her face still flushed crimson.

Her words, 'He's no threat to you', kept reverberating into my ears. Even though I was glancing over the newspaper, I kept pondering that our cold relationship had eventually pushed Amy into isolation, forcing her to suppress her naturally endowed social and chatty instincts.

She was living a life she wasn't meant to. She was a happy-go-lucky girl, a life of any social party. She was now living with me by suppressing her own desires, wishes, and real self. Any woman living this sort of life would be ready to jump the ship at the very first opportunity in search of another companion; in other words, she would be perfectly ripe to engage in an extra marital affair.

We were living like two strangers sharing a roof. There was no communication between us other than the little exchange we would have at the dining table about the children's needs and their on-going activities. Even this short exchange would turn into a war of words, insults, and mud slinging – all on account of my inability to provide funds as demanded to satisfy wants of children, hold social get-togethers, or for upgrading the house. In the end, though, I always had to surrender and fulfil her demands by borrowed funds.

I personally had no problem living quietly, minding my own business, as I had much more on my plate than I could chew. First, the nature of my job was such that it required endless reading of different social, economic, and demographic issues. I could spend all of my time reading books, magazines, and newspapers I subscribed to in order to acquire skills and stay up-to-date. Books had been my best and constant companion in both the good and bad times.

Besides reading my work-related materials, I had to read, compile notes, and acquire new skills to operate the mail-order business. I had to search and select suppliers of goods, set their retail pricing, prepare marketing ads, and compile meaningful and eye-catching catalogues of skill enhancing products including books, audios, videos, and CD-ROMs. I had no time to watch television, indulge into small talks, including meaningless chit-chat with Amy, make unnecessary phone calls, or even attend to such calls.

I was determined to pursue my objective to upgrade my professional skills and standing on the one hand, and successfully run my home-based business on the other, at any cost. The only exceptions were the time spent on caring for our daughters including putting them to bed, reading them bedtime stories, and the upkeep of the house.

While I was single-mindedly pursuing my interests, Amy spent her evenings by attending to regular household chores, including nurturing of the family, and the remaining free time watching television. Since she was an early bird, she would go to bed early and rise up early. I, on the other hand, was a night owl who would go to bed pretty late.

By the time I would hit the sack, Amy would not only be in deep sleep, but almost ready to wake up in another three to four hours. So I would lie quietly on the bed – at a distance from her – in order to avoid disturbing her sleep. Very rarely I would touch her sleeping body in order to initiate sex, and that too would be rebuffed by her mumbling tone full of scorn and rejection,

"Don't disturb me. I have to go to work early in the morning."

Any married woman in her prime wouldn't be happy living in this sort of environment where her husband not only couldn't appreciate her physical presence, her beauty, her nurturing nature, but also failed to appease her physically, sexually, spiritually, and above all, financially. She would always be on the look out to find an alternative to improve her life, especially a man who could lend his ear to listen to her, his shoulder to support her, boost her ego by parroting that she was attractive, sexy, desirable, and wanted – besides spending resources to entertain her and please her with costly gifts.

And this man of her dream or fantasy she would get only by engaging in an affair because her real man was busy fighting day-to-day battles. Since Amy was no different than any other married woman, she was likely falling for the man she had just introduced to me.

Her announcement didn't surprise me at all.

Considering the kind of chill in our relationship, I knew all along that the day would come that she would come across a man she liked and might even decide to leave me. It wasn't me personally as a man, her husband, who had intentionally pushed her to find her satisfaction and happiness in an affair, but my sheer financial inability due to heavy debt load that likely pushed her do it.

I wasn't the only one witnessing my wife leaning towards another man while still living under the roof that I was faithfully paying for each and every month. This sort of thing likely happened in families where the main provider was unable to provide because he didn't earn enough, or earned high enough, but had too many committed payments on mortgage and other debts that nothing much was left for other expenses and entertainment of family members.

Indeed, the size of one's earnings mattered, but how these were disbursed mattered more. The more the number of commitments to be discharged, the less the likelihood of having enough left for personal pleasure and entertainment.

Another reason that Amy likely developed a liking for this colleague of hers was that I didn't take her out for dinner, entertainment, and/or travel, and neither did I buy her any gifts or presents. Since outings and gifts cost money, which I didn't have to begin with, she had been forced to live her life in the four closed walls of the house. And no woman, especially a pretty and attractive one, in her right mind would ever like it – living a desolate life in a pigeon hole.

With this colleague, she was at least able to go out for lunch and taste different foods at a variety of restaurants, indulge into an open, free, and lively chit-chats, and other fun – something a good majority of women enjoyed. Amy had not felt that sort of ease with me for years and years largely because of my financial inadequacy resulting in a too serious and home-bound personality.

The more I self-analyzed myself and looked for reasons behind Amy's crowing and leaning for her new-found colleague, the more I condoned in my heart that what she had done was right for herself. I fully deserved her rejection for not paying much attention to her, or caring and loving her.

On the other hand, I equally justified my actions as no man in his right mind would care, love, or even show affection, let alone have sex, with a wife who never missed an opportunity to nag, belittle, insult, and demean her husband for one reason or another.

As an analyst, I accepted this simple case of cause and effect.

However, I now had to be more vigilant and keep an eye on her activities as there was a third person between us. Although there was nothing I could do to stop her from what she was doing, I had to protect my interests including the well-being of the children, and the house I was maintaining by my blood, sweat, and tears.

Also, I silently condoned her potential affair on the reasoning that if I could have an affair or a romantic liaison at work, why couldn't she? She had the same right to live her life the way she wanted. Being married didn't mean she had lost any of her rights. I had to let her breathe freely.

I firmly believed that in this day and age when women were no longer economically dependent on their married partners, they, as independent earners, could equally manage to run their life and home. With both sexes now potentially independent, there was no reason or any obligation on either's part to live together with visible cracks in their relationship. Theoretically, being married might be construed as a vowed commitment to live together irrespective of the changing state of relationship, but in today's reality, being married meant living together voluntarily, or for as long as the mutual love, desire, and compatibility between the couple lasted.

The presence of children, on the other hand, might influence a couple's decision to stay together at least until children were old enough to leave on their own volition their parent's nest, or temporarily prolong their stay under the same roof. Staying together for the sake of children, on the other hand, could be very unhealthy and damaging for children's development – as concluded by several child psychologists.

Studies after studies have shown that the worsening relationship between the couple in all likelihood is very unhealthy for the growth and development of the children. I knew fully well that the majority of children raised in broken and/or single-parent families had problems concentrating on their studies, were unable to complete post-secondary education, and subsequently ended up holding temporary and precarious jobs. The future of such children was totally bleak.

***

Within days of her bubbling and enthusiastic announcement about working with this handsome and helpful guy at work, I began noticing changes in Amy's tone of communicating with me, her dressing up, and work schedule, besides other things.

"I am leaving for work," one morning she informed me in her commanding tone while I was still tossing and turning in bed.

"Why are you leaving this early?" I asked with my eyes half-open. "The sun has barely risen."

"Oh! There's a lot of work pending at the office," she replied in the same high tone. "I need to submit a month-end balance sheet which is already late."

"But there are twenty days still left in the month." I argued.

"Never mind," she roared. "You just make sure that the children eat their breakfast and board the school bus in time. We no longer have the sitter looking after such tasks."

She ordered me like any army general would talk to a corporal.

"Don't you think I will be late for work, leaving after seeing the children off on their school bus?" I calmly reasoned with her as I sat up on the edge of the bed.

"That's not my problem," she yelled back. "They pay me good money at work. And I have to do my job."

"If you are trying to link the importance of job with its associated earnings level, then don't you think my job is more important than yours as I make nearly three times more than you?"

"Who can argue with you?" she mumbled and stepped out of the bed room. "I may be late this evening too."

She shouted loud enough for me and children to hear while stepping down the lightly carpeted staircase.

I could hear the opening of the garage door. She had driven away to work.

I was still sitting on the bed. I kept thinking about the tone she had commanded me with. I wondered if this new friend had boosted her self-confidence, which in turn, had made her to speak to me as if I was her humble servant.

Not only that, I also noticed this morning, with my eyes half-open, that she had worn a red bra and a matching red panty. This was something new to me. She had always worn the regular white bra and panty for all the years that I could remember. Even her top outfit seemed to be in vogue. What a change? Her interest in this new guy was obviously showing signs of other changes to come.

***

Amy was now leaving for work too early and returning late as well. She convinced me that any time she spent after her regular hours was paid at 'time-and-a-half' rate as the 'overtime pay'. She needed this pay to supplement her income.

Since we worked for the same employer – working under the same administrative rules and guidelines – I was fully aware of the authority approving her daily overtime pay. It was none other than her new admirer. He was blatantly doing her a favour. I didn't want to pursue any discussion on this topic. What mattered to me was that she was home in time on days to take the children to their scheduled extra curricular and social activities and served me the evening meal. The rest of how she spent her time was of no concern to me.

***

"I think Amy is having an affair at work." I told Jen while having lunch together.

"Welcome to the club." She roared. "What makes you think that?" She slyly asked in her typical womanly manner.

"You don't need a rocket scientist to figure out if your wife is having an affair," I tossed back and shrugged my shoulders. "Her work routine has changed, leaving too early and returning too late, even though on the pretext that she's supplementing her earnings by overtime, and that too approved by her suitor. She has started wearing coloured and sexy undergarments, with up-to-date stylish outfits, all to enhance her sex appeal and look good in the eyes of the potential admirer. Not only that, her way of communicating with me has even worsened from harsh to now almost commanding as if I was her subservient. When a woman gets high after getting pumped up by her new suitor, she not only gets too happy and hyper, but also gains self-esteem, and in turn, speaks with more confidence. It's in the psychology of each and every woman on this planet. She likes a man who listens, admires her and makes her feel 'wanted', and provides her a feeling of security."

"You seem to know a lot about the psychology of a woman and how she behaves while having an affair. In a way, you are telling me how I am likely behaving with Peter, as I am having an affair with you." She wondered aloud.

"Well, you are no different than any other woman." I replied sheepishly. "You know the kind of relationship you have with Peter, and what made you to turn to me. In a way, all of these psychological traits have pushed you into my fold. Granted you are financially secure, but there's an element of security outside money that made you count on me, and that's the desire to have a lasting intimate relationship. You know, as colleagues, we are going to be close and working together for years to come. And, you know darn well, as desirous as you are, you are going to be loved hard as long as our relationship lasts."

"Okay, Okay." She raised her right hand, and added, "The same goes with a man's psychology too as he feels emotionally bonded to a woman only after having sex with her. Even though we have been good friends for all these years, you know as well as I do that after our Toronto trip, we are now way more emotionally involved and miss each other's company. If you must know, before the Toronto trip, I rarely thought about you and your problems once I left you at the office. Now I find I can't ignore you or your personal and financial problems as I find myself so emotionally embroiled in your personal life. Now I feel your problem is my problem. I really want to help you."

She placed her right open palm on top of my left hand. I could feel her emotional pain.

"I am overwhelmed," I whispered softly. "Let's not create any scene here. I feel the same for you. After that fateful night in Toronto, we are now emotionally committed to each other. Maybe that's what the affair does – shift attention from a married spouse to someone who loves and cares for you. Maybe that's precisely what Amy too is going through. She likely has found her admirer, and has no feelings left for me. No wonder we are two solitudes under the same roof."

"Don't dwell on something that's beyond your control," she consoled me. "We women will swoon over a guy who would lend us his ear, or lend his shoulder to lean on in difficult times, and above all, will appreciate our beauty, charms, value our company, make us feel uncontrollably desirable. As you likely know, a man always 'wants' whereas a woman wants to be 'wanted'."

"That's precisely what I am lamenting about," I snarled at her. "I failed to give her time and attention, not even conveying her in action or words how much I loved, admired, or desired her. Since I lead a very busy life, and am burdened with financial worries, I think I have knowingly pushed her out of my life. I fully hold myself responsible for forcing her to find a substitute for me. You know I really feel bad when I see her slipping away from me on the one hand, and feel happy for her, on the other hand, that she has found a person who gives her attention, company, and the love and affection she deserves as an attractive woman. You have no idea how guilty I have been feeling ever since I learnt that she was having an affair."

"Look at the positive side," she chided, "she can now at least satisfy her sexual needs like me. If the Toronto night is any example of things to come, I am more than happy to be with you because I know I am going to have the best sex ever. We women are no different than men as far as the liking or wanting of sex is concerned. Men are just more visual and explicit. They have a tendency to brag. We women can equally turn sexually wild with the right, muscular, and virile men. I think with proper precautions and hygiene, we can have the best of sex by engaging in an affair. Since Amy has fallen for a guy who has an Italian descent, she's likely to have a good and banging times. Italians make good lovers. Don't you think she deserves a good time like anyone else?" Winking her left eye, Jen grinned broadly and then let her full laughter out. She had lightened the tight arid air between us. "Sorry, I shouldn't have said that."

She lifted her empty tray from the table and walked up to the standing trolley meant for placing used dishes and trays.

***

Amy's man of interest – Carlos – became an integral part of our day-to-day discussion at home. Whether we were having dinner at the dining table, or driving kids to the shopping mall for shopping, or extra curricular activities, Amy would mention his name and how he helped her in resolving this and that financial or administrative issue, or accompanied her to this and that meeting, or had lunch at this and that restaurant. Even though it was irksome for me to keep hearing his name or about his good deeds helping Amy to advance her career, or about his successful financial investments, I could understand why she would like to talk or brag about him every time we were together – either he had totally prevailed over her mind and thoughts, or she had to downgrade me compared to him and his financial wizardry.

She was spending much more of her time with Carlos. He became her center of attraction. She began bragging about him, his deeds, and his status. Besides talking about Carlos, the only other topic she would talk about was the children's current and potential needs – all leading to demand for more money. How I was physically or financially doing was of least or no concern to her. What simply mattered to her was that the house be running and maintained in good shape and order without interrupting her daily routine and making any demand on her money other than buying weekly groceries, paying the live-in sitter, and the cost of extra social and sport activities that the children were attending.

Now that our daughters were young and had started their elementary schooling, Amy wanted us to drive them to Toronto and Niagara Falls. She wanted to have a short trip, including four nights stay at a hotel, visits to tourist attractions including a visit to see Canada's Wonderland in Toronto and the Falls and Marineland in Niagara Falls to see dolphins in water entertaining the crowds. She wanted me to rent a van so that the children could travel comfortably.

"Since the children are now so used to being driven in a van, I prefer we rent a van for the four-day trip," she demanded.

"Do you realize how much it's going to cost?" I nervously said. "Besides, add costs of three nights in a hotel, daily expenses on food, entry fee to tourist attractions, shopping, and cost of gas. We are looking at a cost of a couple of thousand dollars for four days."

"We can't raise our children within the confines of this house," she emphasized. "It's important for their development to take them out during the summer break. Moreover, almost all children go out on a short or long holiday. When children go back to school, they likely talk about their holidays, where they went, what they did, and so on. Imagine how bad our children would feel if they were to stay at home for the entire summer break of two months, or had no experience to share with their peers. I don't want our children to grow with any inferiority complex."

"I understand your rationale and you don't have to convince me how important it is to take them out even for a few days," I frustratingly replied. "My problem is that I don't have the money to take them around. I even paid our last property tax bill by using the MasterCard, charging close to twenty percent rate of interest. I had no choice other than to use the card to make this mandatory payment. You know the municipality can hold a lien on houses with unpaid property taxes. Couldn't we postpone this trip until next year?" I pleaded.

"No way!" She yelled. "We have to take children out on a short vacation. They deserve the best as both of their parents are earning good enough salaries. In the eyes of our neighbours and everyone else, we are considered a high income family. It's not their fault that we don't have any savings or cash flow to finance their outing. Children shouldn't pay for their father's stupidity about mishandling money or inability to save or invest sensibly. Since you run the house, you are fully responsible for the present mess. Don't blame the children. Consider the cost of such trips as another obligatory expenditure."

She yelled loudly to make her point.

"If that's what you want, so it will be." I garbled.

I had surrendered. Not because of her screams gushing through my eardrums, but she was right. She was arguing for the right cause. As parents, it was our duty to take our children out for a mini break – away from home – to a new city, or tourist attractions meant to interest and develop children's mind, thinking and learning process. Amy was right. It wasn't the children's fault that I didn't have any savings or cash flow. They needed to be nurtured and raised well without any materialistic deprivation – even if that meant sinking more in a debt hole.

Undertaking any road trip requires some good financial planning. There are some families who would finish the trip within the pre-set budget and there are others who would go overboard – spending many times over the budgeted amount. I happen to belong to the latter group of 'over-spenders' because I firmly believe that 'don't get out of the house if you can't afford; but once out, then you don't need to count pennies because you want to travel well, with full comfort, and make an optimal use of time and travel.' The difference in costs may or may not be marginal, but cutting corners on the road to save a few dollars can be harmful to the family's health – like inability to sleep on beds in a cheaper hotel, or eat cheaper, stale, or rotten food causing vomiting or stomachache requiring medical attention. Granted, comfort, luxury, pleasure, and shopping all come at a price, so be it as long as one is on the road.

With such thinking, I knew this trip to Toronto and Niagara Falls was going to cost me way more than I had initially planned. For example, I wanted our children to stay not only at any hotel, but one closer to the sites of interest. For instance, in Niagara Falls, they would stay at a hotel facing the Falls so that they could really enjoy the natural flow of waters and how they fell in a horse-shoe shape from meters and meters of height. Then I had to ensure that they visited each and every site of interest, rode as many rides as possible in the recreational park, and above all, played and fed the dolphins. For me, the bottom line was their utmost comfort and pleasure, irrespective of the cost. In the end, though, I had to pay back every cent that I was so freely spending and subsequently increasing my debt liability.

One can fully enjoy a vacation if paid out from one's current cash flow or savings. However, if it's partly or fully financed by borrowed funds, then say goodbye to all the fun as one is constantly thinking about the rising debt and its repayment. Each and every time one charges an entry fee to a park, meals at lunch and dinner, enter any games, or amusement rides, for fun and pleasure, one becomes too conscious about increasing one's size of debt. It's like a metered taxi – the longer you travel, the more you pay. The debt meter is on from the day one starts out the vacation 'til the day one returns home.

This constant thought that each day of fully charged vacation is increasing one's debt liability depresses the person responsible for repaying the debt. For that person, a vacation causes too much stress and depression rather than any fun, relaxation, or pleasure. And this stress and depression keeps that person on a different wavelength than others accompanying him. While the latter may be having all the fun, with their faces smiling and fully laughing, the debtor in heart is still counting all the beans and figuring how to pay back the debt. Even though the depressive debtor is physically walking, staying together, or even leading his/her family members, he/she is miles and miles away from them. The debtor is accompanying them – all quiet with a depressed and sullen look.

"Does he always look sad like that?" a guard at one of the entry points in the recreational park asked Amy as I let her and our daughters pass the turnstile.

"Not really," she assured him with her superficial grin. "He's serious by nature," she added.

"Why?" The guard showed his curiosity.

"He's a writer by profession," she replied. "You know how writers are always lost in their own little world."

"But right now he's on holidays," he giggled loudly. "He should be smiling and have fun like all others around."

"Oh! Well, you can't change a person, you know." Amy snapped at the guard and moved away from him. She had put up her strong face or she didn't really care about the cause of my melancholy.

"You have a good day, sir." He spoke to me rather softly.

"Thank you." I hissed back and passed him to join my family members.

I really felt bad.

Was my depression and sadness that visible that even a guard on duty didn't fail to read my face? It was obvious that I was unable to hide all the inner doom and gloom caused by the rising indebtedness. As far as my family members were concerned, they had accepted my sad and pensive face as a part of their life. I, as the main breadwinner of the family, on the other hand, was simply performing my duty to be with my family. I was least interested in what I was viewing at this or any other site, or tourist attraction.

I was glad that my daughters were too young to understand the gravity of the situation. As a father, I wanted them to have fun all the time. Moreover, I always wanted my daughters to have the best of the best irrespective of the cost involved or the amount I had to borrow to pay for it.

The trip not only added a couple of thousand dollars in new credit, upping my minimum payment on some cards, but also provided me an opportunity to see Amy's inner state of mind. She accompanied the children on some rides, and sat out and watched them on others from a distance. I, on the other hand, was fully engaged in taking pictures of the park, the children on rides, and other places and buildings of interest.

When I focused my camera on Amy sitting on one of the public benches in the park, I noticed she was sitting ashen faced, with blurry and blank eyes, her hair all dishevelled by

MINIMUM PAYMENT

the hot blowing winds. She seemed totally lost in her thoughts, likely missing, thinking, and fantasizing about her new lover. I was sure she was missing him badly. All along the trip, she had acted like a stranger, had a very limited conversation with me, and when we spoke, it was related to the children's food or entertainment or activity. Even when she shared the hotel's king-size bed with me, she made sure she was out of my reach like she had been for years in our regular bed at home. Obviously, any change in location or type of bed didn't make any dent in her feelings and perception about me.

Renting a van turned out to be both a blessing and a curse. It was a blessing because it provided me with another source of credit. A few days after returning the van, I got a letter from the American Express, one of the financial giants in the United States, with connections with travel agencies, car-rental companies, and airport counters all over the world. The company offered a credit card, under the name 'American Express', to an elite group of travellers all over the world. Its famous marketing slogan to attract more clientele was *'Don't leave home without it."*

When I got the form to apply for this card issued by an American financial institution, I was more than pleased, and felt honoured that I was still in that good financial standing. I could get this prestigious card. Since one's level of gross income was one of the leading determinants used to vet the potential holders of this and any other credit card, for that matter, I was glad my relatively higher earnings were still doing a lot of good to me. The card issuing company wouldn't care about card holder's cash flow situation – until that holder defaulted on any payment. Since I didn't travel that much, I planned to use this card for my other needs.

Within few weeks of mailing the official application form, I received my green American Express card. One of the conditions underlying the use of this card was that the billed balance was to be paid in full by the due date. There was no spending limit on this card; I could spend any amount provided I paid back in full the amount owed by the due date. The card was largely for the convenience of business travellers who would spend varied amounts while on travel, and once back home, or to the work-station, they or their companies would pay up the balances due. Again, the card could be used like any other consumer credit card as long as the balance shown on the statement was fully paid.

On several occasions when I had reached the spending limits on my VISA and MasterCard, I used this American Express card. Complying with the terms of its use, I used to pay off the full balance as well, despite the difficulty it created. For example, I wouldn't be able to make minimum payments on other cards or loans from money left after making payment to American Express.

I had to really juggle making payments on other cards and loans, besides regular monthly bills on heat, hydro, cable, etc. I would make a minimum payment on one card or revolving loan one day, get the statement officially stamped that the payment had been made, then withdraw some amount from the same account the next day to make a payment on the second loan, and after a couple of days, using funds from these combined sources, pay for the third loan, and on and on. I was just getting each of the statements officially stamped that the payment had been made simply to protect my credit rating. I had to go through this juggling exercise each month.

For me, this kind of juggling became an essential act of survival. Making one full payment on one account had tilted the apple cart. I couldn't carry this sort of juggling for too long. The number of payments, their respective mandatory minimum payments and due dates – all had cornered me badly. I was beginning to lose my sanity. I had to manoeuvre within monthly funds left at hand – even if it meant breaking terms and conditions of some cards.

I started to make partial payments on the American Express card, which was contrary to the company's policy. I was fully aware I was not complying with the agreed upon conditions governing the use of this card. The company reminded me a few times, and following that, I again showed my compliance. This on-again-off-again compliance didn't last for too long either because by the mid eighties, the company had introduced another credit card named 'Optima'. This greyish looking card was similar to other credit cards that allowed paying minimum payment on the balance outstanding.

Evidently, the company must have realized that there was a market for such a card as there were many card users like me who paid only a minimum payment on the balance outstanding. And since this minimum payment strictly covered interest charges and almost no write-off of the principal, the use of this new card would further enhance the company's revenue – collected as interest on outstanding balances.

Indeed, banks and finance companies issuing such cards with revolving credit facility would always be on the look out for clients like me. Not only that, they would do their level best to have us on board for as long as possible as we were a steady source of their revenue. This 'Optima' card had a pre-set limit of ten thousand dollars, which in turn meant, I could now manage my life for few extra years.

***

It's a common knowledge that banks and other financial institutions have access, free or for a fee, to information on card users or debtors, compiled and likely sold by major credit agencies. These institutions know darn well the demographics, social, and financial characteristics of card holders or debtors. From such databases, these institutions can easily prepare profiles of card users who are likely to pay full balance each month and those who can't. It's the latter group which likely draws the most attention of card and credit issuing institutions as this group largely contributes to their annual revenues in the form of interest charges on unpaid balances. The group that pays off monthly balances in full is of interest to institutions as well, but not that much, because it's the commission paid by merchants of goods and services who sell on credit cards, or 'vendors', that account for institutional revenue. Card users in this case are simply enjoying a money-free transaction, or sit on their unused money during the so-called grace-period prior to making the payment. This group is the 'real' beneficiary of all the credit freely available during the grace-period – that's the period between the day the sale on credit takes place and the day the balance is due for payment.

***

A few months after I received the 'Optima' card from the American Express I received a VISA card offer, with a pre-set spending limit of five thousand dollars, from another American financial giant. Since I was in a desperate need of funds, I gladly accepted the offer, and extended my lifeline as well. All of these credit cards issued by the American financial institutions were in Canadian dollars as I had to send payments to their named agents located in Canada.

However, since I was in the midst of establishing my mail-order business, and had some of my suppliers of books, audios, videos, and CD-ROMS located in the U.S., I had to use these cards to make payments on goods ordered in US dollars. The transaction would go through in Canadian dollars, using the Canada/U.S dollar exchange rate on the day of transaction – and not the day of payment.

Over time, my inter-continental financial transactions must have been noticed by the Canadian financial institution (FI-I). Or, FI-I might have observed it from the information collated by credit agencies. No matter how FI-I noticed that I was making transactions in US dollars, the bottom line was that FI-I issued me a VISA card in US dollars, with a spending limit of ten thousand dollars.

I could now easily use this card for all of my sales transactions with producers and sellers in the U.S. in their country's currency. That saved me the hassle to see the conversion from Canadian to US dollars, first, on the day of purchase, and then on the day I made the payment – the latter I still had to do. This VISA card in US dollars was no different than other VISA cards, allowing me to make a minimum payment on the balance outstanding.

The flip side of using this card was the complex round-about way of making a monthly payment in Canadian dollars. Since I didn't have any account in US dollars with any institution, including FI-I, the clerk had to do a lot of paper work: first, show a purchase of US dollars as per the amount of payment specified; second, make a draft of that amount; third, attach that draft with the monthly statement. It was quite a time consuming process that I had to face month after month – all because I didn't have a US dollars account.

On one occasion, a bank teller handling the transaction couldn't resist commenting,

"That's a bit of a weird way of making a payment. To my knowledge, you are the only one who makes a payment in a round-about manner."

Even though I felt very embarrassed and ashamed, I simply grinned and replied, "Sorry, that's the only way I can make a payment. I don't have a US dollars account."

"Then you shouldn't use VISA in US dollars," he advised. "Because it costs an arm and a leg; not only you are paying high annual interest of 19.9% on unpaid balance, but also purchasing dollars on the varying conversion rate. Over and above, you are paying a fee for converting Canadian dollars to US dollars."

"I understand all of these details," I frustratingly replied. "Running a business is no fun, especially when you have all of your suppliers located in the US. Someday, when the business picks up, I will have a US dollar account and save myself this agony that I face month after month."

"Well, good luck," he replied with a broad grin, likely finding my words hollow.

He completed the transaction at hand.

While walking back to the office, I kept thinking about how badly I was degraded by a teller. He had no business to comment on the transaction I was making. As a teller, he was supposed to serve me as a customer and refrain from offering me any unsolicited advice. On the other hand, it was also possible that since the teller knew me well, serving me over months and years, he had opened up and showered me with his words of wisdom. He might really be trying to help me to avoid this expensive round-about way of making a payment and save myself some money.

Then my sixth sense showed up and I mumbled to myself, "That idiot doesn't know what it takes to run a business. He's just a cashier, working here for years, and seems to be satisfied and happy with what he's doing. He doesn't seem to have any ambition or drive to improve his job or career track."

While I thought of the teller's career and his limited future prospects, my anger towards him had begun to melt. I rather felt pity for him and his limited future, knowing fully well that only a small fraction of tellers, with the proper mindset on their career, do move up the ladder and eventually hold a senior portfolio at the bank.

CHAPTER ELEVEN

I was in my late forties when I launched the home-based mail-order business to supplement my income. Though this business didn't require any big start-up venture capital, it nonetheless needed some money to purchase stationary to prepare catalogues, their printing, mailing, and a stock of personalized stationary with imprinted company's name to make it look more professional.

Whatever money I had to spend on preparing and mailing catalogues, or on subscribing to different trade magazines focused on marketing was all borrowed either on cards or drawn from the only line of credit I had with FI-II. This low-cost, but physically strenuous business had risks like any other business. Its success depended on how good I would be in marketing and selling the skill-development products. Since I was a rooky who learnt everything about this business from scratch, my chances of success were not that bright – especially when competing against big-name and established printers, publishers, suppliers, and bookstores. It was a calculated risk I took.

With several new credit cards including one in US dollars now at hand, I had access to plenty of money. I was quite confident that I would make it. Since the business was unique in nature, as no one else was selling specific skill enhancement material, I was happily tapping my back that I finally had the product that would sell well across the country. I was happy that I finally had found the way to get out of this poor and miserable life.

The very thought of owning and running my own business boosted my personal confidence and self-esteem. I had my personal business cards imprinted, naming me as president of the company. I left no stone unturned to ensure that the products I bought for sale were of good quality and produced by reputed companies.

Also, these were genuinely useful for buyers. People could order products from the comfort of their home with guaranteed satisfaction. Buyers were even assured to return products, if unsatisfied, at the company's cost. I was so darn sure about the quality and usefulness of the products I was going to sell.

The first catalogue that I compiled comprised of books on varied topics including know-how or how to, inspirational, spiritual, and exercises (as health issues were in vogue at the time). Since I wanted these catalogues to look as professional as possible with a company's logo on the order form, I designed the whole catalogue and then got it printed by a local commercial press. The printing alone cost me a couple of thousand dollars, all paid by borrowed funds.

The very first rookie mistake I made was that I failed to check with the suppliers if they had lately increased prices of their products since our last communication and agreed upon listed prices. Even though the discount rate was still fifty percent, any increase in prices quoted in my final and commercially published catalogue would have cut down my profit margin.

The day I received the batch of published debut catalogue, I received from one of my main suppliers a new price list of its products. The new prices that I was going to be charged were much higher than those already printed in the catalogue. That was not a good omen to start a business.

I pulled my hair and bitterly cursed myself for not checking with suppliers before getting the catalogue published. I had to enter the new prices by hand. Imagine deleting the printed price and then writing by pen the new price for more than thousand copies. It took me several evenings to fix copies of my first catalogue. I had to maintain my sanity, my patience, and drive to march on. I considered it all as a part of the learning process.

I mailed close to two hundred copies of the catalogue all across Canada – mainly to public and university libraries, research, financial, and academic institutions. I used the 9" x 12" size brown envelopes with the company's name and logo imprinted on the top left corner, and affixed a stamp on the right.

I now had to wait for the orders to pour in. I fervently expected their flow in a post box that I had rented from a post office, not too far from home, at an annual fee of close to seventy-five dollars. I didn't want my business mail to be delivered at home and get mixed up with my personal mail. I would rather go to the post office to check or pick up my business mail and parcels of goods ordered.

By the time I mailed out my first catalogue of books and audio tapes, I had eleven credit cards in addition to the line of credit with FI-II. These were cards from department stores namely, the Hudson Bay, Sears, Eaton's, Shell gas company, VISA in Canadian dollars, VISA in US dollars, VISA from another financial institution collaborating with General Motors (I got it as I was driving General Motors' used Malibu van), MasterCard, American Express (green card with full balance to be paid), Optima, and VISA from another US financial institution. Cards from department stores were used to purchase children clothing and household furnishings, Shell's to fill up gas in the car, and all other cards for domestic, business, and other day-to-day needs, including payment of some monthly bills.

One of the reasons I had so many cards in the eighties and early nineties was that department stores and gas companies didn't accept VISA or MasterCard. Each and every department store or gas company accepted its own card simply to protect their clientele or the so-called market share. Since VISA and MasterCard were issued by chartered banks and other incorporated financial institutions, there was quite a competition in the credit card market.

Banks and financial institutions easily won this competition by attracting more and more users of VISA and MasterCard by offering them different incentives including relatively lower interest rates, air mile points for travel, travel and limited health insurance, access to cash advances, facility to pay bills, debt transfers – to name a few. As department stores, oil companies, and other businesses felt the change of winds and noticed a drop in their clientele, sales revenue, and their ultimate profit margins, they all gradually began to accept VISA and MasterCard besides their own credit cards.

Indeed, this competition in the credit card market made the department stores and other businesses to accept VISA and MasterCard cards. It didn't, however, make any dent in the phenomenal annual interest rate that these stores and businesses were charging – averaging close to 30% a year. Even though their sales revenues were beginning to plummet as customers used more freely their new found freedom to purchase goods and services on VISA and MasterCard from any store they wished and felt no more captives of a particular store. Department stores clung to their high interest credit policy. And this in turn further cut down their business, forcing some to even close their long established business.

Since I was new in business, I had no financial strength to sell anything on credit, i.e., on VISA or MasterCard. The only thing I could offer was payment in thirty days, in full after delivery rather than before, and that too, returnable in case of any dissatisfaction with the product. I had absolutely no financial fluidity – something which was a must for any business to succeed, or have good standing in the market. A person who himself was hungry for cash couldn't afford to sell goods on credit or deferred payments.

By running a business, funded entirely by borrowed funds, I had made my life more miserable. This not only resulted in an increased number of monthly obligatory payments, but also the total amount paid out on their respective minimum payments. Business related payments had added a new wrinkle to my already financially dire situation. I was already borrowing from Peter to pay Paul, and now here I was faced with paying business related expenses. That meant more squeezing and juggling with limited cash available.

I bore even this pain with a grain of salt. I convinced myself that this was all a short term pain for a long term gain. My situation would change once I had the business running successfully. After all, each and every business needed some investment, small or large, and also some running costs. There was no reason for me to be impatient or complain.

But it was easier said than done. This additional expenditure along with the rising amounts of other bills that I had to pay from my fixed net income had robbed me of almost every thing including my peace of mind, sleep, as well as concentration on children, domestic and work issues. I was physically moving and attending day-to-day tasks, but inside, I was all lifeless with no desire left to live or do anything. I was a living dead. I hated and cursed myself for putting not only myself, but family members too in this sinking hole of indebtedness.

Even on paydays, when paid workers were supposed to be happy to see the paycheque in their hand, i.e., the remuneration of their work, I would be too sad as I would visit the bank, totally glum-faced, and pay the bills to the last cent. There was nothing left that I could use even the next day, let alone the next two weeks, or until I received the next cheque, which too would have experienced the same lot. I would walk back to the office, all quiet, stone-faced, with almost blurred vision, as I couldn't even acknowledge or recognize my colleagues passing me by on the same footpath.

Back at the office, I would temporarily shove aside my financial miseries, try to focus on work, and keep to myself unless I had to attend a meeting, or Jen wanted my attention on some official matter or simply wanted to whine – since she was close to my heart and knew all about me and my feelings. At times even when some colleague reminded me that he/she saw me walking over to the bank or returning from the bank and I failed to acknowledge his/her 'hello', I would embarrassingly say 'sorry' or apologize to him/her, knowing full well how poorly I had acted – as a prisoner of my own haunting deeds and miseries.

For me, paydays were more depressing as well as distressing, reminding me my real worthlessness on the earth. On such days, employed workers usually put aside a fraction of their paycheque for a rainy day. And here I was who was more concerned about making all the obligatory payments on credit cards, line of credit, and other loans. For most, a payday brought a big smile on their face whereas for me, it brought all the tension and fear. For me, each payday became a day testing my survival skill and ability to survive another two weeks or a month as I had to juggle my way through to make the mandatory minimum payments. Also, each payday reminded me that my expenses were way more than my net income could ever sustain, and if this trend continued, I was indeed heading for a catastrophic, even fatal, disaster.

Even the thought of potential consequences of such looming disaster ran chilled shivers in my body. How was I going to provide for my family including higher education to my daughters, essential for securing better-paying jobs and pursuing successful careers, expenses on their weddings, and other unexpected and unplanned needs? Never mind the potential security during retirement; my other main concern was the cost of my own funeral. Who was going to pay for it? The kids had no means. They were still young, attending school, and fully dependent financially on parents. Even if they were old and had independent means, I wouldn't want them to spend a penny from their pocket on my funeral. Their presence alone at my funeral would be more than I could ever ask or wish for.

Such dreary thoughts, especially on paydays, would drive me wildly crazy, so much so that while alone and in utter desperation, I would rub and hit my head against the wall at times, loudly screaming inside, "Oh God, please, please help," as if such hits to the brain and silent cries to God would generate any solution. Even though I firmly believed in God and His super powers, I never believed that He would simply pull me out of my miseries by a gentle touch of some magic wand.

No; not at all.

I had to be realistic, brave, resilient, persistent, and patient. I had to find my way out. Considering all of my previous efforts to find a source of supplementary income had failed, and the type of skills and job I had, had precluded me to take any part-time jobs like flipping hamburgers, or load grocery bags, wash dishes at a restaurant, I had to find something that was in my alley. As a professional analyst-cum-writer, I didn't think I could ever do such jobs to begin with. Also, I wanted to retain my autonomy to control what I was doing and, in turn, shape my future.

Since I could neither find any part-time analytic work, nor had I the time to become a freelance writer with all the commitments of my current job, the only viable solution that hit my mind again and again was to focus on running my own business with patience and persistence. What more could I do? The business I had started would take its own time to establish and attract the right clientele.

One way to expedite and improve sales of goods and services I was offering was to improve marketing, meaning advertising more in all sorts of newspapers and community, and public spots. And this sort of advertising, again, required a lot of money which I didn't have to begin with. How much of risk could I take with all of borrowed funds? I was already at the hilt of my limits. Running and maintaining the house and fulfilling family needs were the top priorities. I had to finance these before spending on advertising and business operations. The bottom line was that each and every borrowed dollar had to be spent with extra caution.

Amy was totally unaware about the kind of financial tension I was going through. Since our relationship was already fractious and at the lowest ebb, I didn't want to share with her any of my inner feelings, or what kind of financial stress I was facing, and how I was managing both the house and the business. She had her own grievances that I never spent much time with her, never took her out for any entertainment, or on holidays, with the exception of a few days that we took our daughters out during their annual summer break.

***

One evening after dinner, when the children had left to watch TV or attend to their homework, Amy announced, "I want us to separate."

She seriously gazed at my face, from across the table, to read my reaction to her bombshell announcement.

"Why?" I calmly asked her, staring at her full face.

"I don't want to live any longer in a dead relationship," she snapped at me. "You have no time for me or the children. You are always busy with your work, studies, and now business. You don't want anyone around. We don't exist for you. I don't see any reason in living together. Either you leave the house or we sell the house and I can live with the children elsewhere on my share."

She suggested the simple way out.

"Granted I don't spend any time with you or the children," I replied softly, "but I am working hard for the benefit of the family. I don't think you know how badly I need to find a source to supplement our income …"

"Now don't give me that soggy story of yours that we don't make that well, or you can't pay bills because of too much debt. I still think you didn't act wisely in life. If you had acted and spent money wisely or invested in some real estate like many of our friends have done, you wouldn't be in this messy situation. I am just getting tired of listening to your same old record. I don't think you are financially smart." She yelled and cut me off.

"Well, you don't want to face reality, that's your problem." I sneered at her. "I am a realist and don't live in any fantasy world. I did the best I could and will continue to do it until I get what I want. Right now, I desperately need money to improve my cash flow situation in order to pay our monthly bills and other obligations – never mind spending on any unexpected or unplanned expense. Since I can't find a suitable part time job, I have started this mail-order business that, in turn, takes all the time and attention during evenings and weekends. I realize I am not devoting attention to you and the children, but this business needs my full attention and dedication. I am sorry you and the children have to go through this rough patch."

"No, it's not a patch," she yelled, her eyes somewhat moistened. "You have not been paying any attention to us for quite some time. You are never here for me, for the children. If we have to live like that, we might as well part and find our own lifestyle. I think we should sell the house and you just give me my share."

"I have no problem in selling the house, if you so insist." I replied tauntingly and shrugged my shoulders. "The unfortunate part is that you won't get much money out of it as we have owned this house for less than ten years. We still have almost the full mortgage, and along with all other outstanding debts that will be paid after the sale, we are not going to have much left over to split. The very little that you will have wouldn't be enough to pay even a few months rent. I know you earn and can manage your life, but not with the children."

'Never mind about the children," she parroted loudly. "I will take care of them."

"You must be kidding? You can't do that in your current salary," I snapped back. "Unless you are going to live in a publicly subsidized apartment, you are not going to be able to afford renting a decent apartment. And I will never have my children raised in a public housing."

"I will do overtime to make more money in order to take care of them." She rationalized her demand.

"And that would mean paying even less attention to them than what you are already doing." I shot down her rationale. "Leaving aside the issue of time spent on the children's care, just think about the financial side of their care. Even if I don't spend much time with them, I take care of all of their needs and well-being. You know how liberally we spend on the children. Spending time with them is not as vital as fulfilling their material needs. I want them to grow without any financial worry. I want them to focus on their study and put every effort to make their careers without worrying about money, or wasting time on part-time jobs, and so on. By demanding to part ways, you are looking only at your life, likely with some new partner you may have in mind or found, and that, in my opinion, is a selfish way of looking at the situation. Think of the children. How our separation will damage the children's growth, their studies, careers, in essence, their entire future. And I will never let that happen. I can live with our poor, non-existent, uncaring, unloving, and no-sex relationship, but I will never let you play with the children's lives. They still have a father who can look after them."

I was now madly lecturing her. Her suggestion had now hit my rational sixth sense.

"I hate to admit it, but whatever you are saying makes sense." She had thrown in the towel. "What about my life, or our life? First you asked me to adjust to your work demands, now it is business demands. God knows, what will be your next demand?"

"I don't know." I said softly and gazed back into her eyes.

She was wiping the edges with a tissue paper she had pulled from the box sitting at the table.

I placed my right hand on top of hers, and added,

"Just bear with me. I have to take care of this business. You know my nature. Once I decide to do something, then I don't look back no matter what, or question my decision. I go all the way until I have accomplished my objective."

"I am fully aware of that," she concurred with me. "However, I still think you should have opted to write a book of your own since you write so much, and judging from the media publicity that your papers get, you must be doing something really well. I don't know why you want to start a business about which you know nothing about."

"Two simple reasons," I told her calmly, "first, we need money, and that too quickly, and second, I want to do something new, more challenging, as I have been doing too much of writing at work. Writing again at home doesn't appeal to me that much. Moreover, writing a book takes time, and once it's written, one needs an editor, a literary agent, a publisher, and a marketing network. To earn money as a successful writer is a long and unpredictable shot. And I can't afford that. I want a source of quick cash flow. Right now, you just help me and look after the public relations side of this business, the rest I will take care of."

"Well, you know I will do that." She assured me with a grin. "I love to talk to people, in person, on the phone, you name it. What do you think I do at work?"

She patted the top of my hand and walked away from the table.

Amy had simmered down. She had likely accepted the status-quo for the time-being.

I kept thinking how she didn't miss the opportunity, even tonight, to degrade and insult me by saying that I didn't act wisely in life, or I wasn't financially smart. She had never missed any opportunity to pinpoint my weaknesses or degrade me – especially in respect to our weak financial situation.

Even though we were still living as a couple, responsible parents of our children, in the eyes of all neighbours and friends around, we had minimized our weekend outings together for grocery shopping, or for shopping of children's clothes or toys, or home furnishings and accessories. On occasions we were out, I would let Amy and the children do all of the shopping to their heart's content.

If we were at a department store, all of the merchandise bought would be charged on that store's card, and when we were at a grocery store, she would buy things that the kids wanted besides the regular weekly groceries. I would simply walk around and look at shelves full of stacks and stacks of merchandise. Even if I wanted to buy something that I liked, I would not bother Amy to buy it because I never wanted her to spend more – and that too on me – than she wanted to. Since she never believed in budgeting and was a compulsive spendthrift, I, on the other hand, had to keep account of each and every cent that I was spending. With my very light pockets, I had a pretty good control on my desires and wants.

I could see many people in stores walking with proper grocery lists or shopping with pre-set budgets. Whenever I would point this out to Amy and suggest to her to shop with some pre-set budget, she would laughingly ignore the suggestion. For her, all those shopping according to their pre-set lists were just crazy and insane.

While at the checkout counter, I could see many male shoppers opening up their wallets or ladies their small purses carrying stacks and stacks of credit cards. My heart would go to these shoppers, fully empathizing with them, watching them pay by pulling one of their credit cards. Some of these shoppers must be paying by credit cards as a convenient way to shop around whereas others were paying by credit card likely because they had no money or were experiencing a cash flow problem like me. Personally, I hated to see anyone buying groceries on a credit card, and to that effect, I had specifically instructed Amy never to do it – especially when I was with her – as it reflected the family's weak and vulnerable financial situation.

How could I judge if a shopper used a credit card for convenience or out of necessity? Since I had an analytic mind, I would glance at the kind of groceries a shopper had picked and was being charged. If groceries included expensive fruits, vegetables, meats including quality steaks, and other items, I could possibly guess the financial status of that shopper – belonging likely in the upper thresholds of income, and likely used the credit card for convenience. On the other hand, if the shopper had picked up cheaper fruits, vegetables, breads, bacon, packs of sausages, baked beans, and tinned meats, that shopper likely was from a lower end of the income scale, and used the card out of necessity. Even though this was a crude way to judge the financial status of shoppers and their reason behind using credit cards, I could still read and mentally compile a lot of information about people lined up at the cashier's counter.

As I watched people carrying stacks and stacks of credit cards, I often wondered about how they would be making payments on these cards, their financial means, their level of anxiety and distress. I used to console myself that I wasn't the only one who was using multiple credit cards to barely survive. There were many who were likely suffering the kind of financial stress that I was going through. Were most of these people using cards by choice or necessity? I knew I was using out of necessity, so they were in all likelihood. The bottom line was that I really empathized with users of multiple credit cards as I could feel their mental anguish, frustration, and pain. No wonder. Misery loved company.

Another situation that made my heart cry while on a shopping expedition was witnessing a man or a woman pleading and arguing with a young and innocent child wanting to buy a specific thing or a toy. The child would be bursting in tears, screaming loudly, stamping feet on the floor, refusing to budge until slapped hard on the cheek or back by that man or a woman and pulling child's hand, almost dragging the child, and mumbling, "Stop crying, I have no money to buy it right now. I promise we will buy it next time."

And, in the extreme case, whenever I witnessed any one beating or hitting the child in the open shopping center, I felt really bad for both the hurt and crying child and the person giving all the thrashing: for the child because he/she was born in a family with inadequate means, and for the person because he/she was venting out his/her frustration out in the public domain, demonstrating his own inadequacies or financial inability to provide.

I fully recognized that all kids acted that way to get away with toy, game, ride, gum, or anything they wanted, and parents had the right to say 'No' to their child. What touched my heart, however, was the loud cries of their child, uncalled slapping or beating or dragging with a publicly audible plea that they as 'parents' had no money or had no credit left on their card.

Any time I heard such words, I would look at the angry and frustrated parent, and was tempted to ask the parent if it was that child's fault that you had no money to satisfy the child's wants. We as parents have a choice to have a child, and once we have it, we are obligated to provide the child the best within our ability. One shouldn't have a child if one can't afford it because then one is knowingly depriving the child not only the proper nurturing, but also damaging child's future by not being able to provide a proper education, a pre-requisite for that child's career and earning potential. That child with almost no marketable skills was likely going to live in a persistent poverty and eventually become a ward of the entire society. In my opinion, it was no less than a criminal offence to knowingly raise a child in poverty, depriving him/her of basic essential care and opportunities beneficial to his/her advancement in life.

CHAPTER TWELVE

"Amy wants to move out with the kids," I casually mentioned to Jen while we were on our after-lunch stroll around our office complex.

"What? Why would she want that?" She was astounded.

"I am not spending much time or paying attention to her and the kids," I replied. "The fact of the matter is that I am too anxious to see my business rolling and that too, soon so that I can make some supplementary income."

"I really admire what you are doing," she remarked and turned her face towards me.

Our eyes met. I could see her endorsement and the sense of appreciation for my efforts. Her pretty face was partly covered by her furling open hairs due to the light afternoon breeze.

"Thanks," I replied. "I don't think she understands the depth or complexity of the task at hand. It requires a total dedication to start any business. She doesn't think I know much about running a business. Since she knows I write a lot at work, and enjoy writing, she would rather have me write a book of my own."

"I fully agree with her suggestion. She said elatedly. "You are a good analytic writer. You can write a book of your own. Mind you, that doesn't mean I disagree with what you are currently doing. You are a creative and hard working guy. As far as I know you, you are capable of doing anything under the sky."

"Thanks for your confidence and boosting my spirit." I replied with all humility. "I wish I could have the same support from her. But no; I have been belittled and discouraged at every opportunity. Despite all of her negativity towards me, I have been a good provider. I know that much."

"So what have you decided? Are you going to part ways?" she inquired.

"Are you kidding?" I quipped. "I will never do that. She may have found a new admirer to have a good time, but I have to think about the well-being of the children. With her meagre salary, she can't be a good provider and properly care for the kids."

"Don't forget you too have to pay for their support as well as she can claim alimony, besides the social assistance she will get as a single parent. So moneywise, she can perhaps manage," she added.

"Still she can't provide to children what I can." I said vehemently, ignoring her explanation. "And, I am not stupid that for years and years I will be paying her both the child support and alimony, and as a result, I myself will live from hand-to-mouth. Even if I am currently living that sort of life, it's not going to last for ever. My cash flow situation will improve once the mortgage is paid off, and children are no longer dependent. Until then, I have to be patient and keep my sanity even if my personal life with her is all in shambles."

"Our personal lives with our current partners are already in shambles. Don't you think?" she interrupted me. "There's nothing new here. You and I, we both have to be patient to get over the hill. I have a feeling that she's flaring up a bit because of her new found lover. We women are like that. We are always eager to have the company of a male who is ready to listen and adore us, give us a feeling of 'being wanted', even if that meant getting rid of the current man under any pretext. She is just using the century-old excuse that 'I want to leave because you don't pay me any attention'."

"I thought about it, too." I concurred with her concluding remark.

"You don't have to go too far to realize it," she began to explain. "Look at me. Besides our work requirements, I want to be much closer to you, and want and love you way more than Peter – the man I am living with. You know why? Because you are my emotional support; you care for me and above all, want me as a woman. You have injected a new life in me."

"Thanks for lifting up my spirit," I replied with a broad smile. "Speaking of Peter, what's new with him these days?" I inquisitively asked her.

"Well, he's flying high," she started to expound about him. "Did I tell you he got a job offer from Ottawa's newly formed hi-tech company? He's starting his new job in a couple of weeks. This job is in his field, and pays well, has a proper pension plan, and he is allowed to delve into the company's stock ownership plan."

"That's good to know. Congratulations." I looked at her face, and added, "Everything is okay now between the two of you?"

"Not really," she exhaled deeply. "Lately, something has happened that I am even ashamed to tell you."

"What?" I coaxed her.

"It's a long story. I will tell you tomorrow." She replied with a broad sly grin on her face. We had reached the entrance of our building.

While I sat on my chair and tried to focus on the computer printouts I had left open before lunch, I kept guessing what likely could have happened between Jen and her husband, Peter. I knew they were going through a rough patch. Their personal relationship was almost non-existent – like mine was with Amy. Had Peter found out about our affair? Had he assaulted Jen?

I kept guessing. I couldn't concentrate on my work the rest of the afternoon.

After greeting Jen the next morning, I told her, "You know, I couldn't sleep last night. I am still lost on what you said yesterday. Could we go for our after-lunch walk a bit early today? I am dying to know what exactly happened."

"Take it easy," she replied calmly, "nothing serious. We will talk about it."

She started to dial the phone as she had to speak with a reporter from the local newspaper. The person had left a message on her voicemail last evening. I stood close to her desk until she had begun talking.

I tried hard to focus on my work, but couldn't. My head was still swirling around the mystery she had left with me yesterday. My main concern was about her well-being. Had she been found having an affair with me? Was I involved, and if so, to what extent? Was Peter going to see me seeking more details about our affair, or about our trip to Toronto? I felt miserable as more and more scenarios about our affair played on my mental screen.

Finally, the clock struck the lunch hour.

We grabbed a quick lunch together, talking shop about her dealing with the reporter this morning and its follow up. Usually the follow up to such calls required preparation or compilation of statistics as per reporter's specific interest – something not officially published in the standard monthly/quarterly/annual publication.

After lunch, we stepped out of the building and turned towards the narrow walkway, meant only for pedestrians and cyclists, along the Ottawa River. Instead of walking around the office complex – our usual route – we headed to a quieter and serene walkway along the river's bank.

"So tell me in full details whatever happened," I requested her to unravel the mystery she had stored in her head.

"First promise me you won't laugh or get into any comic gesture," she pled softly.

"All depends on what it is," I replied with a smile. "I seriously didn't think it would be anything comical. I have been so worried since yesterday just thinking about how serious and complicated the issue likely was. Anyway, I promise, I won't laugh or even comment until you have spit it all out."

"Good." She smiled back at me. She began recounting. "As I told you yesterday, Peter got a new job, in his own field, with a new hi-tech company. He was happy, thrilled, and I can say, even excited on the day he received his letter of appointment. And you know when a man is that happy and excited, the first thing he wants is sex – as an outlet of such high emotions. So on that night in bed, he approached me to have sex – something I never expected because we hardly have any sex life. I have already told you about it. Anyway, when he clung to my back and spread his arm over my midriff, I couldn't say 'no' to him. Since I am still married to him and living with him, he had the full right to have sex with me. Against my wishes, I surrendered as a cold fish and turned over to face him. Since his approach to sex is not only clumsy, but also totally unsatisfactory, I knew this ordeal would be over in a few minutes. So why upset the guy? Let him have his quick ejaculation – so I thought. But not tonight; before entering me, he knelt on his knees between my half-spread legs. I thought he was going to lick my crotch to arouse me, make me wet enough to enter me, but no. He opened the folds of my pussy with his both hands, stretching each side with his thumb and four fingers. In the full light of the table lamp, he kept looking, and looking deep inside and around my pussy. He ran his eyes on the side lips, inside my pussy as far back as a bare eye could see, looked closely at my clit, my entire crotch. His silence and eyes running all over my genitals made me really nervous and I asked him in a more or less commanding voice, 'Are you checking if I had been to bed with someone else?' He stared at me, making me more nervous. He kept staring. He seemed lost in his thoughts. 'Not ... really,' he replied haltingly. 'I can't tell from simply looking at your pussy if you have been to bed with someone else. Unless I see any sore or any other visible mark on your genitals, it will only be the infection that I might get after fucking you that will possibly indicate that you have been to bed with someone other than me.' Now I was more nervous, knowing how you and I had been involved ever since we were in Toronto. I wasn't regretting over what I had done in Toronto. I just wanted to get out of this very embarrassing situation as early as possible. Imagine a fully naked wife lying with her naked and fully aroused husband kneeling between her legs and doubts shrouding him whether or not to enter his wife. I finally lost my patience. I desperately yelled at him, 'Are you going to enter me or keep staring at me? We can't spend the whole night like that. I am safe. You can enter me.' Even though I knew I was lying, I wanted to get out of this very awkward situation. Eventually, he relented and half-heartedly entered me. He laid on top of me in his one and only favourite missionary position, and as expected, he was all done in a couple of minutes. I quickly pushed him over the side and walked to the washroom. I was angry, mad, even felt ashamed for what had happened. Evidently, my husband had lost trust in me. He thinks I am having an affair. And to further add insult to an injury, he informed me the next evening that he was having some burning sensation while peeing, and he was finding something stuck in his urethra – all signs of a possible STD, or sexually transmitted disease including Chlamydia, herpes, or gonorrhoea. When he told me his symptoms, I really felt ashamed inside and considered myself responsible for all his discomforts. There was nothing I could do. I could only suggest he go see a doctor. And knowing the possible diagnosis, he was reluctant to consult a doctor. It's obvious that he, as a husband, didn't want to embarrass me any further. Personally, I really feel bad for him. You tell me, you also are a husband, would you talk to anyone, including your wife, if you ever got STD after having sex with your wife?"

"Not directly for sure," I replied, "but I would be cautious next time if at all I ever wanted to have sex with her. I think Peter acted wisely and didn't accuse you openly. Because accusing one's wife without any concrete evidence about her having an affair, especially sexual, is not that wise because it may further destroy an already strained relationship between the couple. Not only that, it will show that one no longer trusts one's wife – the trust that binds the partners to begin with. However, I am still puzzled. How did he even suspect that you are having an affair?"

"That's simple," she chuckled, "maybe it was me who gave away the secret by acting too nice to him, cooking often what he liked the most, buying gifts for him, and going out of my way to please him – not out of any love or affection for him, but out of the guilt I carry after getting sexually involved with you. He must have noticed my unusual behaviour and wondered about the reason behind it. Since he knew he wasn't the one who was behind all this change in me, he must have guessed that I was likely involved with another man. You don't need to be a rocket scientist to come to such a conclusion. It so happened that on the night he wanted to have sex, he decided to have a much closer look at my genitals, looking for any kind of physical evidence, and he ..."

"I still find it really disturbing to see you go through such an ordeal," I cut her off. "He couldn't find any physical clue this time, but how can we be assured that you won't go again through this sort of physical scrutiny. We are going to be together, perhaps 'til death do us part, and we are going to have sex, even rough and wild occasionally as per your wishes. How are you going to handle yourself?"

"There's only one way and that's to stop having sex with him, or make sure if he ever wants sex, it should be very short, and in a totally dark room. The other option is to simply tell him that I am having an affair," she suggested. "You know, like you, I am not going to walk away from him as I don't want to deprive my son of all that fatherly affection and care. I have to keep the family unit intact."

"Well, telling him about your affair is not a bad idea," I remarked. "Many couples talk frankly about their extra marital affairs. Such frank and honest talks can either strengthen or totally destroy the relationship between the two – depending on several factors, including the status of their current relationship, their social and economic conditions, presence of children, and their degree of co-dependence."

"Well, this may all be true in a theoretical world," she acknowledged ruefully, "but realistically, no couple talks frankly about their individual affairs and still share the same roof. Reading books about infidelity is one thing and being practical is another."

She had clammed up.

We were now walking silently on the walkway without any other soul in sight.

I clasped her fingers into mine. I wanted to hold her hand, assuring her my full support, trust, and confidence in her, her future actions and decisions.

She pressed my fingers firmly, offering her tacit affirmation.

We indeed wanted each other for our selfish reasons.

We had hardly walked a few steps that she pulled her hand away from my grip, and muttered,

"Remember we are supposed to act as professionals. No touching in the open public place."

"Sorry, it completely skipped my mind." I apologized. "I just wanted to touch and feel the warmth of your body. I wanted to assure you that I am and will always be with you."

"Same here," she replied with her face blushing. "We should get together soon."

"I will talk to my colleague and see if he can allow us to spend one afternoon at his cottage in Aylmer – just a few minutes drive from our office."

I could see how my suggestion had reddened her face and lit her eyes.

"Oh! That would be lovely," she blurted.

She couldn't hide her exhilaration.

***

The second hand Malibu station wagon that I had been driving was now falling apart. I could see each and every day how its engine oil leaked and seeped slowly and steadily underneath on the driveway, and really damaging it. Not only that, I could even smell the leakage of gas and its fumes while driving. I knew such smell and vapours of gas were unhealthy for anyone driving that van or sitting in it. Over time, the rust too had eaten away its rear and side panels. Driving that kind of vehicle was quite risky.

I could take that risk without worrying about its consequences, as my own life wasn't worth anything, but how about that of Amy and children? Their lives were precious and worth saving at any cost. They had their full life ahead of them.

Since I had no cash available and all credit cards were closer to their pre-set spending limits, I couldn't take the wagon for any repair. I was so afraid of the potential repair costs. I knew once I took it in, and the mechanic found several other faults with this old wagon, I would be facing a hefty bill which, in turn, would put me in a messier and financially tight situation. Damned if I got all the suggested repairs done and damned if I didn't. The former because of the amount I had to pay from the borrowed funds and the latter because I would now be knowingly driving a faulty vehicle. And in case of any accident, I might not even get any insurance protection.

I used to buy bottles of engine oil, and after every few days, would fill the oil tank. I knew the engine would catch fire if there wasn't enough oil. By doing this, I was damaging more the driveway – besides all the health risks involved in driving a car leaking gas fumes.

Even my neighbours began observing what I was doing. The spillage of oil on the driveway, leaving smelly vapours, was proving hazardous to their health. They would watch me washing the driveway with all kinds of soaps and detergents simply to protect them from inhaling oil smells. No matter how hard I scrubbed the driveway, no soap or detergent worked to clean the spill. But it had to be stopped. I had no option left. I had to take the wagon for repair, whether or not I had the money.

As I drove the car to the repair shop, I was very nervous. My heart was racing, almost touching my throat, mouth almost dry – all because of the fear about the anticipated high cost of repair. I had a hard time talking to the service manager, explaining to him the reason I had brought in the wagon.

Service managers and mechanics always look for such nervous customers who lacked not only the knowledge about cars, proper names of their functional parts, and what sort of precise repair required, but also lacked the ability to describe clearly and with confidence as to what was needed. Such customers were an easy prey and could easily be ripped off. Almost all car repair shops would financially reward managers and mechanics who were able to sell more auto parts, and sway customers to have high cost required as well as unwarranted repairs. A good majority of customers, once at the repair shop, were likely to accept service manager's or mechanic's recommendations, and pay for all the recommended repairs. For these people, in business to make money, it didn't matter how a customer would pay or how much further he/she would be financially burdened. For them, money simply grew on trees.

In the evening when I got out of the repair shop with my wagon 'all fixed' – using the mechanic's vocabulary – I had incurred debt of another few hundred dollars. I inhaled a breath of relief that the wagon was now safe to drive and above all, I wouldn't be seeing sore eyes of neighbours on account of the oil spill.

Alas! My relief didn't last for too long.

After a few months, the oil began to leak again. When I took the wagon back to the repair shop and complained to the service manager about the poor workmanship, he replied that this was bound to happen as the wagon's body was all rusty and old. No repair would ever be that lasting. He advised me 'not to spend any more money on repairs. Just get rid of it'. I wondered why on earth he didn't offer the same advice when I first brought in the wagon for repair. I really cursed the service manager for playing games with me. He made me borrow more unnecessarily.

This was the second time I had to buy a car on the advice of a mechanic. Since I had no money at hand, I had to weigh in the pros and cons of buying a new or used car. A family couldn't live without a car. It had to be purchased at the earliest because the wagon was falling apart. But it wasn't going to come free. I had to pay for it and that, in turn, meant seeking more borrowed funds.

I was already carrying too much debt on several credit cards, and barely juggling minimum payments on balances outstanding. Taking more debt meant more painful juggling of payments from the income left after mortgage, property tax, and other regular monthly bills.

For me, the amount of debt I could take and able to re-pay was the key consideration that, in turn, determined the kind of car I could buy. All calculations led to one conclusion: buy the cheapest, but some quality and durable model.

One thing was certain though; I wasn't going to commit the same mistake of buying a used car – as I had seriously erred on buying the used wagon which, in turn, required frequent repairs that my thin pockets could ill afford. The new car at least would have full warranty for the year, and another four years on its parts requiring major repairs. Put simply, any repair on the new car wouldn't cost me much at least for one year other than just pay for its periodic oil and filter change.

And to buy a new car, I had to make some initial down payment between two and three thousand dollars. I had no such money at hand other than the money I was about to receive in lieu of my unused annual vacation of a little over two weeks, and some tax refund. The amount remaining after the initial payment was to be taken as a loan, to be repaid in three years.

Amy and I visited one of our local dealers and looked around its car lot. Since prices were clearly marked, along with the additional cost of accessories, if desired by a customer, I paid attention to prices whereas Amy focused on fancy and expensive models. She was totally unaware of what my bottom line was – the price – and the loan I could take.

We got into an argument right at the lot. She wanted to buy an expensive and good quality car arguing that it would last longer. I, on the other hand, was in favour of buying a small affordable car with at least medium quality – if not high. I had to tell her how much I had to pay initially, how much I had, and how much I can pay monthly on the funds borrowed on the car. I told her clearly that we had no choice other than what I could financially afford. I was already in a very tight situation.

"Since when have you not been in a tight situation?" She yelled loudly, drawing attention of other people in the lot. "I am sick and tired of hearing the same crap. You know I have killed almost all of my desires, or what I want do, or how I want to furnish the home – just because you have no money. I really wonder when I see other people in our income group living in bigger houses, driving expensive cars. I don't know what it is that we are doing wrong. It's obvious that you are not handling money right. Since you financially manage the house, buy whatever you want or think is right. I don't care."

She was fuming.

"We are not going to achieve anything by getting mad at each other," I replied calmly to simmer her anger down. "Right now, we simply need a quality car that I can afford. I will get you the expensive model that you have liked in a couple of years. I promise."

"Who's going to finance the car – the financial institution that holds our mortgage or someone else?" She wondered aloud.

"The salesman told me that the company will finance the vehicle at the rate of interest compatible with one offered by the leading financial institutions. I can live with that."

"So which model are we going to buy?" she frowningly asked. Most of her anger had simmered down.

"We will buy a small car with good gas mileage. You can pick the colour you want from the information booklet you have in your hand."

"But kids can't go on holidays in this small car." She was still sulking.

"Don't worry. We can always rent a van; it's only few days a year." I shrugged my shoulders. "Right now, that's all we can afford."

She picked the light silver grey colour.

Once we had selected the car, we went inside the dealer's showroom where salespersons had their offices. We spoke to one about what we had decided to buy.

I let Amy test drive the car on the highway and the main inner street. She liked the car and looked somewhat relaxed.

Since neither of us had the ability to haggle about the price of the car, the salesperson carried all the duly-filled forms to his manager who, in turn, had given us some discount. I made the mandatory initial payment, and then Amy and I signed the loan agreement covering the remainder of the cost (including the cost of some additional accessories like rust proofing, staining of car seats, etc.).

I gave the void cheque in the required monthly amount to be drawn from my FI-II's chequing account. This account was linked to the line of credit that this institution had opened for me years ago. So there was no issue of any cheque bouncing back for reasons of 'not sufficient funds'. I simply had to advise my pay administration to deposit from my biweekly paycheque amount slightly more than the required for car payment to this account.

No matter how poor and volatile my financial situation was, I was very particular to avoid six things in order to protect my creditworthiness and my standing among my family members, peers, and society in general: first and foremost, never ever take debt beyond your affordability, or ability to pay it back; second, never ever miss a monthly payment even if it was just the minimum payment; third, never ever let any cheque bounce because of insufficient funds; fourth, never ever reach a point when some debt collector or agency had to bug me on the phone at home or the office, or knock my door; fifth, never ever think of declaring bankruptcy; and sixth, never ever borrow money from a private money lender.

I could float and buy time to improve my situation as long as I could make minimum payments to get the statements from creditors officially stamped before or by due dates. Even if it required a lot of really painful juggling, it was all worth it to keep away all of the creditors, or give them an opportunity to bug, chase, or disrepute me. I had to ensure that my credit rating was always in good standing.

The acquisition of the new car and its associated financial commitment had cornered me in an almost suffocating situation. Consequently, I was finding it hard to make even the minimum payments.

One month I didn't have enough to make a payment on the line of credit with FI-II. I hated to default on it as it would have tarnished my image or credit rating. Lenders never liked customers who defaulted on making payments and have always been reluctant to lend such customers any more money. In the extreme, lenders could always exercise their right and refuse these customers any access to their line of credit.

With all such haunting considerations, I nervously spoke (nervousness and low-self esteem are pervasive among the majority with no money and sinking indebtedness) to one of the cashiers at the counter, ensuring that others in that vicinity had not turned their ears to listen to my sad saga. I was deceiving myself. Nothing was that inaudible in an open space where tellers worked.

"Hi, I am Robert Vaughan," I introduced myself in a low voice to the cashier. "I have an account here."

I gave her my bank card.

"How can I help you, Mr. Vaughan?" she politely asked with a smile.

"Well, I am having a bit of a problem and looking for your suggestion," I replied.

I gazed at her face; my eyes seeking some helpful solution.

"What's the problem?" she inquired.

"I am short of funds and can't seem to make this month's payment on my line of credit," I told her. "I was just wondering if I can postpone making this payment until the next paycheque without any penalty – like the late fee of twenty-five dollars plus interest."

"You have any money left in your line of credit?" she asked.

"Yes; there are a couple of thousand dollars according to the last month's statement." I replied, in a more natural tone and with some confidence.

"Well, then you don't have a problem," she replied smilingly.

"What do you mean?" I asked sternly

"Well," she explained, "even though I am not supposed to tell you this, you can withdraw from your line of credit the amount of payment due, or more, and then deposit it back. This way, administratively, you would have made the payment even though you haven't paid it with your funds. The machine registers the payment to your account, and that means you haven't defaulted. The only difference you will see in the next month's statement is some increase in your interest charges. I am sure you can live with that, considering the long and winded procedure one faces after defaulting on payment. You want me to do the transaction for you, or you prefer doing it yourself on the machine outside?"

"Please, if you don't mind," I said with a sigh of relief. "I really appreciate your help."

I requested her to go ahead. I kept watching her. I was much relieved that the desired payment had been made. She had gone all the way to help me, even if it meant violating the normal procedure.

"There you are, Mr. Vaughan." She gave me a printed receipt of the transaction, adding, "You know you can always consolidate your loans. That way you just make one payment and save yourself all the trouble of making several payments on your cards or lines of credit. Would you like to do that? I can give you the loan application."

She pulled her top drawer out, tore one form from the pad, and handed it to me.

"Think about it. If you ever decide to apply for a loan, I will be more than happy to introduce you to one of our loan managers."

"Sounds good," I replied with a smile. "Thanks for your help."

With the blank loan application form in hand, I walked over to my office. The major distraction of the month was now over and I could focus on my work.

The cashier had, nonetheless, instilled in me the thought of applying for another consolidated loan. Not that I was against it to make my life easier and less tormented mentally, but at the bottom of my heart I knew this wasn't the right solution to my problem. Granted such a loan would help me save making several monthly minimum payments comprising largely of interest charges with no end in sight. By simply paying interest charges and not any principal borrowed, I was knowingly throwing hard-earned money in a gutter.

As mentioned earlier, this sort of consolidation is good for someone who no longer wants to use credit after paying all of the outstanding loans. One just pays up the amount over a span of three to five years and then can live debt-free happily ever after. But if one has to use credit again, out of sheer necessity, economic survival, or any other personal or behavioural reason, one is likely to cumulate several debts again, and by the time one consolidation loan is paid up, one is ready to take another. It really becomes a vicious cycle: wipe the slate when it's fully written, then write fresh until it's fully written, wipe it again, and so on.

My lifecycle stage and its associated needs and demands costing me more than I earned had totally trapped me in this vicious debt cycle.

In order to buy time and maintain my sanity and social dignity, I had no choice other than to seek, once again, a consolidated loan from FI-II.

One afternoon at work, the phone rang.

"Robert Vaughan." I replied in a professional tone as I was used to talking to users of debt data and reporters from the media and newspapers.

"Hello, Mr. Vaughan," the caller greeted me, sounding rather cheerful. "This is the loan manager from FI-II. I wanted to give you the good news. Your requested loan of thirty-three thousand-and-five hundred dollars has been approved. When can you come to my office to sign papers pertaining to this loan? Also, please bring in all the latest statements of loans, showing outstanding balances so that I could make all the payments on your behalf."

"What do you mean?" I jabbed at him. "You don't trust I will pay my bills?"

"No, no, that's not the case, sir," he replied. "I have full trust in you. I am sure you are eagerly looking forward to paying up all your unpaid balances. I am just following the institution's policy. I hope you understand."

I calmed down. I couldn't argue any more with the poor guy. After all, he was being paid to do his job within the rules and regulations set by the institution. I accepted his explanation and set up an appointment to meet him.

Now I had three main monthly loan payments: mortgage plus property tax, car loan, and the one I had just consolidated, besides paying all the regular bills, and business expenses. I was much relieved knowing that I was now discharging my debt, and would be free in three years time.

Unfortunately this sense of relief didn't last too long. I slid back in the vicious debt cycle as I had to use credit cards to meet some unexpected and unplanned expenses.

These contingencies included installing a new roof because the previous one had been damaged by the hail-storm, the dental treatment I needed that required placing an expensive bridge in my mouth, and then Sarah needed a long-term orthodontic treatment. None of these expenses could be deferred or ignored.

Even though some of these expenses were covered by different insurance plans, I still initially had to pay the full cost. And that meant using the credit cards, forcing me once again to juggle monthly minimum payments. The most ironic part was that any refund that came from insurance companies was spent on other needs at the time rather than pay back the borrowed amount. Put simply, I ended up paying the full costs of services which were even mostly covered by insurances. After few years of necessary and life-supporting spending like that, I was back hanging thin and dry, looking for some institutional help to financially resuscitate me.

***

What I had experienced after each consolidated loan was nothing unusual because of my lifecycle stage and its associated essential and unavoidable expenses. To me, this business of taking consolidated loan became tantamount to replenishing my financial reserves to pay for all big, small, and regular expenses for the next three to five years. Since I paid every cent of the loan I ever took, I considered using consolidated loan as a means of spending my future income.

In other words, I had resorted to using my future income to satisfy my current needs. It was just like taking of thousands of dollars of my unearned income in advance and financing my day-to-day expenses. If I had lost the job for any reason, then I know I wouldn't have survived that long. At times I really wondered if this stable job providing me a steady flow of income kept my life at a bubble.

I undoubtedly needed this periodic reserve to faithfully provide whatever my kids and Amy, even if she were having an affair, asked for under the sky as well as for maintaining our house, lifestyle compatible with our income status, and that of our friends. In fact, their wishes were my command. I didn't want anyone to kill any of their material desire – no matter the cost or expense. As a provider, it was my duty to care for their well-being and needs. It certainly wasn't their problem that I didn't have enough cash flow. For them I earned well enough, being a part of the top twenty percent of all earners on the national income ladder, to take care of their needs, including their annual mini holidays at nicer and expensive tourist spots.

I didn't even think twice when I gave the kids a car to drive to their high school after they were refused to use the school bus because we lived within two kilometres of the school. The School Board wanted to save transportation cost by letting all children living within a distance of two kilometres from the school to walk to school. Rather than argue or fight this totally senseless policy with the School Board, I chose to let my daughters drive independently. That was the only way to protect them from walking in the snow, sleet, and freezing temperatures.

Now that the small car was used by the kids, Amy wanted a car of her own to drive to work. She didn't want to commute by a public transport. This time we bought not only a bigger and better quality car, but also the one that Amy personally liked. I made the required initial payment and the rest on loan paid in monthly instalments.

We were now a two-car family – fitting the national norm of the early nineties for families with both spouses earning. So by buying another car, I hadn't done anything exceptional or out of the way. Since Amy had been promoted on her job and earning more, she agreed to pay the monthly loan payment on the car for the next thirty-six months. Nonetheless, I was responsible for its day-to-day maintenance including repairs and insurance, which in turn, further tightened my monthly obligatory payments.

***

One Saturday afternoon, I drove Amy to a furniture shop in order to buy a small wall cabinet for our kitchen. She was happy with her purchase, as women usually are after buying something they liked.

Since she was in a lighter mood, she innocently or intentionally directed a question to me,

"Can one have a platonic relationship?" She intently looked at me, seeking my affirmation or any other reaction.

Her question shook me. I felt stumped for a moment. I was fully aware, as she also had told me herself, that she was seeing a man at work.

While my eyes were still focused on the road, I asked her, "Why are you asking? What's on your mind?"

"Oh! Nothing in particular," she turned her neck and looked upfront. She straightened her back, started to fidget with her handbag, as if she was searching for some lost article. "I think I told you sometime ago that I like my manager at work, and he equally likes me," she added. "We eat lunch together, go for afternoon walks. Let me say, as colleagues, we interact much more often during the day than most others. Even other people have started to notice it. I am just wondering if we can have a platonic relationship."

"What I know from all that I have read," I began to answer her question, "no two perfectly healthy adults of opposite sex can have a platonic relationship. Once they develop a liking for one another, or are mutually attracted to each other, they are bound to engage in an intimate physical relationship. It's all a matter of time unless some external forces stop them ..."

"Such as ..." she impatiently interrupted me.

She wanted a short and precise answer to her question, likely haunting her for a while.

"Say, if neither wants to lose his or her well paid secure job if caught, or dissolve their family unit, or have some common relative or friend they think will break news about their relationship, or fear of catching any sexual disease, barriers imposed by their culture and religion, and on and on. The list is endless."

I kept elaborating, with stealth looks at her face, monitoring her reaction.

"All these factors that you have cited so far can still allow people to have a platonic relationship. I don't see why not. The relationship doesn't have to be sexual."

She was still looking for my affirmation.

"That's what you think," I said tauntingly. "The law of attraction between opposite sexes dictate that the two will most likely have an affair with just love for one-another and no sex, or engage in sex without any love or affection. The other extremes involve no love, no sex, and both love and sex. These days when more and more women are working outside the home and interacting with their male counterparts or colleagues, they are spending more time with them than say, with their partner at home. Since we are living in a sensitive environment that emphasizes gender equality, and have all kinds of laws against sexual harassment and discrimination as well as laws protecting women against any misconduct, touching, assaulting, etc., most men and women are likely to work together and treat each other with respect as peers or colleagues. Any meeting or get-together of sexes in this group falls under the label 'no love, no sex' affair – comprising normal work-related interactions. On the other hand, there are those who fall in love with each other for any reason including one's attractive looks, too much of personal and intimate interaction, social smartness, ability to gab or chit-chats, compatibility of personalities, willingness to listen and share one another's personal or domestic problems, or even aspirations – anything that will bring together the two opposite sexes. It's the people in this particular group who, over time, may or may not eventually engage in sex – that's what I meant by love but no sex, or sex but no love, or love with sex. Your concept of platonic love applies to this group. And, according to many known psychologists, the majority of both men and women in this group can't maintain platonic relationship. It's just a matter of time when a man or a woman involved can lose him/herself, let down their guard, and express their real and simmering, suppressed thoughts and intentions about each other, and knowingly or unknowingly, drop into each others arms or embrace. Once engaged in sex, then these persons have to decide whether to continue the affair out of love, sex, or both, and whether to keep it under covers or bring it out in the open. That in essence is how affairs take place, and likely culminate into sexual engagement. An affair can stay platonic if one or both are unhealthy, feel no attraction for each other, and simply share and listen to one another's beefing about work or personal problems at home or with one's current partner."

"I am not disputing anything of what you just said," she said with her eyes still focused on the road, "I still think one can have a platonic relationship."

Evidently, I had failed to change her opinion. I didn't think she paid any attention to what I had said. She seemed to have made up her mind. I decided to change the track.

"As you know, the platonic affair simply means having a relationship without sex. Imagine if this relationship turns into an emotional affair where a man or a woman or both are emotionally thinking constantly about each other's well-being, work, personal and financial problems, and completely neglecting their own partner and children at home, or other domestic issues. In this case, the emotional affair damages persons and their families much more than the platonic affair because the heart and soul of those involved are simply focused on each other. I don't know why you keep insisting that one can have a platonic affair; just think about the kind and emotional intensity of this sort of affair. As I said, if a platonic affair turns deeply emotional, it can play havoc and can ruin not only those directly involved, but their families too, including children, unless they end up marrying each other and form a blended family. Even then, it all becomes a messy affair as it may require dissolution of a family, property split, payment of child support, alimony, etc. I firmly believe there's no such thing as platonic between two healthy adults of opposite sexes. Personally speaking, I would rather have someone engage in sexual affair rather than emotional platonic because in the case of the former, one is through with all the built-in infatuation or plain lust. If the first sexual engagement doesn't work out well, that would mean the end of desire for the sought after person. And if the sexual engagement turns out to be mutually satisfying, making partners to have more and more of it over time, then it's a different ball game. In this situation, the issue of platonic relationship doesn't arise; the sexual relationship can go on clandestinely, or in the open, eventually making partners to marry or live common-law. No matter how you look at it, there's no platonic relationship between young and healthy man and a woman."

I again turned to look at her half-face to notice any reaction.

There was none whatsoever.

However, she was now more pensive. I could understand what she was going through – thinking about her and her budding affair with her colleague.

"How well do you know the guy who likes you, and for how long have you two been enjoying each other's company?" I asked her out of sheer curiosity.

I didn't hesitate to ask her this question because she had already told me how much fun she was having in his company.

"I have told you whatever I know about him," she scoffed at me, "I have nothing to add."

She shook her head – in total disbelief, or she had enough of my long winding talk on platonic relationship.

"Well, I just want you to be careful as you hardly know the real personality of the guy. Right now you only know his position, his income, and investments, besides he's good looking, handsome, lends his ear to you, and enjoys your company. You don't know much about his real personality traits including his habits, lifestyle, how he generally behaves or treats his family members, or how he handles domestic contingencies. I don't want to see you get hurt, or end up with a person worse than me. I know I haven't been a good husband, lover, or a provider."

"I am glad you recognized your shortcomings." She turned her neck to graze my face. "I like the guy," she added, "he seems to love me, want me, above all, pays attention to me. He's not cold like you."

"Glad to hear that," I uttered softly. "I am doing the best I can under the circumstances."

CHAPTER THIRTEEN

One late afternoon, Amy called me at work. She had come home early to drive the children to their soccer game.

"Guess what?" She sounded excited.

"What?" I replied in my usual cold tone.

"You got orders from two libraries in Ontario, each wanting to buy one audio-book and one video. Isn't that great? Your efforts are finally paying off." She sounded very cheerful.

"Good to hear," I responded. She had perked me up. "My efforts are finally working. I knew one day they would. I had that much confidence in me. God has been kind," I told her softly.

My heart had begun to thump. The clusters of black spots had shrouded my vision. I was overjoyed. My mail-order business was finally on the way. I was indeed going to have a source supplementing my income.

"I'm really happy for you." She sounded warm and sincere. "I will leave the envelopes at your study desk as I am taking the kids out to their game. Just for your information, I picked these up from the mail box on my way home."

She had placed the phone in its cradle.

I was so excited that I rushed to Jen's office and shouted from the threshold of her door, "Guess what? I got two orders from libraries in Ontario. That means my mail-order business has finally started to roll. Isn't that great news?"

I stood in front of her, resting my palms on the edge of her long table. I was looking fiercely into her eyes.

"Congratulations." She replied with a wide smile on her face. "I knew you would make it. Job well done! We will celebrate it tomorrow at lunch."

"Well, thanks for the confidence and your support." I replied softly as my momentary excitement had levelled off. "We will indeed celebrate it tomorrow. Don't let me disturb you any more."

I got back to my office and glanced over all of the computer printouts spread open on my table. I couldn't concentrate on anything.

I kept thinking how I had started this business, with almost no investment except my devotion, hard work, and persistence in order to simply find an additional source of income. I was sitting on my chair and looking outside the window at the clear blue sky. The past business related events were rolling over my mental screen. I found myself researching at Ottawa's public library, or carrying a box of professionally printed copies of my first catalogue in the public bus. Then my attention turned to the named libraries that had sent orders. I wanted to look at these at the earliest opportunity.

After all of my excitement had trickled down, I got back into my analytic mode. I realized that two orders from more than one hundred libraries that I had sent my catalogue to really meant a success rate of less than two percent. As an analyst, I wanted to measure my own success in quantitative terms which, in turn, can be monitored well over time. This success rate of under two percent was too little or almost negligible. It wasn't enough to cover even the operating costs, let alone any profit or net income that I was desperately looking for. This realization had flattened all of my enthusiasm. *Be realistic*, I said to myself. I had to have a much better success rate if I ever wanted to improve my straitened financial situation.

I was fully aware that almost all libraries across the nation were served by well established publishers and distributors as part of their wide and strong network. These companies and distributors would send out automatically any new release of theirs to all public and private libraries, universities, and other research institutions. I was competing with these commercial giants – and that too with no money.

So realistically speaking, my success rate had to be low because libraries would buy from me only those titles that these publishers or distributors couldn't deliver. Since my catalogue was well researched, and included items available from multiple sources, I realized that it was only my research activity that would eventually save the day for me. Since the undertaking of research didn't cost any money, but simply the time, devotion, persistence, and perseverance – characteristics I was well endowed with – I decided to depend more and more on research efforts rather than money in order to successfully compete and establish my standing in the market.

Within two weeks, I was able to procure and ship out the goods ordered by these two libraries. As expected, I didn't make any net money out of this transaction even though libraries paid all of the shipping and handling charges. This was a norm in the mail-order industry – a customer paid all the freight and delivery charges, besides the cost of goods delivered.

Since I was fully operating on borrowed funds, I decided to use these funds rather sparingly. I could have used these funds liberally in order to compete with giant competitors, but that would have been akin to self immolation. My clients were limited and so was my potential for sales. I had to cut down my expenses.

One way to do that was to save on designing and printing the next catalogue. There was no need to get it professionally done by a publishing press. I realized that the design, format, presentation including proper ordering of contents of goods offered really mattered as these left on potential buyers the first impression about the seller's image, commercial standing, and potential. If a good presentation was meant to facilitate sales on one hand, it was too expensive and beyond my means to produce, on the other. I couldn't spend money I didn't have.

I had to manage with what I had. I had to stay within my means, including borrowings.

I produced the second catalogue on a computer borrowed from the office over one weekend. Since I knew well Microsoft's excel and word softwares, I formatted the whole thing, with the company's logo on the front, on a legal page, and then turned it into a four-fold pamphlet. This time I included items available on audiocassettes and videos on meditation, yoga, spirituality, and religion.

This catalogue had a success rate of five percent – still too low to generate any net income. The only consolation was that it didn't cost me an arm and a leg. I couldn't really figure out if the slightly higher success rate was due to the popularity of contents offered, or the company was finding a niche in the market. Either way, I still hadn't hit my bottom line.

Another thing I learnt from the low success rate of the second catalogue was to reduce the number of mailings, i.e., focus on specific buyers rather than a broad cross-section of them. That way I would have my own genuine clientele and focus attention on them and their needs, and orders. That also would cut down the number of potential suppliers of goods, which in turn, would mean more constructive use of my research time, with a more narrowed focus on choosing relevant contents for a given catalogue.

So starting with the third catalogue, listing audiocassettes and videos on sports and games of all seasons, I opted to sell only to public libraries. This change moved the success rate to ten percent – still not enough to generate any substantial net income.

As a novice running the business, I was learning at every step about preparing more focused catalogues, their marketing, and public relations. I had no control on pricing my products as suppliers had imprinted sale prices on the back covers. I couldn't change those to increase my profit margin. The only way I could do the latter was if suppliers had agreed to offer me a larger discount, say from fifty to seventy percent.

Another way to earn more net income was to increase the volume of sales, and that meant, improving marketing, advertising, and access to more libraries.

Since Amy had agreed to tend to public relations, she had had chances to speak to local reporters. One such reporter had read about our company selling skill development products and wanted to inform the community. This reporter even did a small write-up on the company. I was somewhat contented that the company finally got some public exposure. Slowly and steadily my efforts were being recognized.

I still wasn't making any money to supplement my income. I was working hard, too hard at times, but of no avail. Rather than making money, I was spending more and more of borrowed money on preparing, zeroxing, and mailing of catalogues. I was depleting my borrowed funds more rapidly, firmly hoping the tide would turn my way one day.

Besides using borrowed funds to pay my monthly household commitments, I was now using these to finance business expenses as well.

***

"How is the business running?" Jen asked me one afternoon while we were on our regular after-lunch walk around the office complex.

She looked gaunt. She kept staring at her free hand or distant buildings within her sight.

"Not that earth shaking," I replied. "I am still learning the ropes of running a business. You know, we as analysts can analyze all the numbers and make a good story out of it. To run a business, on the other hand, is a totally different ballgame."

"What do you mean?" She questioned me in a rather soft and depressive voice.

"I mean, I'm a novice who still has to learn a lot about running a business. I have no problem compiling and delivering catalogues, but selling my chosen products is the biggest challenge," I explained.

"You told me you were doing better; one/tenth of all libraries who received your last catalogue sent in orders," she commented, somewhat perplexed.

"These are good for nothing. I can't make any money from such token orders. I need to catch a big fish to make any meaningful returns to my labour," I lamented.

"At least you are putting in the effort to make money to supplement your current income. Look at me. I am likely going to lose soon a good chunk of our family income," she whispered wearily.

"What? What do you mean?" I was astounded.

"Peter has been given a three-month notice that the section he is working in will be closed as the company is outsourcing some of the telecommunication jobs including his." She finally spouted what was getting under her skin.

"Sorry to hear that." I paused and looked at her. "Now I know why you are looking so haggard, sounding depressed. Even your eyes look blank. Did he know at all about this upcoming closure of his section or the likelihood of him losing the job?"

"Even if he did mention it casually," she stammered, "I likely didn't pay much attention because of our lack of communication."

"I thought things were back to normal between you two after he got a job in his own field." I recalled intentionally.

I just wanted to alleviate her tension.

"Having sex occasionally doesn't mean the relationship is back to normal," she replied softly. "Now that he has told me in no uncertain terms that he will be declared redundant after three months, it's really bothering me. I have no idea about the sort of job he will find, where, and for how long as you know how fast the technology is changing and whether his current skills are still good enough to find a job in his field or what he likes."

"I fully share your concern," I said empathetically. "You are right. The technology is changing fast. Not only that, a good number of hi-tech employers have started outsourcing jobs not only to save their wage bill, but also to improve their profit margins. Since wages and salaries as well as production and operating costs constitute the lion's share of business expenditure, owners are taking full advantage of both technological advances and economic globalization. The world is getting smaller every day. Do you know where these jobs are being outsourced?"

"Should it matter to me?" She sneered at me. "These can go anywhere as far as I am concerned. What I know is how their outsourcing is going to affect our family income, standard of living, our cash flow situation, lifestyle, our son's education and future, and our retirement years, besides a lot of other things."

She lamented. I could see her eyes were moistened, as she ran her right index finger on the edge of her right eye.

"I understand how you feel, but isn't this a reality of times?" I gently tapped the top of her shoulder closer to me. "We are outsourcing most of our manufacturing and hi-tech telecommunication jobs with mid level salaries, which in turn, is going to shrink the number of our middle income families. By outsourcing, we are really shifting some of our investments and the spending powers of our families to those in developing countries like India, Hong Kong, China, Taiwan, Philippines, and South Korea, besides several others. As they say, one's loss is another's gain. The majority of producers and manufacturers in the developed and rich countries are doing it not because of any altruistic intention to help these developing countries improve their living standards by providing their populations more decent paying jobs and investment opportunities, but to reduce their own production costs, taxes, and eventually increase profit margins. The rapidly changing technology, improving the means of communication and transportation, is further fuelling this change in the labour markets of both developed and developing counties."

"Yah, but these developed countries are hurting a good number of their own people by making them unemployed, causing them all the mental stress and hardship. We end up caring for such people by spending more on unemployment benefits, social assistance, and health care. What good is that?" she asked frustratingly.

"Well! When you come to think of it rationally," I continued, "there are some benefits that we in developed countries reap out of this outsourcing. Just imagine how families in developed countries including ours are thriving on low cost merchandise and goods imported from low-wage countries. As consumers, we now pay much lower prices than we used to on many goods including cars, household furnishings and appliances, clothing, shoes, garden tools, computers, and electronics – you name it. All such imported goods made in low-wage countries have a much hefty profit margin for our business community. You must have come across a situation where a particular good is sold one day, for example, for one hundred dollars, and few weeks or months later, the same good is put on sale for fifty dollars. Even this fifty dollar price has much higher profit margin for the vendor. So it's not only the owners of businesses or vendors who are adjusting to this new reality of outsourcing and importation of cheaper goods, we as consumers equally are adjusting to this new reality. Of course, this affects our job market, likely resulting in more unemployment. But over time, you will see the job market will adjust to this reality as it absorbs more and more people in a diversity of expanding service jobs."

"You just said the right word – adjust – that I am finding it difficult to accept or live with it," she complained. "You can't understand how nervous I am simply by thinking about the possible loss in our family income. I may not have a good personal relationship with Peter, but he still is making a substantial contribution to family income."

"That's where, I think, you are misjudging me," I commented to appease her. "Who else, if not me, can better understand the pain and tribulations of living with a tight financial situation? I have been living with it for years."

"That's what I am dreading the most," she beckoned. "I don't ever wish to be in your shoes some day. I don't have the patience or stamina to live it."

"Well! We all have to face what comes our way," I concluded. "There are times when one has no choice, but to accept fait-accompli. Let me know if I can be of any help to you or Peter. I am sure he will get a job in some kind of services, if not in his own field."

"I don't think anyone of us can help him. He has to fight his own battle. That's the hard truth," she confessed softly.

***

With my financial situation deteriorating on account of additional business expenditure – costing me way more to run it than the revenue it was generating – I was once again scratching the bottom of my borrowed reserves. My chequing account with FI-IV was now running in deficit. I had been a steady customer of FI-IV for close to ten years. By depositing my biweekly paycheque of reasonably respected amount, I had proven to be a reliable client of that financial institution. But did the institution care or show any respect or understanding for clients like me with an account running in deficit?

One day I got a cheque in the small amount of fifteen dollars and went to cash it at FI-IV. I needed cash to buy some postal stamps for shipping out a couple of catalogues. I gave the cheque to the cashier. She opened my account, gave me a dirty look, and told me to wait as she needed to clarify something with her manager.

"Could you please wait on the side while I serve the other customers?" she ordered me on her return to her seat.

I kept guessing the reason why I had been made to wait on the side. I had a legitimate cheque issued by one of the largest insurance companies in Canada that had refunded some money that I had spent on one of my recent prescriptions. It certainly wasn't a bogus cheque. And I wasn't playing any fraud. Why on earth the teller had not cashed the cheque?

After a fifteen-minute wait, I finally saw the manager walking over to this teller's counter. She announced her decision at the pitch of her voice, intentionally or inadvertently, letting everyone in the room hear, "I am sorry, Mr. Vaughan, we can't cash this cheque."

"Why?" I asked softly, as I gave her an indignant look. "It's a genuine cheque issued by an insurance company."

"No, there is nothing wrong with the cheque," she yelled back as she didn't like me questioning her decision. "It's because your chequing account is currently showing a deficit. This amount will write-off a bit of what you currently owe to us. I am sorry."

"I didn't know the institution had this sort of policy." I pleaded my case. "It has never happened to me before."

"Likely because some managers don't strictly implement this rule when the amount is small, or the client's creditworthiness is in good standing," she explained.

"I believe I am in good standing with this institution. Can't you too be a bit flexible?" I argued, still in a low tone so that others couldn't hear me. "I have been a good steady client of this institution for years. My main mortgage is with this institution. You are really disappointing me or should I say, insulting me by not cashing this small amount."

"Sorry, I am just following the rules." She strongly defended her decision. "To avoid facing this sort of situation again, I suggest you see one of our loan managers and apply for a loan to fix up your chequing account. Would you like to do that?"

Do beggars have a choice? I was in an awkward and most embarrassing situation. I accepted her suggestion before leaving the institution.

I had been publicly humiliated, degraded, and felt kicked in the shin. I cursed and loathed myself. But this self-loathing and pity was not going to resolve anything. I had to face the reality and that too, by keeping my head high.

A few days after this incident, I met the loan manager. It was the same woman who had approved my second consolidated loan of sixteen thousand and five hundred dollars just a few years ago.

"Nice meeting you again, Mr. Vaughan." She greeted me with a bit of sarcasm. "How can I help you today?"

"I want a loan to pay-off my current debts." I spoke as the gun fires a bullet.

"How much do you want?" She pondered.

"Depends on how much you can offer me," I replied. "You know the location, size, and type of the house I own. Since it has well appreciated in value over time, increasing my share of equity, you can easily figure out the proportion of equity that I can borrow."

"Before I do that, may I ask you a personal question?" She hesitated.

She kept looking at my account, and had started to scribble some numbers.

"I gather from the record associated with your property," she paused and kept looking at me, "this is the fourth time you are asking for a consolidated loan against your home equity. The third you borrowed from FI-II was paid out just a few years ago. Why do you seek consolidated loans that frequently? You don't budget well or are experiencing big business losses, or you have some expensive bad habits? I am just wondering."

"To be honest with you," I came straight to her, "I don't like, or should I say, I hate to take such a loan, but trust me, it's purely out of necessity. Such loans give me financial reserves, offering me a false sense of security, and also enabling me to look after the needs of kids, family, and day-to-day life. I don't spend this money to satisfy any of the vices like womanizing, consumption of drugs, alcohol, marijuana, or gambling. Besides the regular spending on day-to-day needs and unexpected expenses, I now have business expenses to take care of. I am running a home-based mail-order business selling skill development products including books, audios, videos, and CD-ROMS. I am determined to see this business running successfully one day."

"Gosh! You have a full-time job and now you are running a business on the side. I am impressed." She was consternated. She paused, and warned me, "You know running a business is a very risky venture. Most of the new businesses are closed within one or two years because the owner either lacks the right know-how about running it or have insufficient funds to operate it. I see such cases day in and day out. My advice to you will be to use caution and spend money on it very carefully. Even though I wish you all the success in your business, but what I have seen, I doubt if you will be able to sustain it."

"Well, I am determined to run it successfully," I re-emphasized. "You may even see me as a millionaire one day. We will see."

Even though I internally agreed with her overall assessment, but I had to defend my pursuit with all the confidence.

"Don't worry; I am not thinking of repaying this loan from my business revenue. My earnings are good enough to repay this loan. You know me. I firmly believe in paying back every cent that I borrow," I reassured her.

"I know you," she nodded, "that's why I ask you right away how much do you want instead of assessing your ability to pay back. You have been what we call, 'a good non-risk client'. The institution has full trust in you. Despite all your financial problems, you haven't as yet defaulted on your mortgage or property taxes."

She had pumped me enough, perhaps intentionally, as she had found a steady source of revenue for her institution.

"Because I take my commitment and responsibility very seriously and discharge these to the best of my ability," I replied with a new dose of self-confidence. I really sounded like an egotist. "So how much do you think I can borrow? Have you figured out?" I asked.

"You can have fifty-two thousand dollars." She replied calmly and looked at me, trying to read my face.

"That's all right with me." I replied with a sense of great relief.

Like the previous occasions when I had the consolidated loan approved, I muttered to myself that I was good to live for another few years.

"That's repayable over five years?" I wanted to reconfirm.

"Yes, indeed," she confirmed with a broad grin. "Here's the formal loan application. Have it signed by your wife as the house is co-owned. And by the way, bring also all the statements showing the latest balances to be paid. I will look after all the repayments. It's something we have to do under the law."

After dinner that night, I placed the form in front of Amy and requested her to sign it as a co-signer.

"Not again." She busted out of anger. "I am tired of signing such forms. It's the fourth time you are asking me to sign it. Am I going to spend my life signing these loan applications?"

I could understand her frustration. I wished she too could understand my situation.

"Well, that's the best I can do under the circumstances," I stated calmly. "Since my net income is still far less than our expenditure, we have no choice other than to use borrowed funds. I hate much more to ask you to co-sign the loan application than you do signing it. I don't feel happy or comfortable asking you to do it, but because you co-own this house, I have no choice. I have to have you sign the loan application – whether you like it or not."

"Why don't you let me run the house?" She demanded. "You just give me your biweekly paycheque. There's no shame if I financially ran the house. Maybe you don't know how to run it. You haven't been good at managing money ever since we have been living together. You really put me to shame, especially when I see those earning the same as you are way better off than us, also leading much happier lives. And what have we to show – nothing?"

She had begun to play her usual tune to belittle and insult me.

"Well, I am quite used to hearing your insinuating and belittling comments," I responded, still keeping my sanity, "but these aren't going to resolve our financial inadequacy. As the key provider, I am doing the best within my current means, even if that means living partly on borrowed funds. Even if I gave you my paycheques, the monthly commitments on mortgage, property taxes, insurance, regular bills, credit cards, and loans – you name it – are almost fixed and have to be paid. It really doesn't matter who pays these. The amount of money is the same. I don't think with twenty to thirty percent of my remaining net income you can run this house. I don't want you to have any financial stress because that, in turn, would adversely affect upbringing of our daughters. As long as I am around, you don't have to worry about anything; you are already taking care of the family's groceries and the kids' activities, and that's good enough for me. The rest, I can take care."

"How much are we borrowing this time?" She asked somewhat bewildered.

"Fifty-two thousand dollars, repayable over five years," I replied. "It's all written in black and white on the form."

"Sorry, I didn't see it. I just signed wherever the x mark was." She handed me the signed form.

The painful turbulence had passed its course.

"As I told you last time," I started to repeat my rationale on taking a loan, "we are trapped in a vicious debt cycle. Hopefully, one day we will get out of it when our expenses are down, mortgage is paid up, kids' education is done, and they are settled on their own. In the meantime, just consider this consolidation loan as part of our future income that we are using it right now. Look at it another way: we have to pay for our needs by current income or savings. Since our current income is not sufficient to sustain our lifestyle, we have no savings either to fall on. But when we are paying back our loan, that's as good as forced savings – the only difference is that these forced savings cost us some additional cost in the form of interest paid on debt which is contrary to the use of conventional savings which also generate some additional income in the form of interest earned. Look at the last loan. We paid thirty-two thousand dollars, of course with some interest. Do you think we could have voluntarily saved that much money over five years – considering our current income and expenditure situation? I doubt it. So consider that as a forced saving, ignoring the cost of interest. Same way, we are now going to be forced-save fifty-two thousand dollars plus interest cost over five years. So basically it's our money: either we first save and then spend it, or first spend it and then forced-save. We are simply trapped in the latter cycle. The only other option to forced saving is to declare bankruptcy, and that you know, I will never ever do it."

"That's one way to rationalize our indebtedness and how our life is debt-dependent," she droned.

"I have to rationalize it and get to its cause and effect aspects," I replied and grazed her face. "I know what I am doing and how much loan I am taking. I will never take a loan if I thought I couldn't pay back. Be honest. Tell me if anyone from the debt collecting agency has ever called you, or visited our home because of any unpaid bill or delayed payment? What does it tell you? That I pay my debts on time and keep the family's image, status, and integrity in tact. We will indeed tarnish ourselves in the eyes of our friends, or neighbours, or society in general if we ever failed to discharge our commitments and declared personal bankruptcy. I agree with you that we have been living on borrowed funds and that's strictly because our income is insufficient to finance our needs. Using debt isn't a sin, as long as it's paid back according to agreed upon terms. We as a family unit use debt; look at small and large businesses that are run on borrowed money, or even look at government's finances, these also are running on debts worth billions and billions of dollars."

"Okay, okay, I got the message." She stopped me from further rationalizing myself. "I can't argue with you." Although she had conceded to my rationale, she added, "I still hate to think that we are living on credit. I find it totally repugnant, derogatory."

"Bear with me. It's all transitory." I remarked, and left her alone.

***

With this loan, I now had to make two large monthly payments: mortgage plus property tax, and this loan. I still had to pay from the small left over net income all of the remaining bills, day-to-day needs of the family, and upkeep of the house. And that meant resorting back to use of credit.

This time though FI-IV had also opened for me a home equity line of credit (HELOC) at a much lower interest rate as well as provided me an over-draft protection of fifteen hundred dollars on my chequing account with a condition that the account must show a positive amount for a few days at least once in six months. The institution charged a monthly fee for this overdraft protection, and prevailing rate of interest on the excessive amount used. The institution likely realized that I was going to need it because of quite hefty monthly payments on both mortgage and this loan, or it could earn more interest income from me, or it did simply out of good will. Whatever the reason, most of my monthly income was now committed on these two loans. I was now more or less working for this institution.

Also, I now had two lines of credit available to me: each with a limit of ten thousand dollars. With this new borrowing accessible from these lines of credit, and that too at a relatively low interest rate, I had stopped using credit cards issued by department stores. Another reason I did it was because such stores had now started accepting VISA and MasterCard to sell their merchandise. The rising dominance of these credit cards in the nineties had given consumers more diversified choices of locations to purchase goods and services, and as a result, markets selling consumer goods and services became very competitive. For many, their survival was at stake.

The financial institutions were also competing with one another to attract more and more clients for VISA and MasterCard. The chief marketing tool was the built-in incentives that these cards offered in different shapes and sizes. These incentives included 'Pay no interest for the first three or six months', or 'transfer balance outstanding from other high interest loans', or 'pay for travel and have free insurance against trip cancellation, or missing baggage', etc., etc. This marketing pitch also touched me and I gained another MasterCard.

The good thing after the fourth loan consolidation in the nineties was that once both cards from American Express were fully paid, the company didn't renew my cards. Similarly, the VISA card, sponsored by an auto company, was cancelled after its balance was paid out. With these cancellations in addition to now unused credit cards issued by gas companies and department stores, I was now using VISAs, both in Canadian and US dollars, a couple of MasterCards, and lines of credit to finance my needs.

Most credit card issuing financial institutions during this competition would increase credit limits on their respective cards without even soliciting a card holder's consent. These companies wouldn't give a damn how such unsolicited increases could sink further some card holders into a much deeper debt hole. Institutions were simply competing to sell more money to make more money and secure a larger share of the debt market.

Such unsolicited increases were advantageous to some and disadvantageous to others. These helped those who paid full balances on receipt of a statement to use more free credit for convenience over the grace period. For those who carried over monthly balances, these increases further tightened the noose around their necks, suffocating and squeezing them to pay more and more of interest income – a major component of revenue of an institution. Since the majority in the latter group was more likely to use these increased amounts out of sheer necessity, these unsolicited increases were largely meant as a trap to catch more of those already trapped in financial difficulties.

After the latest consolidation, I became more conscious about spending, especially on my own needs. I had no control on either the regular monthly commitments, or any spending on unplanned, unexpected needs of the family, or the upkeep of our home. Also, I had no control on essential business expenses like paying for stamps, post box fee, stationary, and so on.

What I could control, however, was all discretionary spending on myself. Even when I was at a store and wanted to buy or eat something worth even a dollar, I would think and re-think before satisfying any of my taste buds or other wants. For me, money became a precious commodity that I was totally divested off by some deity, lady luck, or my own doing. Given a choice of spending even a dollar on myself or on business, I would choose to spend it on business. My personal wants and desires didn't mean a thing to me. I could easily suppress them or postpone them. On the other hand, if my kids or Amy had expressed any desire or even pointed a finger on something they wanted, I wouldn't hesitate to buy it for them on the spot. That's how I felt about my responsibility as a provider – husband, or father.

Like with other consolidated loans, I bought myself some room to breathe with this loan as well. Now that I had this on-going business, I became more and more obsessed to make it successful, so much so, that I could finally make some net income. I knew that like any other business, this business was no magic wand and would take its time to establish and generate income – that too, strictly because I was selling well-researched products to an elite group of consumers. Thus far, a very little net income had trickled from this business. At the year end, I would receive some tax refund against business losses (i.e., expenditure in excess of revenue), and the way my luck was, that refund would be spent on some need of the moment rather than pay off any debt taken for business.

The only other potential source of supplementary income was an unexpected windfall from the weekly lottery that I had been playing religiously ever since it came into effect. That also was my committed monthly expense because its cost compared to its return was all worth it. I was looking for a return worth a million or more dollars at a cost of couple of dollars per week. I fully knew the odds: one win out of fourteen millions (six numbers between 1 and 49 drawn randomly had to exactly match those on the ticket purchased). Each time I bought a ticket, I would fantasize how I would be spending the jackpot after writing off all of my debts. Even though I wasn't living in a fantasy world, each purchase of this ticket, nonetheless, drove me to fantasize for a while. How else a person like me deeply in debts could feel a temporary relief from stress? I always convinced myself that since each and every draw mostly had a winner, why couldn't I be that winner at one of the draws? I had the same chance of winning like anyone else.

***

"Peter was out of job yesterday." Jen whispered to me while we were sitting across the table, preparing for the release of the latest statistics on personal and business bankruptcies.

"Sorry to hear that," I replied softly, and gently tapped the top of her fingers. "At least this didn't happen out of a blue. You knew it was likely coming."

"True," she agreed, "but the impact of the news remains the same. I am really worried and upset right now. We will talk about it later at lunch. Right now, you just go through all of this data carefully. I can't focus. Just make sure there's no error in my component on business bankruptcies."

"Don't worry," I assured her, "I will take care of it. You just relax."

Just past the noon hour, we walked together to the cafeteria.

"How's Peter taking it?" I asked her as we grabbed a corner table. "Since he likely knew it for over three months, has he been looking for a job?"

"Not that I know of," she answered. "You know he doesn't share his feelings with me. I just overheard him telling our son that he had been declared redundant and was out of a job. It bothered me for a while, but then I let it go. You know I feel much closer and intimate to you than him. We at least talk to each other and share one another's problems or needs."

"I know that," I concurred with her.

We were sitting on the sides rather than across the table.

"Still he has to do something; can't simply sit and brood, or watch TV," I added.

"I don't think his prospects of securing a job in his field are that great as he finished his computer degree almost twenty years ago. As far as I am aware, he hasn't been taking any courses or ad-hoc classes to upgrade his skills. Since computer technology has considerably changed over the last two decades, I think he's going to have a problem finding a job he likes."

"That's bad ... really bad," I commented. "In this day and age of rapidly changing technology, automation, globalization, and outsourcing of jobs, it's really important for us all, currently working or those looking, or planning to work, to brush up skills – keep these up-to-date. If we don't, who else will? No employer is going to look after this side of an employee's marketability. The onus is on employees to have knowledge and skills required in today's competitive job market."

"You and I both know it and we have been through these changes," she replied. "You know when we both went for courses on how to use computers, several softwares that we now use in our daily work, and digital technology required in compiling all of the digital data transferred on-line, and so on. Granted, we were sent by our employer, but still a person has to have some initiative to learn and compete in a job market, or even willing to take some risk and open a business."

"Speaking of job market," I added, "it's no longer domestic alone. With the current wave of outsourcing, which unfortunately has swallowed him, the job market has turned global. For some jobs now, one has to compete with well educated and qualified candidates from several developing countries. And that puts even more pressure on those currently working or potentially seeking work to stay up-to-date. We are now living in a knowledge-based economy rather than the conventional run-of-the-mill economy. These days, knowledge is power; the more one has it, the better it is to find a well paying job. And as far as opening an owned business is concerned, it requires, besides all the initiative and risks, some venture capital, sustaining power in the initial and economically depressed years. I don't think Peter wants to open up any business."

"Never mind the business," she remarked in utter frustration, "I will be more than happy if he found a job in his field. Knowing him, he's not going to last for too long in a job that he doesn't like or feel comfortable. The guy isn't that creative, or takes any initiative. He likes a well-routine job of his liking. And that's what worries me. He hasn't kept up with the changing times."

"Well, he can start acquiring skills currently in demand," I suggested. "He has a computer background. I am sure he can build and diversify his technical skills."

"Are you kidding?" she snapped at me. "The guy is running in his late forties. Even if he wants to, he has to pay out-of-pocket costs to learn new skills or upgrade the ones he has. I don't think we have that much of savings at hand. Very soon, we have to worry about our son's higher education. No … no … he has to find a job with whatever skills he has or acquired at different jobs. Moreover, the job has to be in Ottawa as I am not going to quit my job here and relocate elsewhere."

"You are not making things that easy for him with all these restrictions." I chided her.

"Too bad ... too sad," she replied with a shrug. "I don't have to quit a well paying job with a good pension. Who knows if he ever decided to move out and I end up as a single mother with a child who is just at the threshold of starting his higher education? Since he's just about your older daughter, Sarah's age, what's she up to? Do you know?"

"Well, she's planning to go to university in or out of Ottawa, depending on what she opts to pursue," I replied. "Her sister Kerry, who's only one class junior to her, will also follow her. That's the plan right now."

"Wow, you have quite a big expenditure lined up for the next few years," she exclaimed. "With the debt load you are currently carrying, how are you going to manage and finance their university education?" She wondered aloud.

"Well, I am sure I will cross the bridge when I reach there," I replied pensively. "You will be the first one to know. One thing I can tell you right now. I won't let them borrow a cent as I wouldn't like them to start their life with debt. That will be a rather painful start."

"That's all what being a good and considerate father is about." She nodded her head. "I have no clue if I would be facing this sort of situation as a family or a single mother."

***

Now that VISA and MasterCard credit cards had dominated the market, and institutions issuing these cards were mailing out unsolicited application forms to potential households, addressed simply as 'The Resident', and offering incentive to transfer high-interest balances to their card with pre-set limits with no interest charged during the first six or twelve months. I also ended up receiving one such mail.

As the payment of the latest consolidated loan had very much squeezed my finances and I was using credit cards and lines of credit to pay the monthly bills and manage my life, and in turn, making minimum payments on cards, I decided to apply for one MasterCard and use its pre-set limit to pay off the balance on another such high-interest card. I thought it would save me some money for at least six months even if this meant that I was carrying one more credit card.

Since the pre-set limit was fifteen thousand dollars, I simply requested in the loan application that this amount should be transferred to my credit card number xxxx xxxx xxxx xxxx, issued by company zzzz.

After a couple of weeks, I got a note from this new card issuing company that it was able to pay off only one-half of the initially agreed upon amount. This amount would be considered as loan taken on the card and I would be making payments per terms and conditions of the loan.

I didn't want this deal as this would have put me into a more difficult position to spare an additional monthly payment for this loan. In other words, I would now be making two payments instead of one in order to re-pay one card. I immediately sent a request to the new company to cancel my account. I told the company that since it didn't fulfil its stated commitment to transfer the balance in full, I had no choice, but to cancel my account.

In the meantime, however, this new company had transferred the amount of seven- thousand and five-hundred dollars to the institution I had named in my application for loan transfer. The company had cut the pre-set limit to one-half of what it had initially approved. I had put myself in a very messy situation.

Since I cancelled the account with the new company, its issued cheque got bounced at the receiver's end, and the latter wanted me to pay the amount involved – even if I had to use borrowed funds. There was no way I was going to be pushed by these two financial institutions. It was almost like I was going to pay a penalty on behalf of the new company for not honouring its initial commitment.

It took me days and days to negotiate and salvage this mess, besides all the mental stress and sleepless nights I experienced. I normalized my dealings with the old company while I cancelled the entire transaction with the new one. The lesson learnt was: *'never again to fall in the trap of schemes like balance transfer from one company to another'*. Companies offering such promises could always back out for one reason or another, almost crippling the applicant.

***

Over time, I also realized how sweetly and lovingly these credit card issuing companies were tacitly robbing those unable to pay the balance in full. Granted, all of these financial companies had to protect their money and minimize risks, it's how these befuddled card users hit me both as a user and a professional working on indebtedness of households.

For instance, one of the ways these companies protected their money was to make card users, seventy-five years old or less, and carried over their monthly balances, pay for the insurance to cover their balance outstanding. Users had to pay a monthly insurance premium based on xx cents per one hundred or thousand dollars of balance outstanding. The card issuing institutions sold this insurance to the vulnerable card users on the premise that this insurance would give them peace of mind as well as save their families the agony and hardship to repay the balance outstanding after the card holder's death. Put simply, in the event of a card user's death, it won't be the user's estate, but the insurance company who would pay off the balance outstanding. It was one of those fear-mongering tactics that wooed a good majority of financially wringed debtors including me.

Now the minimum payment had to include not only the interest on balance outstanding, but also the cost of insurance. This not only increased the amount of monthly minimum payment, forcing card users to throw more of their income in drain, but the scheme boosted revenue or profit margin of both financial institutions and insurance companies – without making a dent, or subsequently increasing, the amount of credit card debt owed.

***

One day I was at the Hudson's Bay store at the Rideau Center. Since the store had a special sale of women's footwear with no provincial and federal sales tax, Amy wanted me to drive her to the store as she wanted to buy some footwear for herself. She didn't want to drive alone to downtown because of traffic and parking issues. I couldn't refuse her as she had asked me to accompany her after a very long time.

Once at the store, Amy walked over to its footwear section whereas I started walking aimlessly at the second level of the concourse of the center, looking at the large glass windows with nicely laid out merchandise, mannequins covered with attractive and in-vogue clothing, handbags, and footwear – all to entice persons roaming the shopping mall.

Besides looking at these decorated windows, I was observing people passing me by and those at a distance walking towards me. I saw someone with a familiar face, but wearing a uniform of the mall's security corps. I didn't pay much attention to that face as I hardy knew anyone working as a security guard at this or any other mall.

When that familiar face came closer to me, I recognized it right away.

Gosh! It was Peter, Jen's husband, who had been laid off for little over a year.

"How are you, Peter? It's been long since I saw you last." I called out at him, extended my hand to shake his. "How are you doing?"

"I am doing fine," he uttered softly.

He gave me a flat look while I shook his limped hand. His cold handshake had warned me to be very watchful and use words with care, ensuring these didn't hurt any of his soft spot.

"So what's new with you, your job, and family?" I coaxed him.

I wasn't eager to know why he was at the mall, but why he was in a security guard's uniform. I knew he had been laid off from his hi-tech job.

"Not much," he replied softly, perhaps felt embarrassed.

His eyes were shifting around, observing the hustle and bustle around. I kept gazing his face. I could feel his discomfort. He likely wanted me to leave him alone. And it might really have happened if I hadn't called him out. After a lengthy pause, he looked at me momentarily, and sputtered, "I work here as a security guard."

"What do you mean?" I probed him. "Jen never told me you were working as a security guard."

"Because she doesn't know," he explained in his normal tone. He likely had composed himself. "I left her just a few months after I lost my job with the telecommunication company. Since we didn't have much of a relationship, my presence at home was making her more edgy and uncomfortable. She would degrade and insult me rather than lend me a compassionate ear, understand that it wasn't my fault that I lost the job. There are many who like me have lost jobs because of changing technology and current outsourcing of jobs. You know her personality better than I do since you two have been working together close to twenty years. Am I right?"

"Yes, you are," I nodded. "I still don't get it why you are in this job and not in your field, or in any other, for that matter, if I may ask."

"You know," he started to unwind, "ever since I got my thee-month notice, I have been trying to find a job in my field. But I have been persistently refused because what I learnt twenty years ago is no longer marketable today. Every employer wants to hire someone with the latest computer skills, knowledge of soft/hardwares, digital and laser technology. Granted, there are many hi-tech jobs in and around Ottawa; but if I don't have the right skills, I can't blame any company for not offering me a job. I really feel bad that I didn't try to upgrade my skills or attend courses to acquire new skills. Since I had a good job, there was no need or even the realization that I needed to upgrade my skills. I would spend my evenings and weekends enjoying sports, social gatherings, watch TV, and attend to tasks maintaining our house. To be honest with you, I strongly detested going back to school, attend a course, read books, or to seriously study anything. After several failed attempts to get a job in my field, I was getting really frustrated. I hated myself for not taking the action at the right time. As a result, I had started to behave badly with our son, Josh, and Jen. That's the time I decided to leave them in peace and re-start my life on my own. I still love them, but it's in everybody's interest that I stay away from them."

"How often do you see them?" I asked him to satisfy my curiosity.

"Not that often; neither I visit them nor they can visit me as I don't live independently." He explained. "It costs an arm and a leg to rent an apartment to preserve one's independence. I don't make much out of this security guard's job, and the little amount that I got as my severance pay is helping me to sustain my life. I am worried about Josh's future, but there isn't much that I can do. The same goes for Jen too, not from personal, but financial point of view. She is now managing the house on a single income. This onslaught of changes in the job market has destroyed not only my family, but I am sure, many others living across the country."

"Well, that's today's stark reality, my friend." I concurred with his assessment. "I sincerely hope you get a better job one day and join your family."

"I am really concerned about Josh's future," he parroted, "I am not that worried about Jen. I am sure you are there for her. After all, you two have known each other, not just well, but too well, for close to two decades. She is open with you and spends much more time with you at the office."

I sensed that Peter was now beginning to vent out his frustration, and might even start talking about our personal affairs. I didn't want him to indulge into this discussion and that too in a public place. I cut short our meeting by saying, "It was nice meeting you, Peter. I better go. Amy must be waiting for me."

I extended my hand to shake his, but he didn't. For a moment he looked rather tense, beaten by despair, and gave me a harsh look.

"All the best," I said with a small grin. I tapped the upper side of his right arm, and walked away from him.

What I had witnessed was not that abnormal.

The current wave of fast changing technology, automation, and liberal trading with low-wage developing countries have, in turn, been resulting in outsourcing of jobs for largely economic reasons. The latter had started to engulf the most vulnerable, especially those with no or obsolete skills.

It was a rude awakening for all those ill prepared living not only in Canada, but also in several other developed and developing countries. It had separated the labour markets in two segments: one comprising those with no or little skills, and the other with high and up-to-date skills. As a result, those in the former group were earning low wages whereas those in the latter were earning relatively much higher wages – thus widening the income disparity all around the globe. Evidently, changes in economies and their associated labour markets were not only threatening the stability or cohesiveness of family units, but also widening income disparities – among families, localities, cities, and nations. And this income disparity, in turn, was also turning many families to indebtedness, i.e., making them to borrow money to finance their wants and needs.

While driving back home, I didn't share any of my thoughts with Amy. I made no mention of my meeting with Peter. I simply kept thinking about Jen. How was she managing as a single mother of a teenager ready to pursue his secondary education? How was she maintaining her house? I knew she personally wouldn't be missing Peter's presence at home.

The very next morning, I barged into Jen's office, more or less fuming with anger.

"Why on earth you didn't tell me that Peter had left you?" I demanded of her, resting my hands on the side of her table. "I thought we were close friends and talked to each other openly."

She gave me a full stare; kept looking at my face. Our eyes were perfectly locked. We both didn't move for a few moments. I could see her face turning pale. And she could see mine all huffed up. She finally blinked her eyes, got up from her chair, and walked to the door in order to close it.

"Sit down." She ordered me as she walked back to her chair.

"I was too embarrassed to tell you," she said in an almost inaudible tone. "I didn't want to tell you how hurt and defeated I felt at the time. You know my views. I never wanted to break our family. But when his frustration and failures got the best of him and he started to abuse me and physically hurt Josh, I put my foot down and told him to leave us alone. He hasn't spoken to me since then. Nonetheless, he is in touch with Josh and keeps him up-to-date about his well-being. I gather he's currently sharing an apartment." She paused. She now gave me an honest look, and asked, "How did you come to know about it? Did you run into him? I know I personally haven't told anyone about our separation except my parents."

"Yeah, I ran into him yesterday at the Rideau Center." I replied calmly as my anger had subsided. "He was regretting leaving Josh alone in your care. Other than that, he looked all right to me."

"I feel bad for him," she added, "but there's nothing I can do. I have already told you the kind of carefree personality he has. The only thing I am missing with him gone is his share of income. He used to contribute to pay the mortgage and other monthly and on-going commitments. This sudden hefty loss in family income will be more serious and even hurting when Josh is ready to pursue his secondary education. Right now, I am managing the shortfall by using credit cards and cash from our home equity line of credit. It pains me when I use credit to finance my current expenditure. I think about you, your pain, and what sort of mental stress you must have been going through all these years."

"Welcome to the club," I said jokingly to cheer her up. "Now at least I have someone who can really feel the pain and suffering that I have been through all these years. And this battle is not over yet. Like you are concerned about Josh's secondary education, I am equally worried about my daughters'. That way, I have twice the level of your worries. But we can't and shouldn't live with such anticipatory worries. We have to face the situation as it comes. Living with borrowed funds is not that reprehensible as long as we can repay these to the last cent. You will be fine as long as you keep making the desired minimum payment by due date."

CHAPTER FOURTEEN

I was running my business on a shoe-string budget. I had no borrowed money to spare in order to take any risk, or spend it freely on advertising or promoting the business. On the other hand, I was fully aware that if I wanted to see my business flourish and successful, it needed a good exposure not only in one city, but in all major cities across Canada, and that sort of exposure, in turn, would require extensive high-priced publicity and advertising.

I used to follow intensely the glamorous and enticing ads, both in newspapers and on television, of several other mail-order companies selling garden and machine tools, clothes, and other merchandise. I very much wanted to emulate these companies, but didn't have money to spare for such commercially designed ads. I needed money to make money – perfectly in line with the famous adage that '*money begets money*'. No business ever became successful by simply wishes or wants alone; it needed, besides the right ideas, concepts, and know-how, a lot of crafty and pricey promotional campaign.

Rather than throw in the towel, I decided to take one small step at a time. I decided to start gaining some exposure right in the city I lived in. I thought if my efforts were successful and brought in some revenue, I could easily spend that on more commercial ads in newspapers across the country. I knew I could never afford to air ads on television and its supplementary infrastructure (like an automated telephone system where viewers would right away place their order and also pay by credit card). Both the response and returns to ads aired on television differed from those in newspapers; for example, in the latter's case, people would have more time to think and decide about the purchase, and also pay by cheque, money order, or credit card, whereas in the former's case, people would instantly place a purchase order and pay by credit card.

I started to write ads on the desk-top computer, have it print on a jet-ink printer (way inferior to laser), and then would make its zerox copies on papers of different colours (as I had read that a coloured paper drew more and quicker attention than the plain white paper). Depending on the nature of goods I was advertising, I would then go to places with potential buyers of these goods to hand deliver these ads. I was just following the simple rule: go where your potential market is. For example, if goods included videos on improving a game of golf, I would deliver these ads at all golf clubs and grounds in and around the city rather than places like elementary schools or community centers.

Besides visiting potential locations, I would also place ads on lamp posts of major streets, downtown, or other thoroughfares. If the lamppost was wooden, I would use thumbnails to stick on it, and if it was of concrete or cement, I would use scotch tape. All of such campaigning was done on the weekends or on statutory holidays between the months of May and October as I had no time during the work-week. Also, the onset of wintery conditions wouldn't permit it. Other places I used were the public bulletin boards in grocery stores, shopping centers, gyms, and community centers because advertising at these places was free. And, that's what I wanted.

These ads on coloured papers, left on locations with potential customers or walking crowds in general, were no guarantee that these would result in any sales because a good majority of people would hardly read it, let alone respond to it with an order. Even if a few read it, some among these were likely to throw it back in a trash can. Knowing all such outcomes, I was still pursuing my mission, hoping that even if a fraction read the ad, I would consider myself successful in promoting the name of my company and what it does.

To further enhance the awareness about the company, I decided to have a big ad in large blue letters imprinted on a white vinyl plated thick black foam sheet with a magnetic back. I paid for two such ads on vinyl plates. I could stick one on each side of the car that I drove around the city, enabling people to read about the local company's name, and selling products from coast-to-coast – as I was selling audios and videos to libraries across the country – from Halifax in the East (on the Atlantic Ocean) to Vancouver in the West (on the Pacific Ocean). And, the local newspaper had already informed the community by doing a short write-up on the company. So I was working intensely to promote the awareness about my company and what it sells in the nation's Capital – all meant to improve sales.

***

One Saturday afternoon in early August, I was coming out after placing an ad on the bulletin board of a grocery store off Merivale Road that I ran into Jen. She was pushing her cart full of groceries. She was wearing a white cotton blouse with a white skirt with green polka dots. She had her hair tied in a pony tail.

"Oh hi Robert," she called to me loudly, with a broad smile on her face. "What are you doing at this West-end store? Don't you have a grocery store in the neighbourhood in the East?"

"I was here in relation to my business," I replied without a hitch. "I had to place an ad about my new catalogue on the store's bulletin board. I see you are pushing quite a load."

"Yeah, just the necessities of life," she responded with a smile, and started to walk with me. "You have time to have a cup of coffee?"

"I have all the time for you," I chuckled and gave her an affectionate look.

She turned her neck and looked at me. I could see her lightly blushed face.

"I just want to reach home in time to mow the lawn," I said.

"I mowed the lawn this morning before coming here for groceries," she informed me.

She had started to transfer groceries from the cart to the trunk of her car.

"So we can drive down to McDonald's for coffee?" I asked her.

"No, I was thinking of having it at my place. You know I live very close by," she added.

"All right; as you wish." I readily accepted her offer and walked up to my car.

"I'll follow you."

I parked my car behind hers on her driveway. She opened her garage and unlocked the entrance to her home. I lifted bags of groceries from the trunk of her car and in two runs, placed everything on her kitchen table. In the meantime, she had put the kettle on.

I pulled out one of the dining chairs away from the table and sat not too far away from her. I just wanted to watch her actions and attractive face, a face that I had not kissed for a long time.

"Where is Josh? I don't see him. Isn't he at home?" I showered her with questions about the whereabouts of her son.

"I just dropped him at the Harvey's. He's working there from two to eight today." She replied without any hesitation. "You just have a seat. Coffee should be ready soon."

"So he's working these days. How come you let him work knowing he's in the final year of his secondary school?" I wondered aloud.

"You know my finances are tight ever since Peter left me," she explained. "I let him work so that he can have his pocket money without bothering me."

"I agree with your view point," I replied. "In my opinion, however, he should be focusing more on his studies since he's at a make or break situation. You could have managed to pay his pocket money for another few months so that he could focus his efforts on getting good grades. These are very important to get admission at some good university."

"I understand all that, but he insisted," she replied. "You know how kids are these days. If they don't get their way, they can easily make parent's life very difficult. Now that his father is no longer here, I let him do whatever he wants to do to maintain peace and quiet at home." She paused. "Would you care to have something with coffee?" she asked.

"A cookie or two would be fine. You know I am a cookie monster." I said laughingly.

I was now trying to lighten up the environment, cheer her up a bit after lecturing her on Josh's future. She had gotten somewhat tense.

I soon realized she didn't call me here to discuss Josh's future. She wanted to have some quality and relaxing time in my company. She was living alone and had no fear of anyone disturbing her. She had all the privacy to do anything as long as Josh was away from home. She might even like to connect with me as it had been a long time since our bodies had greeted each other.

"I see you have mowed the lawn well. It's looking nice." I remarked, as I looked outside from the big glass window of her kitchen.

"I am getting better doing these household chores. In fact, I no longer mind doing them," she replied with some sense of pride and satisfaction. "All in all, I am doing fine except one thing and that is my physical vacuum. There are times I really crave for sex, even masturbate, but that still leaves me unsatisfied. With age, I feel I need more and more of physical satisfaction. Even though we have been together for almost two decades, and even sexually involved for years, it still has been rather spotty – just three to four times a year at the most while we are together at a conference, or at your friend's cottage, or during our office get-togethers like picnic or Christmas as we slip away during our official afternoons off. I have always enjoyed sex with you. Now that I am free to have as much as I want, you are still tied up with your family. How is Amy's affair coming along? Do you think she's going to leave you?"

"I have no clue about her affair or what she plans to do," I replied.

She was now walking towards me, carrying a tray with mugs of coffee and a plate of 'Digestives' cookies. As she bent and placed the plate on the table, followed by a mug, then another mug, I looked at the deep cavity between her breasts and their sides. It had been too long that I had even touched her breasts, let alone sucked on them.

I could resist no more. And who else was there to stop me? She herself had signalled her desire to be fondled and even engage in sex. Moreover, her talk about how desperately she needed me at times had stirred up my emotions, had even aroused me a bit. She had awakened my lust for her.

I pulled her in my lap.

I held her lightly in my arms and whispered in her ear, "You are not the only one who feels sexually starved; I feel the same. I too miss you all the time." I gently rubbed her back, as she lay comfortably in my arms, with her feet firmly placed on the floor. I hissed, "I am always hungry for your body, but, unfortunately, I am not as free as you are. You have to bear with me."

"I know that," she whispered back.

She tried to get out of my embrace.

"Let's finish coffee first," she suggested. "I know you don't have much time to spend with me today. We will just have a quickie. That will at least keep me level headed for some time."

She sat on the next chair and passed me one of the coffee mugs. She held the plate of cookies in front of me.

"You know life as a single mother isn't that easy," she began to pour her heart out to me. "Even if I am leading a pretty busy life, and have all the financial means, there still are times when my heart really cries out for a man's company – husband, a common law, or a friend. I don't know if it's just me or it's common among single mothers. Then I have this boy who is still much closer to his absent father. He hardly listens to me or cares for me. He speaks to me only when he needs something, including money."

"You aren't experiencing anything abnormal. All young kids these days are behaving like that in almost every family – conventional with a couple, or a single parent. We as parents have to cater to their needs, still preserving our own needs, respect, and dignity. My daughters act the same way. There isn't much that I can do except to comply with their wishes."

As soon as we finished our coffee, I pulled her back in my lap and put my arms around her.

"You know I have to leave soon," I reminded her softly "Let's just focus on ourselves, our current need to connect, even if it's for a short while."

"Any while suits me," she tightened her arms around my neck, with her feet resting again on the floor. "Let me warn you though," she muttered, "that since I sweated much while mowing the lawn this morning, my body may still smell of dried sweat as I had planned to take a shower after dinner. So my body may taste all salty or rotten right now. Had I known about our encounter this afternoon, I would have taken a shower."

"Don't worry," I assured her, "you always taste sweet to me, or should I say, too sweet."

I planted a kiss on her dimpled cheek.

Indeed, I smelt her dried sweat, odour released by her armpits, and my lips even felt a sour and salty taste of her sweated body. I simply overlooked the odour and taste of her sweated body because that was nothing compared to the heavenly physical satisfaction we both were about to get. The fragrance of her hair was another catalyst charging my body. Her upper body clasped in my arms was very intoxicating as her hardening nipples began poking my chest. I was thinking of one and one thing only: how to fuck her to heighten our mutual satisfaction?

"Shall we go to bed?" she asked in a seductive voice.

"No, not today," I replied, "I only have time for a quickie."

I kissed her open lips and slowly walked my hand on her still fully covered breasts.

She lay quietly in my arms. My right hand was now roaming slowly and softly on her body – from face to knees – and occasionally pressed her crotch.

"Let me draw the curtains." She demanded after a while. "Let's undress. I don't feel that comfortable lying angular in this position."

She released herself from my embrace and walked up to draw curtains of all of the windows of her kitchen and dining area. She made sure that no neighbour of hers would be acting as a 'Peeping Tom'.

After possibly blocking all the sun light in the room that was filtering through the glass windows, she stood in front of me.

"Don't you want to undress? she demanded.

"Do I have to?" I replied jokingly.

I stood up in front of her.

I watched her pulling her top over her head and roll down over her arms. After she threw the top away on the dining table, she stretched her hands at the back to unbutton her bra with her thumb and index finger. She tossed that too on the table.

She was now standing naked to her waist in front of me.

I too had removed both my shirt and the vest.

We both were now standing half-naked, facing each other.

She gently rubbed each of her breasts with her open palm, and then lifted each up by the curvature between her thumb and index finger.

"Don't you think these are sagging?" she remarked, likely wanting me to look at her erected nipples.

"Not really," I replied. "I will just give them a massage to bring them to a proper full shape."

I moved closer to her and gently lifted each of her breasts. I rubbed the tip of each of my thumb on her nipples, and then lightly tweaked each between my thumb and index finger in a more or less circular way. While I was focused on activating her nipples, she had opened the belt of my trousers and pulled them down, covering my feet.

"You can now remove your underwear and sit on the chair." She ordered me.

She walked to the adjacent room and brought back two back cushions from her sofa and a large beach towel folded in three layers.

She signalled me to get up for a while as she placed the layered towel on the black vinyl seat of my chair. The towel covered all three sides of the seat.

"There you go; you can now sit comfortably." She bristled as if she had done something out of the way.

She unbuttoned her skirt and rolled down her panty over her feet.

She stood all bare naked in front of me.

I could see her full crotch, with pubic hair, her covered clit, pinkish red area under her lips, and the opening of her sacred spot.

"You are looking beautiful." I commented, looking all over her in awe. She was standing as a live statute.

"It's not the first time you are looking at me fully naked," she replied with a ravishing smile.

"No, but to a man, it doesn't matter how many times he has seen his woman naked," I commented. "The fact is that he relishes very much each and every time that woman strips off in front of him, or stands or lies bare-naked with him. Her nakedness always arouses him, charging his desire to explode into her." I explained as if I was an expert on sexual matters.

"But your dick isn't fully erected yet, even if I am standing all naked before you," she pointed out.

"It's getting there," I vehemently replied. "You know well that I don't believe in a shot-gun approach."

"I know how to speed up the hardening of your joystick. It's quite simple," she replied smilingly.

She came closer to my chair, and knelt between my legs, placing her knees on the cushions. She placed her hands on my inner thighs and widened my legs. She held my dick in her hand, and began to move gently her right thumb on its gland.

"You want me to open up my pony tail as I know you want my hair well spread on your dick and thighs while I give you a blow job." She gave me an enchanting look.

"I am glad you know me so well," I replied with a smile, and let her hair free. "I am sure you know another thing that I like while you suck my dick."

"I know, I know," she replied, "you don't have to worry. I will take it right up to my throat. I know you like to be sucked deep – full length. Just give me a minute."

She placed my dick into her mouth and started to suck it very softly.

As she intensified her sucks, she slid the shaft closer to the deep end of her mouth. She knew her limits. She didn't want to choke herself.

As soon as my dick was fully erected and was hard as a rod, I pulled it out of her mouth by pulling a fistful of her hair.

I placed my hands under her armpits and signalled her to stand up.

She stood up, impatiently looked at me, and waited for my next move.

I held her hands, pulled her closer to me. I made her sit, facing me, on my thighs and slid my hard rod in her pussy. She whole-heartedly welcomed the visitor she had been eagerly waiting for.

She placed her legs across the seat of the chair. We were now both sitting on a chair – two bodies perfectly joined and synchronized with each other. She had firmly placed her hands on the top curve of the chair.

"Oh! It feels so good." She hissed. "I have been really craving for it. I am glad I ran into you this afternoon.

"Me too," I muttered.

I tightened my grip on her upper body, almost squeezing her, kissing her cheeks and lips sporadically.

"Just make sure you don't come until I want you come." She whispered this command. "I want to enjoy holding your dick inside me as long as I can."

"You are the boss," I assured her, "since you are the one who's going to make all the movements, up and down or circular, how hard or soft thrusts you can take it, and eventually tell me when to fill your crack."

She made her first up and down slide in a very gentle manner.

"I want to glide on your prick on my own pace in order to optimize my pleasure and sensation, especially when it gently knocks my G-spot. It really feels good and relaxing."

"I am glad to hear that," I bubbled and kissed her passionately. "Just keep in mind that this is a short session."

"I know that," she snarled, "but I want to satisfy my longing for a while. You have to bear with me."

She placed one of her hard nipples in my mouth to nibble. Either she was now too excited or wanted me to stay quiet. She gradually increased her rhythmic motion of gliding up and down.

While I held her nipple between my lips, I started to gently knead her other breast.

I sucked hard and intermittently bit her nipple.

She started to coast up and down on my rocky shaft faster and more vigorously.

I knew she had quite sensitive nipples; even a soft rub or a lick would sensate her entire body, making her slither and jerk her body with heavy pants and loud moans.

The only way to cut short this session was to play hard with her nipples, causing her extra stimulation to slide much faster on my hard dick for a perfect climax – not only for her, but for us both.

I began to suck her nipples alternately with more intensity, at times bit them, and slapped hard on her curvy bums. I wanted her to touch her physical limits.

"I ... like ... it ... I ... like ... it ... let ... me ... glide ... hard," she cried out hysterically, and intensified her slides on a hard solid pole.

She started to jump all over me.

She began to wheeze. She tried to squeeze the walls of her pussy. She wrapped my body much closer to hers. She started to pull my hair. She began rubbing vibrantly her face against the side of my neck, and at times, on top of my chest.

With her eyes closed, she began to sob, and grunted feebly,

"O yeah ... OO yeah ... OOO yeah ... OOOO God ... you ... can ... come ... now... come ... please ... I ... am ... tired ... done ..."

She was gasping.

I let myself go and filled her honey hole.

I tightly squished her upper body while I was relieving myself, eventually placed my head on her full breasts. She fastened her arms around my neck.

We were now quiet and motionless.

We had thoroughly satisfied our mutual hunger for one another – at least for a while.

I felt my inner thighs were all soaking wet with a mix of warm flowing juices – hers and mine. We both had unloaded ourselves at the same time – as she wanted, and had specifically ordered me.

"It was good ... really good." She broke the silence with a broad smile. "I wish I had it more often ... There are times I really miss you."

She tightened her arms around me, and nestled her face on my chest. I felt her honest plea and I was sure she felt mine too. It was rather unfortunate that I was not accessible to her at her own choosing.

She half-heartedly got up from my wet thighs.

She walked up to her kitchen drawers and fetched a couple of clean towels.

We both dried ourselves.

"Where's your powder room?" I asked her.

"Why? You want to wash up?" she queried.

"Yah, I want to wash my dick," I explained. "You know I am going home and I don't want anyone to smell the odour of yours or mine sexually released hormonal juice. Don't forget I have two grown up daughters and Amy at home."

"I understand."

She led me to her powder room.

After cleaning myself as best as I could, I walked back to face her.

"Thanks for everything; see you on Monday at the office," I said smilingly.

"Sure." She walked with me up to her entrance door. Before opening it, however, she gave me a warm hug, a passionate kiss, and cheerfully uttered, "Thanks for the lovely afternoon. It was really rejuvenating."

***

All of my efforts to place ads on bulletin boards, or distribute personally at potential locations in and around the city failed miserably. I didn't gain a single new customer. And if there were no customers, there was no sales revenue either.

Even if the business were to run initially on borrowed funds, this wouldn't last for too long either as these funds would, sooner or later, be depleted as well.

Thus, for a business to survive and compete successfully with giant publishers and distributors, large sales revenue was a must. To generate this revenue, I needed to attract a broad base of customers and that was possible only by a good pricey and crafty marketing campaign, and that too run by a professional marketing agency. As human beings need oxygen to breathe and live, business needs effective marketing to survive, compete, and thrive. Marketing oxygenates business. I learnt this mantra from books and periodicals on marketing.

Knowledge alone could never successfully run any business. It required means of sustenance. I didn't have any other than borrowed funds.

I was well aware of this stark reality even before I started the business. Nonetheless, I took a calculated risk and was now watching my dream fading away. Even if I could write a good and persuasive ad, it wasn't going to earn any revenue until it reached and persuaded the right kind of people through the right media. It was just like I had the vehicle to drive from point A to B, but in order to actually drive it, I needed to fill it with gas first, and for which I had no money. No gas, no movement – it was that simple.

I haplessly watched all my efforts wasting away. My time, energy, dream to change my financial situation – all were turning into ashes. Despite such setbacks and their associated frustration, painful and sleepless nights, I didn't give up my hope to see the business running successfully one day.

I decided to enlarge the current base of my customers – mostly public libraries – as I not only had improved my focus on these, but also increased their numbers, hoping to gain more orders, and more revenue. That meant spending more on stationary as well as mailing out of catalogues – all using borrowed funds.

Over time, I was back to where I was before I took the fourth consolidated loan. Since I had accounts and made payments at three financial institutions – FI-I, FI-II, and FI-IV – anytime I faced a teller at the counter of anyone of these institutions, I heard the unsolicited advice that I should consolidate my loans.

One day, I really got pissed off and told in an emotionally controlled tone to one of such tellers at FI-III, "Look, consolidation is no guaranty that I would no longer be living with any debt. It's good only when one totally stops using credit, or use it to the extent that can be fully paid on receipt of its statement. Consolidation, in fact, places needy debtors in a more precarious situation as they pay off not only this debt, but also pay on newly cumulated debt. I am old enough to tell you from my personal experience."

"No, I still think consolidation will help you," she insisted. "You won't be making so many minimum payments."

Now I was really angry and almost scolded her.

"Why don't you just focus on the payment I am making? Let me decide what I should do or how to handle my debt liability. I don't like to be pestered to follow the same suggestion. You are really embarrassing me in front of other customers. Could I speak with your supervisor, please? I really don't like this persuasive selling of loans each and every time I am here to make a payment."

"No reason to get angry, Mr. Vaughan," she replied calmly. "I am simply doing my job promoting services that this institution offers to help customers. We like to help them anyway we can, including lending money. If you ever want a loan in the near future, I will be glad to arrange a meeting for you to see our loan manager about consolidating your loans, and easy debt payment plan. It's your decision. I am just making a suggestion."

"I understand," I replied in a much softer tone. "I work and analyze debt market and am fully aware of your institution's role including yours as a teller. I also understand that you people are paid extra bonuses for bringing in more clients seeking loans as you are helping your employer to increase its revenue to pay for your salary."

"Well, I am just doing my job," she chortled. "Our job is to help customers attain their financial goals."

"You are doing your job well," I replied sarcastically, "but since each customer has his/her own individual needs, only he/she can decide what's best for him/her. I was telling you from my experience that loan consolidation doesn't help everyone, especially those who use credit because of their poor or no cash-flow situation. Such people will continue to use credit at least until their day-to-day needs have subsided for one reason or another. You may have noticed from my account that I am just about to finish paying for both my mortgage and my last consolidated loan. I am sure I will be seeking another loan, if I have to, without all of your persuasive talk."

"I am glad to hear that." She replied with a grin. "That's what we are here for."

***

In the beginning of the twenty-first century, the Finance Minister of Canada finally introduced some altruistic legislation to help Canadians use credit with a better understanding about the rate of interest they were paying on their different sources of credit, and the number of years it would take to pay off each loan if they continued to pay just the minimum payment. The lending institution had to clearly specify the rate of interest charged – annual as well as daily. It also had to specify the number of years it would take to pay off the balance outstanding, if one continued to pay just the minimum payment – simply to make the debtor fully conscious and aware of the situation he/she was in.

Besides these changes, the legislation also had tempered with the initial down payment for the first-time home buyers, amortization period to pay off mortgage loan in order to boost the housing sector, and in turn, the nation's economy.

This legislation also included some terms and guidelines for private lenders or companies, including the maximum annual rate of interest these could charge to their customers – mostly those with a low income.

The government of the day wanted to boost the economy by kick-starting the housing sector. It made home-ownership easier for Canadians by allowing them to own a house with no down payment, or on full one-hundred percent mortgage, to be paid in forty years instead of the usual twenty-five. Over time, this plan back-fired as families who bought high-priced houses overburdened themselves with heavy mortgage debt, besides paying relatively higher insurance and property taxes.

Such families, most with limited and mid level income, and with high mortgage debt, began to feel the heat. These families had not much money left for other day-to-day expenditure, and as a result, resorted to depend on credit cards and newly opened lines of credit. Families had no room to save anything, and imagine if they were to live in such straitened circumstances for forty years – almost their working years – they would likely have ended up with no savings for, say their children's post-secondary education, or for their own retirement.

After a strong public outcry, the Finance Minister relented and introduced another legislation making first-time buyers to make a minimum payment of five percent of the value of home (meaning ninety-five percent mortgaged) with amortization, first reduced to thirty-five years, then to thirty years, and eventually to the conventional twenty-five year term.

***

Since I was almost at the end of paying off my mortgage, all of these legislative changes didn't affect me. As far as my non-mortgage debt was concerned, my gosh, I was loaded with that, I was fully aware about the rate of interest I was paying on each and every source of debt I owed.

The only thing this legislation did for me was to remind me each and every month about the number of years it would take me to pay off a particular debt. For example, if I owed, say $9,500 at 19.99% rate of interest, the monthly statement would clearly imprint the estimated time it would take to repay this debt would be 73 years and 6 months if I simply paid the minimum payment (that roughly translated to paying seven dollars of a monthly minimum payment to pay off the principal, the rest would simply be interest charges). And if I used the same card to make additional purchase, its next month statement would show even larger estimated period of payment because of the increase in balance outstanding. Imagine getting several statements per month telling me the estimated times to pay off different debts – at times, showing me even one hundred or more years of time to pay off a particular debt. I didn't think I was going to live that long.

Nonetheless, the information was alarming, often driving me to insanity. I couldn't blame the institution for rubbing it deep into my skin. It was simply obligated to remind me, even if I was totally helpless to do anything. I could only afford to pay minimum payments irrespective of the number of years it would take me to pay off the debt.

Despite all the piercing reminders about the time to payback each debt, what could I, as a debtor, do? Nothing really – simply ignore such reminders. Even if I marginally increased the amount of monthly payment, which I couldn't do, nothing much was going to change. The only option was, like it had been over all these years, to pay off in full by taking a consolidated loan.

These monthly reminders simply added insult to my already deeply bruised and frustrated ego, mind and soul. At times, such reminders touched the bottom cores of self-loathing. To maintain stability of mind and stay focused on work was quite a challenge. It really tested my grit.

One day I was reading an article written by one of the so-called experts from one of the private companies managing bankruptcies. Considering my own expertise in this area, and all the knowledge I had about household indebtedness and how to manage it, I really didn't have to read this article, but still out of interest, I went over it.

According to this expert, one method to live a debt-free life was to start paying off first the lowest debt; increase its monthly payment while paying monthly minimums on others. After this loan is paid off, take the next lowest, and increase its monthly payment, keeping minimums of all others, and so on and so forth. Over time, one would be debt free.

On the surface, the whole concept looked simple. In my own case, however, how could I increase payment on any one loan when what I was doing was simply paying just the minimum on all accounts? Moreover, what would I do if debt were to rise on one card or another? Even if I didn't use the card I was trying to pay off, I was still increasing the amount of debt on another card, and that meant, increasing minimum payment on the card used. The plan proposed by this expert likely assumed no more taking of new debt; it simply focused on paying off the current debt, which in turn, was rather unrealistic for debtors like me.

***

Since the business wasn't generating any significant income, I was still in the throes of finding means of supplementing my income. As I mentioned earlier, I hadn't been successful in finding any part-time work that would have been in synch with my main job. That left me with the only possible remaining source – and that was to win any windfall from the 649 lottery I faithfully played twice weekly. Even though the odds of winning were one in fourteen million, I still played it and hoped for a complete turn around of my life. Like any other winner in most draws, why couldn't I be too?

Not only a lottery provided a chance to buyers to fantasize about their enriched lives and unexpected overnight spins in their life styles, fulfilment of several personal and buried dreams beyond their expectations, this also provided governments an additional source of revenue. Governments, in turn, could use this revenue on opening up new recreational and amusement parks, rinks, entertainment centres, etc. for public, and as a do-gooder, gain public support and votes. For governments, revenue from lotteries was, in economic terms, an indirect voluntary taxation. People wouldn't mind buying more tickets and contribute to such revenue as they were the potential beneficiaries as well – provided they had three and over matching winning numbers. As the human greed dictated, the larger the jack pot, the more the number of tickets sold, and hence the more the revenue for governments.

Considering that both the public and governments benefitted from lotteries, Canada started another national lottery called 'Super 7', later changed to 'Lotto Max'. The initial cost of this ticket was two dollars, giving buyers three rows of numbers from 1 to 49, with a jackpot much bigger than that of 649. Anyone with a ticket matching randomly drawn seven numbers in any one of three lines was eligible to claim the jackpot worth two or more million dollars. This lottery was drawn once weekly on Fridays and the odds of winning the jackpot were one in twenty-eight million.

As a resident of Canada, I now had three chances of winning a windfall worth one or more million dollars – Wednesday's 649, Friday's Super 7, and then Saturday's 649. Even though I hated to gamble at any casino or even play poker on cards with friends, I had no choice, but to buy religiously tickets for 649 and Super 7.

As a result, each and every Thursday, Saturday, and Sunday morning, I used to wakeup with a hope that today was the day I was going to become a millionaire and was going to lead a debt-free life. I would open the newspaper and the first thing I would look for were the numbers drawn the previous night. My hopes crushed into pieces when my ticket numbers didn't fully match the randomly drawn sequence of six or seven numbers.

Despite such thrice weekly disappointments, I never missed buying lottery tickets. I considered their cost as an essential expenditure, knowing full well the long shot to win a jackpot. Still it was worth taking a chance, considering the amount of potential windfall. Again, that was the only source left for me to see any change in my financial situation.

I was in one hell of a financial mess.

After years of religiously purchasing lottery tickets, only once I came very close to winning a jack pot of fourteen million dollars. This was in one of Wednesdays' draw of 649.

One Thursday morning, I was matching numbers of my ticket with those officially drawn the previous night. The first five numbers were on the dot, matched perfectly. My heart had started to jump out of sheer joy. My body felt an electric shot running through it. My fingers had begun to shake as I kept matching number after number until my eyes stumbled at the sixth number. I looked at it again and compared it with the one on my ticket. HELL. NO. The number didn't match. I had 47 whereas the printed number was 42.

Oh! What a painful moment it was?

So instead of winning the full jackpot of fourteen million dollars, I had won close to twenty-three hundred dollars only. This mismatch of one number alone – 42 against 47 – deprived me of winning the full jackpot. This miniscule amount was of no use to me.

My very first reaction to this calamity was a silent cry, cursing myself, even the Almighty God, and everyone else around for what I had experienced, and how close I had come to seeing my life changed. God really had been very cruel to me, so I mumbled to myself. Time and time again, I cursed Him for bringing me so close to salvation and then pulling back all of His backing and support. Why? Oh ... Why? I needed just one more matching number. Why couldn't it be 47? Why 42? I kept hitting on the numbers printed in the newspaper as if the newspaper had intentionally done this to me.

After I calmed myself, I realized that no such cursing or complaining was ever going to change what had happened. Life had to move on. I had to face the day-to-day reality.

It took me a couple of days to recover from this monumental setback. My inner strength kick-started my physical, mental, and spiritual powers to fight my daily battles. The only word of consolation I got from Amy was that I wasn't destined to win. According to her, there was someone much needier than me who had rightfully won the jackpot.

Evidently, the Lady-luck didn't support me or some deity was dead set to see me go through all the pain and suffering and continue to live on a never-ending hope of a financial recovery. Hope, after all, was the only oar I had left to help me keep rowing my life's boat in very turbulent and choppy waters. I had both the patience and stamina to hold on to the oars in order to manoeuvre my boat sail steadily through these rough waters.

A persistent hope for the better kept the flame of my life's candle burning, lightening my way to a more fulfilling and sane times yet to come. Hope was the only catalyst driving my life.

***

"You are looking at a man who lost fourteen million dollars for just one darn mismatched number," I announced as I walked up to Jen's desk on Friday morning.

She looked at me, gave me a blank stare, and bewilderingly asked, "What are you talking about?"

"In the day before yesterday's 649 draw, I had five matching numbers," I stuttered. "Just missed the damn jackpot by one mismatch number – 42 against 47. How cruel the fate can be?"

"It's really disheartening," she replied in a sympathetic voice. "Still, you must have won some amount. How much did you get for five numbers?"

"Measly close to twenty-three hundred dollars," I replied. "This amount isn't going to salvage me ... pay off my debts."

I was in a way crying on her shoulder, looking for her full sympathy.

"I fully understand," she straightened her back. She said in a consoling tone, "You still won something. Winning is winning. Congratulations."

"Thank you." I replied.

I turned away from her desk in order to walk back to my room.

"Are you free this evening?" she called out. "I was just wondering if you could come to my place this evening. I want to talk with you. Or, say, I want to unload some of my stress."

"What's the matter? Are you all right? Is everything okay?" I showered her with question after question.

I was quite concerned about her well-being. I tried to read her face.

"Not really," she replied.

I noticed her face looked somewhat sad and pale.

"We will talk in the evening. Can you make it?" She asked.

"You shouldn't even ask this kind of question." I replied. "You know how co-dependent we have been and still are. Let me know when you are ready to leave. I will follow you."

After I sat on my chair and reached for the computer printouts, my mind and thoughts were focused on guessing Jen's stress rather than my work of the day. I kept thinking about the kind of stress she was likely going through.

I could hardly wait to hear what was stressing her.

CHAPTER FIFTEEN

As I turned my car on Jen's driveway, I saw her opening the garage door. She had slowly driven and parked her car inside the garage. I saw her put the key in the lock to open the door to enter the house. It was evident that her son, Josh, was not at home.

"Where's Josh?" I queried as soon as I was with her in the kitchen.

"He's at work – late night shift on Friday," she replied dimly. "You care to have a cup of coffee or any other drink – soft or hard, considering this is Friday evening."

"No, nothing for me," I replied. I spread my right arm over her shoulders. I gently pulled her body closer to me, and said, "I am here to share what's bothering you. Your sad face tells me something is really eating you inside."

"Thanks for coming over," she rested her head between my neck and the shoulder top, "I really wanted to talk with you not just on one, but a horde of issues," she woefully replied. She faced me eye-to-eye, placed her right hand on my shoulder, and added, "You are the only one I can share with my family related or personal issues. Let us just sit at the table."

We sat facing each other across the dining table.

"A few days ago, Josh told me that his father had to eat last weekend at the Sheppard of Good Hope located at Murray Street, and also he goes to Ottawa's food bank to take some free groceries. Even though Peter doesn't communicate with me, he keeps Josh up-to-date, knowing well that Josh, in turn, will convey the message to me. He is simply using our son to communicate with me."

She had started to unwound what had been eating her inside.

"How has he gotten to this stage?" I wondered aloud. "I thought he was an employee at the Rideau Center and was reasonably well-paid."

"Yes, but paid only at a minimum hourly wage rate," she clarified, "and you know one can't make a living on a minimum wage. He was sharing a room and paying half the rent. Now that his roommate has moved out, he's living alone and has to pay the full rent. He is hardly left with much cash to sustain his day-to-day life. Since all of his old credit cards have been cancelled, he can't apply for any new one because of his low income. Ever since I have heard this about how he's sustaining himself, I have really been disturbed. I still consider myself married to him. At times I even blame myself for causing all this misery to him."

"Your concern is natural, but you can't blame yourself for putting him in this situation," I consoled her. "As I see it, he himself is responsible for not only putting himself in this situation, but also for walking away from home, leaving you and Josh on your own. That really was a cowardly act, totally uncalled for. He's well educated. As a responsible and matured man, he should have put in every effort to upgrade his skills the moment he came to know that his employer was about to outsource his job. Complaining and sulking about the inevitable changes weren't going to help him. He should have paid attention and work hard to acquire marketable skills. You know how a person of any age without such skills is doomed these days, has no future not only for him, but also for those who depend on him. I think there's still time. He's only in his early fifties. He can turn things around provided he's willing to do what it takes to be gainfully employed."

"I am fully aware of all this," she nodded, "but who can teach him to do all this. This is all self-motivational. The guy is not that keen to go back to school or college in order to upgrade his skills. Now he has another reason. He's short of money – can't afford it. Even if he gets borrowed funds from any government source to upgrade his skills, he has to pay it back sooner or later. As I see it, not only he has ruined his own life by acting stupidly, but also of his family. His actions have impacted Josh as well. Like father, like son. Josh too has been unable to secure an admission to university because of his poor grades. Granted, Peter loves him and is in touch with him, but he still can't guide or monitor Josh's development on the phone. Since Josh doesn't communicate with me that much – maybe he thinks I haven't been good with his father – Peter's absence has really left him totally unchecked, hung dry. He does things in his own ways, or as guided by his peers. Now that he's earning money, I have a feeling that he has befriended a girl at the workplace, and is also smoking marijuana. I often smell it when he's talking close to me. I won't be surprised if one day he told me that he's married. And that would completely nail his life down without any future."

"Considering the age he's at, he is likely looking for some love, affection, and companionship with his peers including his girlfriend – any void that your poor relationship with Peter has likely left in his life." I tried to rationalize Josh's behaviour. "Right now he's leading a life with no parental care, and meandering his way through all these critical turns at adolescence."

"I understand," she nodded, "but you know how Peter and I – each one of us – had to fight for our individual survival. He was totally lost in job search and finding his own identity whereas I kept tending to my struggles as the primary breadwinner. I treated you as my support and managed to fight my battles, but Josh had nobody. Now I feel what he must have gone through. Obviously we didn't act as good parents and raise our son with proper care and supervision like you and Amy have been raising Sarah and Kerry. Parents' roles do help nurture and raise good and well-behaved children, focused on their studies and career paths. I am sure Sarah and Kerry know what each one wants to do. By the way, how's Sarah doing? Has she gotten admission to university?"

"Yes, she has," I replied, "but with a lot of conditions. As you know she has been good with her studies, always got excellent grades, and is perfectly bilingual. She wanted to pursue her studies in law at one of the four major universities of Canada – McGill, Queen's, Toronto, or Vancouver. I told her I couldn't afford to pay for her residence and other expenses out of Ottawa. She brooded for a while. Both Amy and I felt bad too. But there was nothing I could do. Luckily, Amy supported my decision. Eventually Sarah reluctantly agreed to join the University of Ottawa with a condition that I would let her complete her final semester at one of the European Universities – in France, or the United Kingdom."

"Would you be able to afford it?" she asked me bluntly. "You still have lots of debts to pay in spite of four consolidation loans you have already taken."

"True," I concurred with her. "All this indebtedness or the number of consolidated loans I have thus far taken, don't deter me to spend on my daughters' education, helping them to acquire all the possible skills to ensure well-paid career paths. Even if I have to take another consolidated loan to do it, I will not hesitate for a moment to do it. And by doing it, I am not doing them any favour either. As a parent, it's not only my responsibility, but also a moral obligation to see them grow as productive and contributory members of our society. If I can provide them a car to go to a high school, I can always provide them anything under the sky as long as it's within my reach. My job will not be complete until we as parents have seen them settled down with a job, in or outside of Ottawa, financially help them settle in their own living space. I simply don't want them to start their life like their parents did. They must have a debt-free start in life. What they do after is their business. As kids, they don't have to know my financial situation or how I am fulfilling their needs and wants. Their focus has to be on pursuing successfully their chosen careers. Helping them achieve their goal would be my greatest reward. Money comes and goes, but any missed opportunity to help a child at the right moment is never going to come back. To me, producing children is not a big deal or a challenge; the real challenge is to nurture and raise them with proper education and skills so that they and their potential families can make a good start. Borrowing for such a noble and worthwhile cause, and that too for one's own children, shouldn't ever enter any parent's mind."

"It's all laudable. I am really impressed," she commented. "I really get nervous, even scared at times, when I have to use credit or borrow from my line of credit. You know ever since Peter left me, I have been piling up debts too. Now I have to worry about Josh's future. Even if he's not going to any university, I will still have to pay for his continuing education likely at the Algonquin College, which by coincidence, is much closer to our home. This should save me a lot in both transportation and out-of-city living cost."

"Has he decided what he plans to do?" I queried out of interest.

"I have no clue," she retorted, "I am sure he'll tell me at some point, especially when he needs money. Who knows? Like you, I may have to borrow to finance his education."

"Well, borrowing isn't a sin that you have to be nervous about or scared of, and that too for your son's future," I remarked. "As long as you pay it back without a hassle. We both know that using borrowed money is tantamount to using one's future income with some added interest cost. There eventually comes a point in a lifecycle stage when expenses are way less than income and one can pay off all the debt outstanding."

"You know I have often wondered how you have managed to survive with load after load of indebtedness, and still maintain stability of mind, focus on job, business, and maintenance of home, and above all, keep your lust and libido alive. Normally, a stress of any kind kills ones libido or sexual performance, but not in your case. I shouldn't be saying it, but as a woman, I can testify that you're one hell of a seductive pumper. I know you have kept me going for all these years."

"Thank you for boosting my male ego." I bowed my head a bit. "Don't ever forget, you too have been contributing to our lasting and fully satisfying sexual relationship. You know darn well that such a relationship is always a two-way street where participants adjust to each other's needs," I shot back. "I will tell you some other time how I managed to live with indebtedness and kept my sanity. Tonight is not the time to get into those details." I placed my right open palm on top of hers, and added, "You know all about our initial agreement, commitment to satisfy each others physical and sexual needs to make each of us energetic enough to fight our daily battles. Granted, over time, we have become so dependent on each other – physically, spiritually, and emotionally. We may not have lived as a married couple under the same roof, but we have lived one hell of a mutually-supportive life. I am by no means ashamed of it."

"Neither I am," she interjected. "Moreover, what's there to be ashamed of? As two human beings, we chalked out our own way. Unwavering support of one another in both high and low times has been the adhesive that kept the relationship going; over time, sex between us became secondary."

She whole-heartedly defended our sexual liaison and steadily increasing co-dependence.

"Why are we getting so nostalgic?" I asked her light-heartedly. "I thought you wanted to share what has been stressing you out. Now that I know it was all about Peter and Josh and your concern about their likely future on which you have almost no control, I would only suggest that don't let that bog you down. There isn't much you can do. They both have to fight their own battles. You can at the most provide each one of them some financial support."

I tapped her open palm still placed on the table top. I pushed back my chair to stand up and leave.

She leaned forward and firmly squeezed my palm. She gave me a pleading and sad look.
Her face turned very pale, eyes glistened, and she stuttered, "I haven't yet told you the real reason I invited you this evening. Sit down for a while," she ordered me.

"And that is?" I queried nervously as I sat back on the chair.

"I ... have ... a ... breast cancer," she eventually spit out.

"*What?*" I shrieked out. I kept shaking my head in total disbelief. "When did you learn about it?" I kept gazing her face. I sat frozen on the edge of my seat.

"Yes. My doctor told me a couple of days ago," she calmly replied.

She was still bluntly gazing my face, seeking some sympathetic and supportive response from a person who had been a pillar of support to her.

"I am truly sad to hear that," I sputtered out. I pressed her palm more firmly. "Oh ... no ... Jen ... it ... can't ... be ... true." I finally jumped out of my chair and rushed to her side.

I encircled her upper back with my arms. She rested the side of her face between the lower portion of my stomach and the crotch. She placed her arms around my lower waist. She sat still while I softly moved my palm over her coiffed hair.

"How come you have known all about it for a couple of days and you are telling me tonight?" I wailed.

"I didn't want to tell you at work," she whispered, "because I didn't want you to be shocked at work and let others know about my condition. We still have to focus on our work and manage our lives, including our families."

"Don't worry; you will be all right." I whispered, still moving my open palm over her head. "I am sure it can be cured as medical science has made a lot of progress in treating cancers, especially the breast cancer."

"No, the doctor told me that it's quite at an advanced stage," she commented with her face still resting on my lower body. "It has been spreading fast in both breasts. He estimates I may at the most live for another couple of years."

"That's still an estimate," I repeated, and tapped the top of one of her shoulders. "Your doctor's estimate can go wrong too."

"I know." She now looked at me. "The bottom line is that I am not going to be around for too long. Now you know the reason why I have been going over our life this evening." She looked up at me with a grin. She was likely pretending that this whole episode was too light and not really that worrisome.

"I am going to need you as long as I live." She added, and pressed her face more firmly against my body. "Promise me you will be with me in my final moments."

"I will always be with you," I assured her. I slowly moved my hand over her back, trying to soften her pain and fear. "I am really and truly sad to see you in this situation. Please don't hesitate to let me know if there's anything I can do for you, including driving you to a doctor or hospital for any tests or treatment," I added, assuring her of my undivided attention and commitment she needed.

"Thanks for the offer," she whispered. She removed her hands from my waist, also her face away from my body, and added, "I haven't yet told anyone in the family including Josh, Peter, not even my parents. You are the first one to know and please keep it to yourself. Nobody at work should know about my condition. I would like to carry on as if nothing has happened. Since you are with me at work, I can always ask you to drive me for any medical appointments or tests or treatment as these take place during the regular business hours. I know I can depend on you."

"Without a doubt," I assured her.

I fully embraced her upper body, and kissed her forehead. I could see her welled-up eyes, tears strewing down her beautiful face, a face that had kept me going through all kinds of pains and tribulations for years and years. I could see her uncontrolled tears streaming over her cheek-bones, down to the arcs of her neck, soaking the top edges of her blouse, but I had no nerve or strength to wipe or dry these – even though in normal times, I would have nipped these in bud. She was too precious to me to see her shed a tear.

Unfortunately, it was the reason and ill timing behind these tears that had totally drained my strength to help her out in this most harrowing moment. I let her emotions flow – even if she was seeking solace from a person whom she herself had shielded from all sorts of ill winds.

While driving home I kept watching on my mental screen the flashes of times Jen and I had spent together. We had been supporting one another in both good and bad times for more than twenty-five years. Granted, we were colleagues, and I had liked her and wanted to bed her ever since the day we joined the office. It was a bad luck or a coincidence that we both were scorned by our respective souses. As a result, we made an unwavering commitment to sexually satiate each other, something really essential to keep our sanity, job, and health to fight our battles, and over time, became really co-dependent. Even though we were not a married couple, we still managed to live like a couple, close confidantes, and always ready to rub each others back on both work related and personal issues. And now she was struck with a terrifying and terminal disease, allowing me to have her companionship for another couple of years at the most.

Not only she became a victim of totally unexpected terminal disease, I also became a victim of her indisposition. From now on, I wasn't going to be able to have sex with her – sex that had kept me energized to face all sorts of personal and financial problems. I wondered how I was going to manage without her as an intimate, supportive, and trustworthy friend.

She at least knew for how long she was likely going to live in pain and suffering whereas I, on the other hand, had no clue for how many years I was going to continue to live a painful life without her. Even though our source of pain was different, but still pain was a pain. I had to find a coping mechanism. I could see my work as the only possible refuge.

Then my attention turned to Jen's son, Josh. How was her sickness going to affect him? As a teen, still at the threshold of starting his post-secondary education, he might or might not be able to finish his studies before his mother's demise. The future of this poor kid was already not that bright, and now, with his mother's terminal sickness, it looked more and more pathetic.

With his mother now facing certain death, he wouldn't have any more financial support left to pay for his education. And if he were to continue working on low wages, flipping hamburgers, and over and above, say, he got married out of sheer want of love and affection, and had a family of his own, it was a sure bet that not only would he be heading for a divorce, but also would be certain to lead a life in abject poverty. Even though he never got along with his well-earning mother, he still had his financial needs met. He was not only losing his mother, but also the likely prospects of making a decent living by his inability to acquire the right mix of skills he would need to land a good lasting job.

I didn't think he had learnt any lesson from the failures of his father. Perhaps, he was abandoned at a much earlier age. Father's love and affection on the phone must have served him right during those early years. But when he really needed his father for a proper guidance and support, he wasn't around. I really felt bad for Josh.

Even if I wanted to tell Josh as to what was likely going to happen to him over the coming years, I couldn't do it because Jen had particularly stopped me doing it. I had to respect her wishes.

In the same vain, I thought of Peter who was likely going to lose his estranged wife. Even though they had lived apart for years, they still were a couple – not yet legally divorced. As a couple, not only they owned a son, but also a property that I was sure Peter would move into or sell it after Jen's death.

I couldn't help thinking about Jen. At the time she married Peter – a well-educated man with a potentially good future – she must have loved him. She had agreed to spend her life with him. She must have had some great expectations about the kind of good, loving, and prosperous life she would have with her chosen partner. Nothing wrong with that as women, compared to men, always married with much higher expectations. I was quite certain that she never ever expected the kind of life she ended up spending without a man she once so loved.

It was ironic to see what the time cycle had done to this couple. I didn't think any one of them had ever expected that their family unit would break, not due to any fault of theirs, but strictly due to the kind of changes that had swept the labour market affecting, and even eliminating, certain jobs altogether over a very short span.

Peter must have been happy to finish certification in computer technology as it was in vogue at the time. What he likely failed to realize was that this technology changed so swiftly, and if one didn't keep skills up-to-date, one was bound to lose one's ability to hold on to a job in this field.

Coupled with this tidal wave of change in technology was another dramatic change of rising globalization which had instigated manufacturers in economically advanced countries to start minimizing their production costs, or increase their margin of profit by contracting out several computer and other labour-intensive jobs to countries with relatively low labour costs.

It wasn't just Peter, but millions of others like him who became victims of these turbulent changes in the labour market. They all either lost their job for which they were likely trained or settled for one at much reduced wages. And the loss of job meant not only a loss of earnings, the primary source of one's family income, but also a loss of self-esteem, more stress, increased dependence on credit, and in extreme cases, dissolution of one's family unit. These changes in fact crashed hopes and lives of millions and millions of families caught totally ill prepared to face the challenges of a new labour market and the economic upturn.

Peter turned out be just one of these unfortunate ones. The saddest part was that he himself was to be blamed for not only his own suffering, but for running away from his family, destroying both his wife's and son's life by shirking his responsibility as the primary breadwinner of the family. Had he kept his skills up-to-date and found another well-to-do job, he would have preserved his family unit in tact. This in turn might even have saved Jen succumbing to cancer. Who knew?

***

"Robert Vaughan here," I spoke in an authoritative tone as I picked up the phone at work.

"Hi, Mr. Vaughan," the caller responded and identified himself, "this is Ed Holt, one of the loan managers at FI-I. How are you this afternoon?"

"Just fine," I responded, "How can I help you?" I thought he was one of our data users and wanted some information on personal bankruptcies.

"Mr. Vaughan, the reason I am calling is to inform you that in order to help you manage your financial needs, our financial institution has approved a home equity line of credit for you," he explained to me in his slow and sweet tone.

"I don't think I even asked for it, or ever applied for it at your institution," I replied instantly.

"True, you haven't applied for it," he concurred, "but we as loan managers periodically review records of our card holders as well as of those carrying loans with us. I have noticed that you have been making a minimum payment on one of your VISA cards. You know it will take you more than your lifetime to pay off the balance outstanding on your card if you simply continued to make a minimum payment. I thought you might like to payoff the card by using funds from this newly created line of credit, or you can make a partial payment and use remaining funds for your future needs. Since we are here to help our clients, we are always looking for ways to help them, especially when it comes to financing their personal and family needs."

"How much is this home equity line of credit worth?" I impatiently asked.

I didn't want to carry on with this sort of conversation, and that too involving my finances, out in the open public environment.

"It's fifteen thousand dollars." He replied. "If you want, you can pay off twelve thousand dollars currently outstanding on your card and keep the other three for future use. Keep in mind though that this line of credit comes with a life insurance up until you are seventy-five years old, and your monthly minimum payment on this account will include the cost of insurance premium. You will also be given cheques to help you draw funds from this line of credit in order to pay other bills or obligations. Above all, the cost of borrowing from such line of credit is way too low compared to what you would normally pay on regular credit cards. The only catch here is that the interest charged on these funds varies and is tied to the latest prime rate plus two percentage points. What do you say?"

"Sounds good to me," I replied in a more pleasant tone.

By this time, I had figured out the reason he was calling. I had two VISAs with this institution: one in Canadian dollars for day-to-day use, and the other in US dollars for business use. And both of these had high balances outstanding.

"When can I come to sign the paper?" I finally inquired.

Considering my dire financial situation, I badly wanted access to any amount of readily available cash.

"You can come anytime tomorrow. I will have the paperwork done." He happily cut off the connection.

Since this wasn't the first time I had a line of credit established, I wasn't that over-excited to have immediate access to another fifteen thousand dollars. This amount was just a drop in the ocean of debt that I had been floating in, with water waves hitting at times my nostrils, making me gasp for air to breathe.

I realized that this loan manager was simply doing his job. He wasn't doing me any favour, but simply generating more business and revenue for his employer. This 'do good' deed would give him more brownie points and help him earn a promotion after exploiting the most vulnerable debtors like me.

Even though I didn't like the concept of paying a monthly premium on mandatory life insurance on any card or loan balance outstanding, as this always gainfully worked for the lender and protected all of its loaned capital. As a borrower, however, I had no choice, but to abide by the terms and conditions of the loan I had accepted.

Jen likely overheard the conversation.

No sooner had I finished talking to the loan manager, she barged into my room,

"Was he the guy from the financial institution FI-I selling home equity line of credit?" She wanted to know.

"Yes. Why do you ask?" I questioned her.

"Because he sold me one too yesterday," she quipped. "He offered me the same amount of fifteen thousand dollars."

"Interesting, the guy seems to be doing his job well," I added. "I am sure there are many like us out there looking for cheaper credit."

***

"You know years ago, I had almost left you," Amy sputtered out of the blue while we both were in our bedroom. We were getting ready to turn in after a long day. I had just finished buttoning up my night shirt.

"What do you mean?" I lightly mumbled. I gave her a sharp pensive look. I was hoping to hear her complete sentence.

"I mean for all intent and purposes, I was ready to move out." She had rolled her white cotton nighty from her neckline down to her knees. "Even though I was physically here, but mentally and emotionally, I was out of these four walls." She finally completed her sentence as she sat on the edge of her side of the bed.

"You don't have to tell me this as I have known all along how emotionally far apart we have been for quite some time. The way you sleep at a distance from me tells it all." I reinforced her claim by the factual evidence that she could hardly refute.

I sat on the lone chair placed in the corner of the bedroom, fidgeting with the sleeves of its arms.

"That's interesting. You have been reading me so well," she sneered at me. "Considering the kind of self-centered life you lead, I didn't think you would ever notice the widening emotional gulf between us."

"True, I have been so immersed in fighting my own battles," I concurred with her, "but that doesn't mean I am totally oblivious to what has been happening between us. Ever since you started singing praises of your well-liked colleague, and also started to belittle me more than I really deserve, I have let you live your own life. You are an independent woman. You know what you are doing."

"I wish I knew," she murmured. "I wouldn't be discussing the issue tonight."

"Is something the matter? You want to talk about it?" I looked at her, almost invading her eyes. Silently, I was inviting her to open up and share with me what was bothering her.

"Let me put it this way: one looks for something better than one has at hand," she replied, with her eyes now searching for something she had lost on the light blue bed-sheet. "I was happy when I met this colleague of mine. He always lent me his shoulder to lean on. Over time, however, he has started to reveal his true self, his beliefs, gender bias, and his personality traits. The more I learn about him, especially as a potential long-term friend or even a partner, the more I am turning away from him. I am so used to the way you have been treating me with so much care and compassion, even making sure that I am fully insulated against any heat of day-to-day squabbles – financial or else in nature. You have really treated me no less than a queen of this castle. No, when I look at all the pluses and minuses, I have realized that what I have at hand is much better than what I have been pursuing. I am sorry it took me all that time to figure it out. ... Mind you, as an independent woman, I had to try to change my lot."

She had rested her case.

She was now waiting for my response – condoning or disapproving her actions, and her eventual choice.

"Thank you for honestly sharing your thoughts," I calmly replied. "And, thank you for opting to stay with me despite all my limitations, weaknesses, and vulnerabilities. There really has been no issue between us except our lack of cash flow, which in turn, has soured our relationship, my communication with you and the children. I have been trying hard to find a source supplementing our income so that I can pay off my monthly obligations without accessing borrowed funds. In my heart, you are still a beautiful woman I loved and married, and have blessed us with two loving and adorable daughters. I didn't let you leave me even when you tried to move out years ago because I still love to see your beautiful smiling face, still good enough to make my day. It's rather unfortunate that I haven't seen that smile for ages."

"I am fully aware of that," she interrupted me, "but it's your day-to-day cold attitude towards me that has really pushed me away from you. I understand you have been too worried about money matters and trying very hard to be the best provider and caretaker, but as a woman, I need your attention, care, affection, emotional support, and above all, physical and sexual satisfaction. Show me any woman who hasn't spent any private moments with her husband outside the walls of her home for close to twenty-five years. Indeed, patience has limitations. I did venture out looking for a better companion, better life. I don't think anyone can blame me for that. I haven't been successful – that's my lot. Maybe we are destined to live with each other. If that's the case, then we definitely need to adjust to each other's needs and try to re-connect. You know when I really look at the situation I am in, I hold you responsible. You are the one who has pushed me into it."

Her voice began to tremor. She was just about to sob. I could see moist corners of her eyes. She was visibly moved.

"You know that turning back the clock isn't going to be that simple," I calmly replied. "It will take time and a lot of understanding. We will have to learn to trust each other. How do I know that tomorrow you won't find another man to try out with as I am still no good to you? Does that mean that after few months or years, I would be listening to the same soggy story that I heard tonight? I think let's give ourselves some time to heal. Let's not do anything that would create any problem for the kids as they are in the midst of working on their careers. Right now we can simply let bygone be bygone, and live our routines including looking after our kids and business. I still depend on you to take care of its public relations side, including answering of any phone calls."

"There haven't been that many lately," she lamented. "I personally don't think we are reaching anywhere with this business. I don't think we are even recovering our day-to-day costs, let alone any profit. You seem to be working for nothing, really."

"You are right," I fully concurred with her. "Indeed there are times when I question myself why I am wasting time on this business with very little potential to succeed. Then I convince myself that this business, like any other, needs time to find its niche in the market. Even though we have no money to promote its reach to a wider segment of buyers, I still firmly believe in my own efforts to make it run successfully one day. Put simply, it has become an albatross for me. It's challenging my male ego. You know me. I don't give up anything that easily. It's part of my personality."

"It's a good personality trait," she replied in a more controlled and strong voice.

She likely had gotten over her personal ordeal.

"You should apply this trait, nonetheless, on something that you think would result in some more tangible returns, not necessarily monetary, but also that will give you some sense of personal accomplishment, help you savour the returns to hard work and devotion," she suggested.

"What are you alluding to?" I impatiently cut her off.

I sensed she wanted me to pursue something else in order to supplement our income.

"I mean you have been a good analytic writer at work for all these years. You can use your writing skills to write a fiction or a non-fiction under your own name and make money instead of trying to run a business you don't know much about. You will at least be doing what you really like. As far as I know you, writing makes you happy. It's your real passion. Why not pursue it and do something more creative and constructive rather than spending time and effort on selling a few books, and that too on some knowledge acquired from textbooks on business or magazines. I think we all will be better off if you did something you are passionate about. That's just my suggestion. I know in the end, you will do whatever you alone would decide."

"Thank you for your suggestion to write a book," I graciously accepted her suggestion with a broad smile. She had pumped me sky high. "And above all, thank you for reminding me about where my real passion lies. Keep in mind though that any return on a privately published book will take time, and even there, there really is no guarantee. It's still worth a try. What can happen at the most? Like all of my other ventures, this may also fizzle out."

"You may be right," she replied. She lay on her side of the bed. "Time alone will tell. If you are destined to earn a supplementary income, you will; and if not, then it isn't going to happen no matter how hard you try," she sagely remarked.

She switched off the nightlight closer to her pillows.

I was still sitting at the chair, watching her dishevelled black hair curled around her upper back. Since we had been sharing the bed as two strangers who simply needed a few hours of sleep to freshen up to face the next day's challenges, Amy had stopped putting any effort to get properly dressed before hitting the sack.

Any normal mid-age woman wanting to be close to her husband, on the other hand, would have likely worn sexy lingerie, or a short sexy negligee, brush her hair, and spray herself a few touches of perfume to entice her husband for a lovemaking session, or even just for a quickie before getting lost in a dreamland.

I, on the other hand, would change into my pyjamas and lie down on my side of the bed. Even occasionally if I ever wanted to have sex with her, I had to kill my desire because I knew she wasn't going to be a willing participant, or I would be rebuffed. And I hated to have sex with a cold fish, or against a woman's wishes. And at times when she agreed to have sex, it would be obligatory rather than out of passion for one another. It was like a married woman relenting to let her husband quickly get over his arousal. Over time, I had gotten used to her silent treatment as well as rebuffs – especially after she began her affair with her colleague.

What she had suggested tonight, however, made perfect sense to me. Our business wasn't generating any income – not even recovering its running cost. We were unable to promote it because of its shoe-string budget, and that too drawn from different lines of credit, or credit cards. So instead of making any net income, we were increasing our debt liability. In the beginning I considered it as all a part of short-term pain for a long-term gain, but this process couldn't last forever. It had started affecting the monthly minimum payments.

And the final nail in the coffin was the advent of Internet in the nineties. Now almost every bit of information, research papers, and other material on personal development was freely accessible at various sites. Why would one pay for something downloadable from a given site at no charge? This downloading and online access had turned away hordes and hordes of paying-shoppers from several businesses, eventually forcing many to close their business or declare bankruptcy.

Our small mail-order business, with no financial support, had no chance in hell to survive in this newly automated and highly competitive market of books, videos, audios, and CD-ROMs. Even my research efforts, the ones I was so proud to offer to our clients, turned pale and ineffective compared with what people could find with one click of a button at one of these Internet sites. One simply needed a few key words to start the research process.

In my heart, I really thanked Amy for drawing my attention to what was really happening to our business and its likely doomed future. I, on the other hand, still strongly believed that I would eventually pull it through one day and make it a success story. I must have been a high class fool, still nurturing my own baby on borrowed money.

What really changed my thinking and forced me to close it was the day-to-day news about the speed in which well-established businesses were closing down, putting their employees and their families into serious economic hardship. I thanked the Lord that for me, closing the business was not that painful or costly because it was my secondary activity – working only during evenings, weekends, and holidays.

Her suggestion about writing a book of my own baffled me a little. Granted, I knew how to write. I loved writing. I had a great passion for it. But what could I write on? At my job, I had done a lot of analytic writing analyzing finances, including indebtedness, of households in Canada and those in the United States and other advanced European countries. I didn't want to write any text book on this or related topics including distribution of income or income inequality in general.

I kept mulling and mulling over the type of book I should be writing until my eyelids got heavier and heavier. I got up from the chair and moved to lie on my side of the bed.

A sudden surge of desire to simply hold Amy in my embrace shook my entire body. I stretched my hand to place on her mid-riff before pulling her over. I wanted to hold her and softly kiss her just to express my appreciation for her very helpful suggestion she had offered this evening. I had no desire to go all the way to poke her.

I pulled my hand back to my side and let her stay asleep. I had controlled my emotions in time. It was too early to have any physical contact with her after what we had gone through this evening. I didn't think she was ready to receive me either. We both needed a healing that time alone would do.

***

"So how did the appointment go?" I asked Jen.

I was driving her back to the office after her medical appointment at the Ottawa Cancer Assessment Clinic.

"As one would expect," she replied with a shrug. "Doctor wants me to go through all kinds of treatment including radiation, chemotherapy, and oral drugs. Any surgery is ruled out because the cancer has spread in both the breasts as well as in the periphery of my lungs. I am just wondering if any of the proposed treatments is really worth it. We all know the end result – the almighty death that no treatment can stop."

"True, but we still should have the proper treatment and hope for the best," I counter-argued.

"Sorry, I don't see any sense in going through any of the recommended treatments when in the end I am just going to live for a few more months. I might as well die at the earliest opportunity before becoming bed-ridden and dependent on a family member, or a friend. Look, how I am making you go out of your way, almost forcing you to drive me around. I don't want you to take care of me or be at my service round the clock. I still have a husband who is no good, a son who has no time, and parents who live far away in Hamilton. Under these circumstances, what good it is for me to extend my life?" She vehemently put on her brave face.

"It's not the time to dwell on your circumstances," I advised her. I placed my hand on her shoulder, and added, "Just don't worry about anything. Do whatever pleases you because in the end, you live with your own choices and decisions. And, don't worry about me. As I promised you, I will do the best to help you out and be with you as long as it's within my reach. We have been good friends, firmly supporting one another for a little over a quarter of a century. You don't know how much I love you and care for you. I get chills even at the thought of losing you."

"I know that," she replied. She placed her left palm on my right thigh, and muttered softly, "I feel the same for you. But nothing is in my control. However, you still have a family to look after. So be realistic. You can't be around me all the time."

"By the way, speaking of my family, I want to tell you that Amy is done with her colleague," I sputtered out.

"What? How did that happen?" She snarled. "Has she been jilted?"

"No. I think it's the other way round." I sounded like a devil's advocate. "She has opted to get out of the relationship as she didn't like her friend's true colours including some of his personality traits. As she put it to me, she has decided to live with the one at hand rather than risk living with a new found one. According to her, I treat her like a lady, a queen of her castle, have given her full independence, and have never bothered her about any issue ranging from managing a home to fulfilling of the kids' needs. She has been leading a carefree life."

"Indeed you are a nice person. I would say too nice," she added. "Too bad she came to this realization after that long. Why do you think I have been with you for all these years? Any woman with a right head on her shoulders would have done the same."

"Stop saying that, Jen," I pled with her. "I am just an ordinary man who happens to treat a woman with all the care, decency, and curtsey. And when it comes to financials, I make sure I don't bother my spouse and demand or make any claim on her money. I let her fully control her hard-earned money whereas I, as the primary breadwinner, control mine to manage home and needs of my family members. Even though we are two earners in the family, I have been managing home and paying from my own earnings for everything except groceries. I have never ever asked Amy to chip in for any regular or unexpected family expenditure. This is likely one of the reasons that I have spent my life on credit, paying one consolidated loan after another. And the life is not over yet. I don't know how many more loans I have yet to take."

"That's what really intrigues me." She gave me a penetrative look and continued, "You remember I asked you once before about how you have managed life paying one debt after the other. It really bothers me and makes me nervous anytime I use credit. I think by using credit I am digging my own grave; the more credit I take, the deeper I go under, and more likely I am to stumble while re-paying it. Now that I am just about to die, I just want to ensure that I die debt-free. It hasn't been easy to manage a home on one income."

"I fully understand how you feel," I sympathized with her. "Personally, though, I don't think using credit to fulfil one's needs or as a stop-gap measure to resolve a cash-flow problem is all that bad provided one handles credit responsibly and not frivolously. It's not like I take credit on one hand, and then declare bankruptcy on the other in order to avoid paying it back. My thinking and attitude about using credit is way different than of many others because I work as a professional in this area and consider repaying any debt as my moral obligation. I have been earning well enough to make the necessary monthly minimum payments to protect my credit rating. I never defaulted even when I was at the lowest ebb. As a result, I have never been contacted by any agent of a credit or any collection agency reminding me to make any missed payment. I think I once told you that as far as I am concerned, using credit is no different than using one's future income as I am paying every cent of it back to the lender with additional cost as interest on borrowed funds. With this stringent thinking about treating credit as future income, I don't get nervous when I use credit or request any consolidated loan. To answer your question more specifically, three key factors kept me going on this credit path: first, my well-paid stable job, enabling me to make minimum payments; second, owned home with steadily rising equity, enabling me to use it as a collateral for more and larger loans; and third, my undying patience and hope that one day my life will take a turn for the better. I have used my own money – current or future – in all such transactions. Mind you, as a professional educated consumer, on the other hand, I always felt bad and even uncomfortable each and every time I sought a loan. So from that perspective, I feel no different than you when it comes to seeking credit. I also would like to die debt-free."

"I understand your rationale behind treating borrowed funds as using future income, and I have been living with it too," she interrupted me. "What I want to know is how you personally felt about debt's day-to-day ramifications, fears, inability to focus on more important issues, etc."

"Seriously, I would be lying if I ever told you that living on borrowed funds had been totally worry-free, or has no repercussions on my day-to-day life, or the thinking process, or on my personal goals. You know when one owes money and constantly thinking about its repayment, one's mind is very much distracted, which in turn, certainly affects one's ability to focus on accomplishing life's other goals, on day-to-day work performance, and on and on. This distraction can also breed fright and fear that can make one to live a life of a timid and low self-esteemed person. You know the adage that a deep or heavy pocket makes a person happy and more confident whereas an empty or thin pocket not only weakens the person, but also robs one of all the human dignity and peaceful and happy living. Also, this distraction is likely to cause mental stress and other health related issues, which may even enforce a person to perform below one's real potential. To tell you the truth, this financial stress and its associated worries have been affecting my work performance. Even though in the eyes of everyone around, I have been a very creative and productive analyst-cum-writer, but the fact is that I haven't been performing at my full potential. This has been my greatest regret."

"I can't believe what I am hearing," she replied with her jaws open. "You of all people around saying that you haven't been able to perform at your full potential is incredible. What else would you have done? The entire department is impressed with your creative contribution and productivity. And here you are telling me that you have been under-performing."

"Well, you wanted to know the truth about how I have been feeling," I retorted, still seeking her affirmation. "Now that I have told you, there really is no reason for you to distrust me. I firmly believe that all human beings should perform according to their real potential; not to do that is really sinful, or a crime committed wilfully."

"I never think about such things," she acknowledged. She shook her head sideways. "What would you have done if you had lived without any stress or distraction?" she wondered aloud.

"I could have pursued a side career as a writer and written a book," I replied calmly. "In that case, no one else would have suggested for me to do it."

"Now who has suggested you to do it?" she questioned me.

"Amy," I promptly replied. "She thinks I am wasting my time and effort on a business that has no chance in hell to lift off successfully. Now that almost everything is available on the Internet, no one is going to order any product from us. She wants me to close this business and focus on writing my own books."

"I think she has a good point here," she crowed. "To be honest with you, I myself have been thinking for quite some time to persuade you to start writing books of your own. You are a good writer, have a strong passion to write. Why not try your luck in this area instead of spending time, efforts, and resources on something you know very little about? I think Amy has given you a good suggestion. That also shows that not only she wants to remain your partner, but is also encouraging you to do what's good for you. Don't you think she is sincerely trying to help you find more stable means of supplementing income that you have been so desperately looking for?"

"True," I confessed, "but earning any money from a book isn't a sure shot. I earnestly want money now."

"There's no guarantee of anything in life," she promptly corrected me. "We still have to take a chance and do our best to accomplish our goal. You know these things better than I do. Why can't you accept it as another challenge? What's the hitch?"

"I have no problem complying with both yours and Amy's wish," I replied submissively. "Right now the problem is to pick some meaningful and saleable subject matter with an eye-catching title. Can you suggest any?"

"You're such a creative person," she parroted, "I am surprised you are asking me to suggest the subject matter and the title. As a starter, you can write on Canadian households in debt – a topic in your professional alley – elaborating on their different sources of debt including mortgages, use of credit cards, different lines of credit, and how do they manage to repay these back, stresses and strains they feel, and so on. Or, you could write on the changing face of our labour force – how both the technology and different trade agreements among developed and developing countries have been affecting workers all over the world. I can go on and on. The bottom line is that you write on a subject matter you know well and feel comfortable writing about."

"I don't want to write any thing in a textbook format," I argued with her. "As you know, the market is already saturated with such books. Many publishers have now stopped printing textbooks. Nonetheless, these are still open to printing fictions and non-fictions of personal, financial, political, or historical significance."

"Go for the fiction as a starter then," she drew the conversation to close as we had entered our official parking lot. "And, good luck." She got out of the car and slammed its door behind.

We both were now silently walking to our office.

***

Since my financial reserves, including the latest line of credit offered by FI-I, were shrinking with each and every day, my desperation to find a source to supplement income was crossing the bounds of my patience and tolerance. I knew I had to soon look for another consolidation. The only remaining unknown was to pick the financial institution willing to lend me the amount I was still somewhat vague about. There were still some months left to pay off the last consolidated loan, besides paying for the mortgage on the house, its property taxes, and several other monthly bills and debt obligations.

To buy myself some time, I decided to look for a part-time sales job during evenings and weekends. Now that I had run a mail-order business selling books in print and on audios, I thought I had gained enough knowledge and insight about books in vogue, their publishers, and also could conduct a meaningful conversation with potential customers about the upcoming new and old well-known authors.

I was quite confident that any bookshop would be happy to hire a person knowledgeable about books and magazines. Above all, I had experience of running a business for ten years, even though my clientele included largely public libraries across Canada.

Carrying an abbreviated version of my résumé, highlighting knowledge and experience relevant only to this part-time sales job, one evening I visited a local bookstore situated in a big mall. I spoke to the lady attending the cash register, explained the reason why I was there.

She looked at me from head-to-toe, and smilingly replied, "Sorry, the manager of this shop is away tonight. You can leave a copy of your résumé with me. She will contact you in a couple of days."

Days turned into weeks, and months and I didn't hear a word from the store manager. I realized I was never going to hear from this lady as I was likely a total misfit for that sort of public relations, customer pleasing, or customer enticing job. I, as a middle-age man, could never do a job to attract business what a pretty girl in her teens with a beautiful smile on her face could.

Moreover, I was a man with a serious and depressive look. Never mind the knowledge about books and authors I had. It was the personal presentation and appeal of sales rep that really mattered not only to this shop owner, but to all other vendors eager to sell their products and make money.

This rejection didn't really deter me. Even though I knew that I wasn't going to get any part-time job putting me up front or allowing me to interact directly with incoming customers, I decided to look for a job where I could work behind closed doors.

Coincidently, around the same period, I found an ad in the local paper that one of the local grocery stores owned by one of the nation's leading businesses was looking for part-timers over the weekends to help place produce including vegetables and fruits on shelves, or in baskets, or made-out open trays.

I thought it was an ideal job for me – working on the weekends and without coming in contact with customers. I was active and healthy enough to cart out boxes of produce from the store's warehouse, open them, and spread them at their marked locations. No exceptionally advanced skill was required to do this job. I had to submit a formal application along with a short résumé.

I seriously mulled over this job opening. True, I was in dire need of quick cash and this opportunity to earn it looked like a god-sent. When I sat down to draft my application and an abridged version of résumé for the job, I felt really miserable. I cursed myself. I found myself totally out of place.

What was I supposed to write in the application that I had such and such advanced degree and was currently holding a well-paid professional job with the federal government, earning even more than the company was likely paying to its high-level managers. Any one seeing such details would have thrown my application in a waste basket. Not only that, that person would have likely taken the whole thing as a joke, cursed me as well for wasting his/her time.

But I needed money to manage my day-to-day life; to keep the wolf away from my door. My financial circumstances had finally brought me this low that I was now ready to do any unskilled menial job.

I wrote the application in a broadly vague format, intentionally hiding facts about my education, current job and salary, and analytic papers that I had published and gained professional recognition. Half-heartedly, I mailed out the application.

Guess what? I didn't get any response to my application. Not a word from the potential employer.

Evidently, I wasn't considered good enough to carry and open boxes of produce and place these in marked trays. People making selection of candidates must have realized that I was over-qualified or totally unfit for this job. This hit me and my ego very badly. I really felt deeply bruised. Time and again I felt I was good for nothing. How low could I stoop to earn some extra money to run my life? Each and every effort of mine to earn it had thus far failed miserably. I wasn't reaching anywhere.

After I calmed down, I really appreciated the staff of the store for ignoring my application. Considering that these people were likely well experienced in recruiting staff on almost daily basis, they might have read my vague application accompanied by an equally vague résumé, conveying them my half-hearted desire to find a job with them.

By not responding to my application, they likely had done me a favour by silently protecting my professional dignity. I myself would have been embarrassed to tell them the truth about the real me.

Moreover, I didn't think I would have lasted there for too long either.

CHAPTER SIXTEEN

"Good afternoon, Mr. Vaughan," the loan manager at financial institution (FI-IV) greeted me with a broad smile. "Please be seated. How can I help you today?"

"I am here to seek a consolidated loan," I replied.

I could see a dossier under my name on the top of her desk. I had arranged to meet her a week in advance.

"As I look at your record, you still have a couple of month's payments left on your last loan of fifty-two thousand dollars that you took almost five years ago."

"Yes, I realize that," I humbly acknowledged. "I am just wondering if I can pay off the remainder of the previous loan from the new one I am requesting today."

"Certainly," she quipped, "there's no problem. You just have to file a new application. You know the amount you want?"

"I am looking for one hundred thousand dollars," I replied without a hitch. "This amount should be enough to not only pay off the balance of the previous loan, but also the remaining portion of the mortgage on the house as well as other outstanding balances on credit cards and lines of credit."

"Good thinking," she commented. "By taking a consumer loan, you can pay off the rest of the outstanding mortgage as well. Since you have been paying the mortgage on a weekly basis, you know you have been saving yourself a lot of interest. And now by paying the remainder, you are in fact saving a lot of interest charges. In fact, you are paying off the mortgage in eighteen instead of the conventional twenty-five year period."

"Well, you are the one who suggested to me to do it when I moved my mortgage from the financial institution FI-I to your institution," I pampered her. "If the system allows it, then why not use it? It's a plain common sense."

"If I am not mistaken, this is the third time you are seeking a consolidation loan from this institution." She reminded me after turning pages of my dossier.

"Actually, it's my fifth consolidation, third at this institution," I corrected her. "It's almost every five years that I have been seeking a consolidation loan. Since I have a serious cash flow problem, I more or less have been managing my life on such loans. There is always a convincing and legitimate reason that I have to ask for it. Besides the need to spend on some unexpected or unplanned expenditure, there is some looming in full view that as a responsible family provider, I have to fulfill. For example, this time, there's an urgent need to do some upgrading at home as it's eighteen years old now, and then I have to spend on post-secondary education of my daughters along with their job-related settlements away from home. It's all a part of being financially prepared for any move."

"So you are one of those who like to cash in equity in their home," she chided. "Now that you are going to have a mortgage-free home, its market value is all your equity, your saving for any future use or for retirement years. You are a rich man."

"I know what you are getting at," I interrupted her. "The media is also writing openly that homeowners are using their homes as automated teller machines (ATMs) to finance their needs. As I see it professionally, it's true and not true as well. True, in the sense that any rise in home equity is accessible and can be used as collateral to secure a bigger loan, and not true because cash in the form of loan available is not that free. Any loan one takes against equity as collateral, one has to pay back with interest. It's not like one withdraws money from ATM with or without a service charge."

"But you know we have a system where you can borrow money against home equity and don't pay back. Under the Canadian Homeownership Income Plan (CHIP), for which you would be eligible in a few years time, one can get up to fifty-five percent of one's equity in cash without paying back provided you hand over the ownership of your home. You and/or your spouse can still live in the house until you both die, or can re-gain the ownership by paying back the loan. Mind you it's a new scheme and only a fraction of the elderly homeowners use it."

She explained the CHIP program. I, nonetheless, was fully familiar with it because of my work involvement.

"If you personally ask me," I interjected her, "I would never ever think of using this program to hand over a mortgage-free house worth thousands and thousands of dollars and still likely to appreciate in value over time, just to have fifty-five percent of its current market value as interest-free cash. One would be foolish to divest one's life's major asset just for a petty cash one needs to finance one's planned or unplanned expenses. It's always better to keep the home as an asset and pass it over to the kids or any other family member as the transfer of home, as principal residence, is tax-free in Canada. Why not transfer the home to children or loved ones as a legacy? In my professional opinion, this whole plan is simply misleading and really robbing the financially vulnerable elderly home-owners."

"You seem to be quite knowledgeable," she commented. "Do you work with household finances, indebtedness and other debt related issues?"

"I am really ashamed to admit it," I embarrassingly replied, "I work and write about finances of households, and in the eyes of the media, I am one of the experts in the field, but look at me, I have not been able to manage my own finances. I have lived my life on borrowed money. Thank God, I earned well enough to pay back every cent of any loan I ever took, and that too, within my reach and affordability, and lived a dignified life in the eyes of everyone around. It could have been a real disaster for me, my family including our kids if I were not earning enough, or had borrowed more than I could pay back, or had turned to any private lender for help who, I am sure, would have eaten me alive by this time."

"Oh well, that's life." She exhaled and pushed herself against the back of her chair. "You know there are doctors who are well experienced to cure anyone's disease or sickness, but their own. So don't feel that bad. Who says life is sweet for us all; it leaves a bitter taste for many – even immutable scars." She paused and gazed all over my painful face. "Take this new application form and get it signed by your wife as well as she co-owns the house. We can meet tomorrow to finish the rest of the paperwork."

Before Amy fully changed to turn in for the day, I asked her, "Could you please sign the loan application that I want to return to the loan manager tomorrow?"

"Are you asking for a loan again?" she questioned me angrily. She held her long nighty close to her breasts. "I am really getting tired of signing these loan applications. Now, why do we need this loan?"

"Well, there are four reasons," I replied calmly. "First, we need to have reserve money not only to send Sarah abroad to finish her last semester of her degree, but also to send Kerry away out-west to pursue her higher education; second, to pay off the remaining little portion of the mortgage on the house; third, to do some upgrading in the house as it's getting old; and fourth, to pay off all other outstanding debts we owe to department stores, on credit cards, and lines of credit. Just imagine living in a mortgage-free home with some upgrading like installing a new fire place and a floor."

I had sweetened the offer in order to pacify her anger.

"How much are we asking this time?" She shot another question at me.

"One hundred thousand dollars," I replied slyly.

"That's quite a sum," she replied. "Do you think you can handle its payment besides all other monthly and annual obligations?"

"I wouldn't have asked for it if I thought I couldn't," I assured her. "Everything is taken care off."

"That much I know," she replied confidently as she pulled her nighty down to cover herself.

After she had opted to live with me, she appeared to have mellowed down a bit. I could sense she was now controlling her anger and frustration, even though there hardly was any change in her nagging attitude.

"I can't change your spending habits. Just give me the loan application," she demanded, "and show me where to sign it. You know what you are doing."

I placed the application on her dressing table; gave her the pen and showed her the place to sign.

While she was signing, I re-emphasized, "Aren't you happy that you are going to live in a mortgage-free house? Not only that, we will have sufficient funds for both Sarah and Kerry to wrap up their studies. As good parents, we don't have to give them the slightest of hint that we are unable to finance their needs, especially when it comes to pursuing their career paths. I think I have it all planned."

"You are good in planning such things," she replied, shrugging her shoulders. "I live day-to-day life. I am glad at least one of us thinks about the future. You are the one who promised to support both Sarah and Kerry to pursue their chosen career paths. What about the expenses on their upcoming weddings? Have you thought about it as well? Or, we will ask for another loan at the time?"

"Well, let's take one step at a time," I said and tapped her shoulder after she had imprinted her signature on the form. "I will do the best at the time of their marriage as well, even if it meant to take another loan. I want to see them happily settle down. I want to do everything in good taste and style. I will never ever give them the impression that their parents are unable to support any of their material needs and wants."

"I know you better than you do yourself," she remarked. She placed the pen on the dresser, and added, "You don't have to brag or impress me."

She walked to the washroom to change.

I put back the signed application in the brown manila envelope.

I was all set to face all of my forthcoming financial obligations. My biggest joy and heart-warming self-satisfying thoughts were that I was finally going to live in a mortgage-free house and was able to see my daughters successfully pursue their post-secondary education goals and careers – despite all of my financial worries, life on borrowed funds, and my miserable failures to find any source to supplement my income.

***

I was really glad that I had pre-arranged funds for my daughters' education. When Sarah was ready to fly out to Paris to complete her last semester, the French Embassy wanted to have assurance backed by my financial institution that I had enough funds for her travel, tuition, boarding and lodging and other day-to-day expenses while she lived as a student in Paris. She was not supposed to look for any employment in that city in order to finance her expenses.

Since I had my newly re-financed line of credit with no balance outstanding, the institution had no problem issuing a signed assurance, which in turn, helped Sarah to get a visa and other travel documents.

In the same way, when Kerry moved out to the west-coast, I was ready to spend any amount on our travel, and few nights stay at a hotel with daily incidentals, besides spending on Kerry's boarding and lodging, books and furnishings, and other incidentals. Before returning to Ottawa, Amy and I ensured that our daughter was settled comfortably at one of the student hostels in the campus to pursue her studies.

And when Kerry got back to Ottawa, she wanted a car to visit homes of clients as part of case studies she had to work on as a professional counsellor. Considering the importance of personal visits and above all to save her commuting time, I agreed to lease for her a small compact car available at the minimum monthly payment.

One day, I saw an ad in the local newspaper, with such a car available on lease for one hundred forty-nine dollars a month. I thought it was something I could afford with my replenished reserves.

However, when I visited the dealer to have a look at it before its purchase, I ended up committing to two hundred fifty dollars a month with all the necessary bells and whistles. According to the dealer, the advertised cost of the one hundred forty-nine dollars was simply meant to lure customers to the dealership – as the cost included a standard model with no extras, which no one would ever like to drive. This compelled me to withdraw annually an extra twelve-hundred dollars a year, or six thousand dollars over the five-year lease agreement.

Since I had no personal savings and managed almost everything with borrowed funds, I was too conscious about spending even a dollar above the tightly planned expenditure. I had to spend such funds with extra care as I never knew where the next more essential expenditure, and how much of it, would be incurring.

I was fully aware that borrowed funds were not a bottomless pit either; these were bound to finish sooner or later. I wasn't going to go too far if I had to spend each time thousands of dollars more than the pre-budgeted expense. On the other hand, I could never put any of my family member's life in risk, or overlook any of their need or want.

I had been walking on such a razor thin wire for decades and decades.

***

Our daughters were now pursuing their own careers. They also were working like other kids of their age for few hours a week to make some extra pocket-money. Over time, monthly and annual household expenses had stabilized. With house value appreciating over time, and no more mortgage to pay, its rising equity gave me a sense of future security. Also, I now had some financial room to manoeuvre.

With this easing of the financial pressure, I seriously began working on improving two vital areas of my life: first, to improve the relationship with Amy as she and I were now spending more time under the same roof like complete strangers with no physical and/or emotional connection; and second, to find a stable source of supplementary income.

In order to fix our relationship, I decided to take Amy away from Ottawa, thinking that a change of location, scenery, environment, and above all, private walks and time spent together in more romantic surroundings would eventually rekindle our old flame and bring us closer. After all, we were deeply in love at one time, cared and respected each others needs, values, and feelings. In my eyes, she was still a beautiful woman. I was glad that she had agreed to marry me. It was rather unfortunate that I was not able to fulfil her expectations because of my financial inadequacies, and as a result, she had turned her back to me. I could understand her disappointments and frustrations, but there was nothing intentional. I simply became a prisoner of my own circumstances.

After a little over twenty-five years, I was finally able to take Amy away from home, from the city itself, on a long three-week trip to Europe. I didn't care about the cost of the trip – close to twenty-five thousand dollars.

My objective was to make the trip as enjoyable as possible for her. I wanted her to stay at good hotels, visit popular places of interest, and make the best of the trip in every sense, including breaking any of her personally imposed barriers, inhibitions, prejudices, and regrets about marrying or living with me.

Unfortunately nothing worked out. No matter if she was at the popular Vatican City, or Trevi Fountain or Fontana della Barcaccia at the Spanish Steps in Rome, or visiting Museums showing works of Leonardo de Vinci and Michelangelo in Florence, or at the height of Eiffel Tower in Paris (France), or Trafalgar Square of London (England), or roaming through

Scottish Mountains, Amy kept her silence or spoke very little during the day and spent nights lying far away from me like she had been doing at home. Her *'Touch me not'* attitude remained the same even after crossing the North Atlantic Ocean.

The most ironic part was that as an extrovert and with good people-oriented personality, she spoke as little as possible whereas I, mostly introverted and reluctant to talk shop, had to do most of the talking as we walked to different places or at lunches in the afternoon or dinners at night.

The trip miserably failed to open any of our personal barriers built over the years. It was abundantly clear that she, like any other woman, was finding it to hard to erase the old memories, sufferings, let-downs, fights, naggings, etc. And unless and until a woman had cleared her mental blockages and was at ease, she was never ever going to indulge into any sexual or intimate relationship.

Following this trip, I made sure that I took Amy out, even for just a week, each year, hoping that sooner or later, we would be able to re-establish our communication, mutual trust, physical and emotional relationship. But nothing changed her.

It was evident that she had been deeply hurt and frustrated by my inability to provide her the life she had perhaps expected after marrying me. Her unmet needs and expectations had badly soured our personal relationship. She even fell for one of her male colleagues, who lent her his ear and emotional support, because she couldn't take me and my presence any longer. Her extra marital affair with him didn't last long for one reason or another was a separate issue altogether. The bitter truth was that even if she had compromised the situation, she wasn't happy living with me.

Amy's unchanged cold behaviour coupled with almost non-existent communication had really bolstered my resolve to focus more on my second goal, and that was to find a stable source of additional income. This time I had to find a path that was also fully aligned with my skills, desire, and passion. I didn't want to fail this time. My repeated failures of the past might also have contributed to Amy's disdain for me, re-enforcing her opinion about me that I really was no good at anything and deserved her silent treatment.

I knew I was a creative analytic writer. She had acknowledged it. The media had publicly recognized it. My peers and colleagues had appreciated it, even if with a bit of resentment out of professional jealousy. Above all, both Amy and Jen were now more or less pushing me to write a book of my own. They both held the opinion that that was the better way to earn any supplementary income. At least I would be doing something I liked and had passion for.

I couldn't afford to ignore pestering of each of these two women, who I loved and cared for, and who were virtually a part of my life. The only unknown here was whether to write a fiction or a non-fiction, as the writing of each required some preparation and a different mindset.

Even though Jen had offered me some vague ideas about what to write about, I still needed to learn the art of transferring these in the form of comprehensive books. Ever since I had discussed with her the choice of book's topic and genre, I was more or less inclined to debut my career as a writer with a fiction.

To that effect I turned back to the resources available at Ottawa's public library. Now instead of reading books on running a mail-order business and its associated details, I began to read on writing of a fiction.

Over the next few months, I went over all kinds of books and materials on the craft of fiction writing by genre. I also read works of rich and famous fiction writers. The more I read about them, the more determined, excited, and hungrier I became to leave imprints of my own foot-prints.

I had the choice to write historical, crime, political, war, legal, mystery, thriller, or some fantasy fiction, but I eventually opted to write about people, their day-to-day life, struggles, inter-personal relations of men and women, their romance, behaviours, etc. – something that readers could easily indentify themselves with a protagonist, or issues of the day tackled, or resolved. I wanted to write a fiction that also conveyed some message, encouragement, motivation, drive to overcome self-imposed fears, inhibitions, or obstacles – something a reader takes way from a story – even if it's a small message to pursue or persist when required instead of just walking away from life's any opportunity without a thought.

There finally came a realization that writing a fiction was not only a means to earn income, but was equally a means of spreading a word, a thought, or sharing with readers an opinion, a message, an experience from which they can learn something to improve their behaviour, life, or well-being. Writing a fiction was no different than what I was currently doing at my job writing papers on finances of real persons and families.

Each and every paper that I had written not only included specific statistics or financial analysis, but also touched on their spending and saving behaviours, their personal, and motivational psychology behind it, and finally offering them some cautionary advice about keeping up their day-to-day well-being. I was already writing about and communicating with live people. I was going to do the same in a fiction likely in a more personal, open, and frank manner as governments' guidelines to write official papers would no longer inhibit my thought and writing process.

***

"What's the prognosis today?" I asked Jen as she sat in her passenger seat in the car.

I had driven the car from the parking lot to the entrance door of the Ottawa's Cancer Care Center.

She was all quiet and ashen-faced.

"Nothing new," she replied curtly. "My doctor doesn't think I am going to live for another year. My life is coming to an end. He has advised me to quit my job and stay at home from now on."

"Don't say that, please," I begged her and gave her a merciful stare. "We both know you are living a limited life. So ... when ... do you ... plan to resign?"

"Now that the doctor has told me point-blank, I should stop working in a few days time. I have been wrapping up at work for a while now. Give me another few days. Once it's done, I am out." She replied in her feeble voice.

"Let me know if you need any help at work," I muttered softly.

I gently placed my arm on her shoulders.

"You don't have to say it," she scolded me. "You have been dedicatedly looking after me for all these years. We must have been related in out past lives. Maybe you are repaying me for something good that I might have done to you in our past life. Do you believe in reincarnation?"

"No, I personally don't," I replied, "but I respect your views and thoughts on it. Right now I know how important you are to me and I want to do the best to save you from all this pain and suffering."

"Oh! Don't worry. I am not afraid of dying," she assured me. "Considering the kind of stress you have lived through your life, did you ever consider taking your own life? And, if so, what sort of feelings you went through? I just want to hear about the feelings one usually goes through while dying young."

"I am sorry I can't be of any help to you here as I personally never ever contemplated finishing my life," I replied vehemently. "Irrespective of the magnitude of stress, tension, and helplessness, this is something I never thought of. In my opinion, it is really cowardly to take one's own life. If God has given you life to live, He also has given you the strength to cope with all its ups and downs. Only you know how to cope with it. Neither ups nor downs stick with you forever. One simply needs to face these with patience and resolve. It so happens that we always remember our downs and continue to brood and wrap ourselves around with these. Very rarely someone thinks of all the ups. Look at you. Even at this stage, you are more focused on downs rather than ups. Don't you think we two at least have seen some good times together?"

"Indeed, we have," she concurred. "I have spent my life by simply relishing those happy moments. I don't know if I ever will have another time to say it, but I want you to know that I really enjoyed the good times we had, and I want to thank you for that."

She moved closer to me and gave a soft peck on my cheek. Her sad face suddenly brightened up like a momentary flash of lightning followed by complete serenity. I was sure she was simply lost in her thoughts about her upcoming end.

"Thank me for what?" I softly questioned her. "We did the best to support each other when we both were in doldrums. We listened, respected, and trusted each other. Even now, I am following your suggestion to pursue a completely different career of a fiction writer."

"What do you mean?" She again perked up for a moment.

"I have started writing a contemporary romance fiction," I broke the news to her. "I really don't know if you will be able to read it, but I just wanted you to know that it's under way now. I work late at night and over the weekends."

"I am really pleased to hear it," she replied softly. She was now pensively gazing all over my face. She uttered softly, "It really doesn't matter if I will ever be able to read it. For me, what matters is that you are at least going to live a bit happier because you are now doing what you like best – and that's writing. Never mind the money part; if you are destined to make it, you will, and if not, nobody ever will be able to create it for you. It's that simple."

"That's what Amy says too," I quipped with a dim smile.

"Speaking of Amy – how's she?" she asked. "Has she changed? Does she now go to bed with you? I know you have been taking her almost annually on a short vacation. I am glad I am not leaving you without a sex partner."

"No, she hasn't changed a bit," I lamented. "I don't think she ever will. So you are not leaving me with any sex partner. As far as I am concerned, I don't think anyone out there would be able to replace you. I think I have had my share of sex. As far as my relationship with Amy is concerned, we will indeed live cordially, respecting and caring for each other *sans* any sexual intimacy. That shattered part of our life will never ever revert to normalcy. It's like a crack in the mirror that can never be fixed."

"Don't ever give up," she advised me in her feeble voice. "People change over time. She may as well." She suddenly turned to me and said, "Drive me home, please. I don't want to go to work right now. And I don't want you to come with me inside the home as I know my weakness. I would fall in your arms and cry and make you miserable as well. I want you to simply drop me at my driveway and leave. I want no scene."

I fully complied with her wishes.

She alighted from the passenger side of the car. She looked somewhat uncomfortable and unstable. In her shakier voice, she mumbled, "Goodbye – 'til we meet again. Where? Only God knows."

She closed the car's door and slowly walked up to her garage-door. I didn't move until she had totally disappeared from my sight.

On my way back to the office, I kept thinking about the manner and the words she had used to say goodbye to me. Did these mean that it was a goodbye forever, or was she personally so badly bitter and hurt after hearing from the doctor that she had less than a year left to live.

I wished she had let me in, talk to me to share her personal pain. I knew she had nobody at home to share her feelings. She was all alone, despite her son still living with her.

My heart cried for her just by thinking about what she was going through – fighting a terminal sickness. Her life's clock was ticking away. There wasn't a thing I could do to comfort her in her most tragic phase. This was the time she needed someone's shoulder to lean on, but she had preferred to fight her own battle. She was a strong-willed woman.

The very thought of Jen and what she was going through had overwhelmed me. I was now driving with eyes almost full of tears, so much so that I very narrowly hit the rear end of another vehicle waiting at the red light.

***

A couple of days later, I got a note from the division's director informing me that he had accepted the resignation of Jen and until we found her replacement, I was to look after her section's work. In other words, I was to act as the department's spokesperson on both personal and business bankruptcies.

I had no problem handling double the workload. Especially doing Jen's work gave me some consolation that I was helping her out in a way in her most critical period.

Any excessive workload never killed anyone. What was really killing me was the simple thought of Jen's suffering and pain. How was she managing herself? When I could no longer control my emotions, I dialled her number at home.

"Hello," I heard a weak voice, hardly audible, of a woman from the other end.

"How are you feeling, Jen?" I whispered on the phone's mouthpiece. "I gather you have resigned effective today?"

"I am feeling no different than the shape you left me in two days ago," she replied. "And, as far as my resignation is concerned, I told you what my doctor wanted of me. I am now simply supposed to wait for my time."

"I understand that," I replied in a very sympathetic tone. "Is there anything I can do for you? I am really worried about you. You are all alone at the moment."

"Everything is fine." She replied in a bit more stronger voice. "Don't worry about me. I am all home-bound now. Anything I need from outside, Josh can get it. He can drive me to any medical appointment or to the hospital emergency. The rest, I have to face as it comes. There is nothing you can do. That's why I didn't even invite you to come inside the house when you dropped me a couple of days ago. I am strong enough to face it, even ready to die any minute. No one including you needs to worry about me. You just take care of yourself and your family. And, thanks again for everything."

With that she cut off the connection.

Obviously she didn't want any one to bother her. She simply wanted to be left alone.

***

Almost seven months to the day I left Jen on her driveway, I heard on the morning of Tuesday, September 30th, 2003 from the division's director that Jen had peacefully passed away. He likely had heard the news from her son, Josh, or husband, Peter.

I was deeply saddened to hear that my beloved and most trusted and intimate companion was no more in this world. I was devastated. I felt totally desolate. I felt I had lost a vital organ of my body. I felt listless, all empty and hollow. The grief caused by her death had totally swallowed me, left me handicapped, and mentally tormented.

Even though I hadn't seen her over the last seven months, I still felt her presence all around me. I still felt I could reach her in my moments of need, despair, and frustration. She was still there to support and advise me on my personal affairs.

On Thursday, a day after she died, her family including her parents, who had arrived from Hamilton, held a wake for her for two consecutive evenings at the Pinecrest Cemetery off Baseline Road in Ottawa. Since the family had decided to hold a private funeral, I decided to go to her wake on the very first evening.

In the sombre and serene atmosphere of the room, I noticed Jen's dark coloured wooden casket placed along the side of one of the long walls of the room. There were some bouquets of flowers, mostly roses, lilies, carnations, orchids, daffodils & tulips, etc. – some placed directly on top of the casket, some in large vases on tables, and some fixed on the wall.

Since the family had decided to keep the casket closed, I didn't even have a chance to see for the last time the beautiful and so ever pleasant and smiling face of the woman I so deeply loved and cared for. I went there especially to look at her face and retain its image for ever in my head and soul. Now with the casket closed, I was divested of any opportunity to see her departing face. I could only guess how she must have been looking inside the casket.

Even though her picture of eons ago had been placed in a 12" x 12" frame standing on the nearby round table, it wasn't what I was looking for. Standing near her casket, I was trying to feel how much pain she must have endured, how much she must have cried in pain, scars of her tearful face, and total helplessness. I cried for her in silence.

I stood there close to her covered body – a body I had closely held physically, romantically, and spiritually – until I felt someone tapping my shoulder, and talking,

"She meant a lot to you, didn't she?" I heard Peter's voice.

I didn't even hear his footsteps likely because of the fluffy carpet in the room.

I gave him a silent stare. "Well, it's natural when you have worked with a person for close to thirty years," I murmured. I shook his hand, and gave him a gentle embrace. "Please accept mine and my family's sincere condolences. And please convey these to Jen's parents and other family members as well. God bless Jen's soul."

While Peter and I were talking, I saw Josh walking slowly towards us. He came and gave me a casual light hug.

"I am sorry, Josh, you lost your Mom," I said in a tattered voice. I tried to place my arm around his shoulders.

He just moved away, as if he had some personal grudge against me. Might be he didn't like me because I was often visiting his home, or was too close to his Mom. After all, he was an adult who understood the intricacies of a relationship between two adults of opposite sexes.

"Don't mind his bad behaviour tonight," Peter said in his defence. "He is quite upset on losing his mother."

"I understand," I replied. "So now you are going to take care of Josh and look after the house, I presume." I added.

"I am not sure as Josh is getting married with a girl he met while he worked part-time at a burger joint," he replied. "I personally don't want to move in there because of old memories and the time I spent with Jen. I think I will continue to live where I am and lead my own life. I will indeed look after the house until it's sold." He paused. "Could we speak for a few moments outside this room as I want to clear some air between us?" he asked.

"Certainly," I replied. "I didn't think there was any bad air between us. But, please, feel free." I encouraged him.

"You know, Robert," he started to unwind his suppressed frustration or his inner-self as we slowly walked outside the meeting hall, "I am fully aware that Jen was more than a colleague to you. You two were quite intimate with each other, or let me put it mildly –you two had quite a lasting affair. I accepted that reality. She spent way more time with you than with us as a family. She always used to speak highly of you, comparing me with you, and nagging and putting me down at every opportunity she got. Even though it made me really envious of you, I began to hate her. The more she belittled me, the more I became determined not to improve myself for her sake. I didn't think I owed her anything. I began to live and pay more attention to Josh."

"Granted you didn't owe her anything, but you still were responsible to improve your own career, pay attention to the changing job market, what was happening to your company, about out-sourcing of your job, and so on," I interrupted him.

"Absolutely," he concurred with me, "but you know when you start hating your spouse, you don't want to do anything, even if it involves improving your career. I felt I had lost everything. You can accuse me of all the dereliction. Besides that, I had no desire to start all over again to build or update my skills. With my fixed mindset, I thought I was well educated and had high skills to pursue an uninterrupted career path. Not even in my dreams I could ever visualize that the skill set I had would be obsolete in a matter of few years. The realization to upgrade my skills, required by the rapidly changing automation and technical changes in the job market coupled with liberal international trade agreements causing outsourcing of jobs, came to me very late. By that time, I had no money to invest on myself. I had to accept what was available – even if it meant a job of a security guard. What really can I say? I am not proud of myself. At times I wish I had a growth mindset like you – always on the look out to improve knowledge and skills. I know you tried to run a business, and after it failed, you are now trying to write a book of your own. I wish I had your resiliency and creativity. Anyway, it's too late to worry about such things."

"It's never too late for anything," I replied softly. "Learning is a continuous process. It's really important for each one of us to be prepared to the best of our ability to protect interests and well-being of our families from any sort of anticipatory changes – be these related to job, commercial, or financial markets. You could have still stayed at home and taken care of the house, your wife, and provided proper guidance to Josh. Your wife was earning good enough. So what if you were working as a security guard? A job is a job." I counter-argued.

I was now really controlling my suppressed anger on his dereliction.

"The very fact that my wife was earning way more than me really put me to shame, giving me a feeling of total worthlessness," he sputtered. "I couldn't accept it for the life of me. You may consider me as an old fashioned male chauvinist pig with a big ego, but the fact remains that the majority of baby-boomers of my generation would have problems accepting this situation. I didn't want to be supported by my wife. I simply didn't want to play a secondary role."

"Well, it's all personal," I replied with a shrug. "Whether you like it or not, your wife has still left you with almost thirty percent of her income and that too indexed to the annual rate of inflation that you will get as long as you live. See. She hasn't left you penniless even after her death." I remarked sarcastically.

"I realize that," he mumbled.

He started to move one of his feet sideways on the carpet. I realized he had had enough of my lecture and was likely getting annoyed.

"Let me sign the guestbook before I leave," I begged leave of him.

I knew he had spit out all of the venom – his hurt feelings, pride, and suspicions.

He walked with me to the table where the guestbook was placed half-open. Before I reached for the pen, I extended my hand to shake his,

"Once again I am deeply sorry to see Jen leave us," I said. I firmly shook his hand. "Take care of Josh and everyone else."

"Thanks for coming," he replied, and turned his eyes to the meeting room.

He walked away from me.

I took the pen tied to the guestbook and inscribed on a fresh page, "God bless you, Jen. I will miss you and your friendship forever, Robert."

I stepped out of the cemetery with a very heavy heart. I felt like the worst loser in the entire world. I had lost my one and only soul-mate.

***

With both Sara and Kerry now settled in their chosen professions and that too, away from the parental nest, and Amy's relationship with me as cold and distant as ever, and with relatively lesser financial distractions, I had all the time to focus on my writing.

My life revolved around three key activities: home to work, taking care of home, and reading and writing. Since our social life was very limited, almost non-existent, I had nothing else to do, but just read, read, and read, or write, write, and write, or mix the two.

It took me close to two years to finish the script of my debut contemporary romance fiction.

His Almighty had finally relented and agreed to bless me and my efforts. The tide of my life was beginning to change. A few months after the release of my fiction, I received my first royalty cheque.

Hurray! I had finally earned my long fought and sought after supplementary income – income that I had been struggling to earn for the last three decades.

The amount of royalty cheque didn't really matter to me. It was the thought that as a new and freelance writer, I had been able to draw attention of some readers, who in turn, had willingly purchased my fiction. For a novice writer stepping into a competitive publishing world, I was profoundly happy to have found my niche.

Following the widely popular adage, '*success breeds success*', I was really encouraged and decided to pursue this new career as a writer with full vigour. This happy and self-fulfilling accomplishment also proved that what really contributed to this success was not only my resilience, skill, creativity, and mindset, but the real passion for writing that I had gained at work over decades and decades.

No wonder it's said again and again that if one worked with passion in any area of one's choosing, the success, sooner or later, is bound to come.

That's the power of passion.

***

"I am glad to see you are gaining popularity," Amy said jubilantly.

She had been listening to the interview I had just completed with an announcer at one of the radio stations in the United States.

"Well, it's nothing new," I replied casually. "Announcers at radio stations and journalists in the media need people like us as badly as we need them. It all comes with the territory. I am glad though that the book is gaining publicity, which in turn, should generate some supplementary income for us. You know all my life I tried to earn some extra income by taking any part-time job. Now when I come to think of it, no such job, irrespective of what it had paid, would have given me any public recognition. Moreover, just think about the kind of legacy I would be leaving behind as a writer. Working on a part-time job wouldn't have given me this opportunity. Maybe some Deity or God finally led me to do what is right for me."

"I am really happy for you that you have found not only the source of extra income, but also readers who likely would be following you and your work. Isn't that nice?" she added.

"Indeed it is," I affirmed her conclusions. "I still have to win someone who matters to me way more than money."

"Who's that?" She was inquisitive.

"You ... your real love and affection," I replied.

"What's wrong with me ... my love and affection for you?" She looked all puzzled.

"On the surface, there's nothing wrong," I clarified. "It's our cold relationship beneath the surface that I am talking about. We live like two solitudes under the same roof."

"Have you ever thought why we live like that or have a cold relationship?" She snapped back at me. "Look at yourself, your full immersion in your own work and other pursuits. Look at your face – always looking sad, struggling and worrisome. You are so self-centered. You have no time to even speak to me properly, never mind as a husband or a lover. How can a woman who sees her self-centered husband in such a miserable and round the clock grouchy situation express her love or desire for him? I even think twice before talking to you about me or any family matter, let alone any loving, intimate, or sex talk. You are never at ease, or have that inviting contented and loving look that would excite or incite me to come closer to you. At times I get so frustrated that I begin to nag you because that's the only way I can vent out my anger or convey a particular message. I have been living with you very patiently, hoping that some day you will come out of your depression and craze of work. You know even after the short affair I had had, I opted to live with you because I firmly believed that you were a much better and loving man underneath than what your exterior conveys. And, speaking of our sex life, you know very well how quickly I melt when I am in your arms. Even your simple touch makes my genitals sprout as a fountain. And you still have the audacity to tell me that I am cold to you. I want sex as much as you do. There are times I get so frustrated that I want to initiate sex and really devour you. If as a man, you don't initiate it, how on earth would I know you want me? You know how badly a woman wants to be wanted. How on earth can I express my desire to a man who's depressed all the time? If you want us to have a normal sex life, you have to change your personality, your mood swings, show some interest in me, foreplay or excite me outside the bed – you know all these things. I don't know why I am wasting my breath."

"I am truly sorry," I replied.

She had really embarrassed and shocked me with her honest revelations. And she had assessed right.

"I have been bogged down by financial problems all our life. I have been trying hard to provide you and the kids the best of everything that life has to offer, neglecting, I suppose, the other important part of our life as a couple – the amount of time spent together and our sex life. Now that I know which route to follow for the rest of my life, you will not see me in the same tight and depressed mood or engaged in any rigid work routine. You have been patient for that long. Just bear with me a bit more. One day all these clouds of gloom and doom will be pushed away with the bright sunshine. Trust me. Our good times are just around the corner."

Following this hearty and open conversation, Amy must have felt good and relieved of all the possible tension that she had been silently cumulating over all these years.

That night, as soon as I lay on the side of my bed, she promptly moved closer to me and spread my arm around her waist. She wanted to be hugged, and hugged tightly.

I pressed her body firmly against mine.

"Love me tenderly tonight," she whispered naughtily.

"I will be glad to, dear," I replied lovingly, and held her in a tight embrace.

I was happy that my old ebullient Amy was back into my arms.

ABOUT THE AUTHOR

In this second fiction, Raj Chawla, penning as Paul Shona, writes an emotional tale of families ravaged by the rising level of indebtedness and the transformation in the job market arising from the rapid automation including computer and digital technology, and international trade agreements facilitating outsourcing of jobs from high to low-wage countries.

Like his debut romance fiction *Quest for Second Sex*, published in August 2016, drawn heavily on his study and job related travels in different continents, the author weaves this heart-wrenching tale by drawing heavily on his professional knowledge and analytic experience he gained while he worked as a research analyst for more than four decades at Statistics Canada, Ottawa (Canada). In his job, the author analyzed earnings, incomes, assets, debts, wealth, and labour market participation of households in Canada, the United States, and other advanced affluent countries.

A complete list of author's publications can be found in Appendix III of his second book, *A Writer's Journey Through the Bureaucratic Maze: A True Account*, released in June 2017, or at his site at http://www.rajchawla6.com. The latter also includes a detailed bio of the author.

The author's books are available at
https://www.amazon.com/author/paulshona.

The author is a member of the Yahoo's Indie Romance Ink writers group as well as a few other selective groups of writers on Facebook.

Please feel free to reach the author at rajchawla6@yahoo.ca.

www.ingramcontent.com/pod-product-compliance
Lightning Source LLC
Chambersburg PA
CBHW052235220526
45471CB00001B/59